Hackerspaces

Hackerspaces

Making the Maker Movement

Sarah R. Davies

polity

First published in 2017 by Polity Press

Polity Press
65 Bridge Street
Cambridge CB2 1UR, UK

Polity Press
350 Main Street
Malden, MA 02148, USA

ISBN-13: 978-1-5095-0116-8
ISBN-13: 978-1-5095-0117-5(pb)

A catalogue record for this book is available from the British Library.

Library of Congress Cataloging-in-Publication Data

Names: Davies, Sarah R., author.
Title: Hackerspaces : making the maker movement / Sarah R. Davies.
Description: Cambridge, UK; Malden, MA, USA: Polity, 2017. | Includes
   bibliographical references and index.
Identifiers: LCCN 2016029144 | ISBN 9781509501168 (hardback) | ISBN 9781509501175
   (pbk.)
Subjects: LCSH: Makerspaces.
Classification: LCC TS171.57 .D58 2017 | DDC 658.3/8–dc23 LC record available at
   https://lccn.loc.gov/2016029144

Typeset in 10 on 12 pt Palatino
by Toppan Best-set Premedia Limited
Printed and bound in the UK by Clays Ltd, St Ives PLC

For further information on Polity, visit our website: politybooks.com

Contents

Preface

When I first heard about hackerspaces, and became interested in them as a research topic, I knew that I had to get one of my colleagues involved. Dave Conz had written his PhD on the amateur technologies of biodiesel, and in the process had become an expert in the technique. If anyone was a hacker and maker – if anyone had a natural affinity with the art and craft of making stuff work – it was Dave. In 2012, funded by the research centre that employed us (the Center for Nanotechnology in Society at Arizona State University), Dave and I teamed up to carry out a research project on hackerspaces across the US.

Dave and I carried out the research and collected the data together, but I am writing this alone. Dave died in 2013, suddenly and very tragically. He was – well, so many things, but amongst them a passionate researcher, thoughtful analyst, and maker *par excellence*. His enthusiasm for all things making leave their trace on the work that we did together and the arguments in this book. I hope that it can serve as a celebration of him and some of the things he cared about.

Acknowledgements

This book is for Dave. It goes without saying that his thinking, practices and research work have immeasurably influenced my writing.

I am extremely grateful to all the hackers, makers, tinkers and community builders who talked to us about their hacker and makerspaces and what they did there. All of our interviewees were generous with their time and with their spaces, allowing us to ask all kinds of impertinent or ignorant questions and to poke around in dark cupboards and forgotten shelves. This work couldn't exist without that generosity. Similarly, the Center for Nanotechnology in Society at Arizona State University provided the funding for Dave and me to visit hackerspaces around the US. I'd like to thank the Center, and particularly Dave Guston and Cynthia Selin, for their support.

Since starting this project I have switched continents and jobs and lost a fantastic, knowledgeable collaborator. I therefore owe a debt of thanks that is even larger than usual to all those who have discussed hacking and making with me or who have commented on my writing, including the anonymous reviewers provided by Polity, whose comments were instrumental in improving the book at all its stages. David Gauntlett, Andrew Schrock and Aubrey Wigner were thorough readers whose opinions were extremely important to me. More generally, I have learned much from the growing body of scholarship on hacking and making, including work by Jeffrey Bardzell, Shaowen Bardzell, Carl DiSalvo, Silvia Lindtner, Daniela Rosner, Johan Söderberg and many others. Ana Delgado, Denisa Kera, Martin Malthe Borch, Morgan Meyer, Christo Sims, Karin Tybjerg and Louise Whiteley have all been important interlocutors as I have thought about hacking and making. Talks at the European Commission's Joint Research Centre, the Center for Science, Technology, Medicine and Society at UC Berkeley, the Center for Nanotechnology in Society at Arizona State University, and the Centre for Science Studies at Aarhus University all provided me with opportunities to test out my arguments with audiences of scholars, hackers and makers. Another useful audience was comprised of members of my extended family, who read some early text and provided comments, grammatical corrections, and strong discouragement from overusing the word 'affordance'. Finally, I'd like to thank Raffael Himmelsbach for reminding me that, while the hacker spirit of Do! Plan! Make! is valuable, so at times are other, quieter, ways of being.

1

Introduction

There Are a Number of Places This Book Could Begin

There are a number of places this book could begin.

It might start with me, in my kitchen, stirring a jar of sourdough starter. Sourdough is a thick batter-like home for wild yeasts that, when at room temperature and in its active growth phase, foams happily and releases a rich, hoppy smell. For millennia it's been used to bake bread that has a slightly sour tang – hence, sourdough – and which generally requires longer to rise, but which is delicious and, by some accounts, better for you than breads made with instant yeast. I hadn't heard any of this stuff before a year or so ago, but today I am stirring my own culture, feeding it with flour and water and setting it on the kitchen counter to let the microbes grow and develop. Tomorrow I'll mix some of the starter with more flour and water to begin making bread dough, kneading it for 15 minutes or so before leaving it overnight to rise.

Or it could start in a hackerspace – any hackerspace, it doesn't much matter which one. It might be tiny, like one student-run hackerspace in Boston I visited, which was squeezed into a few square metres in a basement of a university building. The walls are filled to bursting with whiteboards, piles of humming servers, books, notices and posters, and shelves of wires and plugs and tools and spare computer parts. There's also what appears to be a small flying machine, labelled 'McFly'. In the centre of the room, student hackers sit around tables or on a battered sofa, talking in groups, focusing intensely on laptop screens, or plugging, welding and building. The air, in the manner of air in densely populated basement rooms the world over, has a thick, moist fug to it.

Or we might be in a much larger space – a TechShop, or the 40,000 square foot ex-factory makerspace that is just down the road from the students in Boston. These kinds of spaces might feel emptier: they're probably less crowded, and tools and materials are balanced less precariously. But they're still full of stuff, from laser cutters to 3D printers and CNC routers and, importantly, the finished or half-finished projects these tools are being used to build. You can see anything from beer brewing systems to exquisitely fine jewellery and hacked bikes with glitterballs attached to them. There's more space, so there are more comfy chairs, plus a library of sofas, armchairs and bookshelves in the centre.

But we might also begin in the media, with the UK's *Guardian* newspaper launching its 'Do Something' campaign in early 2014. This was, as the paper wrote in its 'Do Something Manifesto', an invitation to 'try something new'. Through a monthly magazine, journalists present stories and discussion about easily accessible and low-cost opportunities for readers to try something different. Articles give advice on everything from places to learn how to upholster your furniture to unusual ideas for a date or whether it's possible to learn Russian in a day; the tone is chatty and friendly, with reader feedback and sections like 'The Do Something Challenge' and Beginner's Guides. The campaign, the Manifesto explains, is motivated by the belief that the experience of novelty adds value to people's lives. Whether it's trying out new things, meeting new people or learning something different, living life such that you accrue new memories and new experiences means that you will live more intensely. If you 'broaden your horizons, learn new skills, or implement more beneficial habits', they suggest, your life will be more satisfying (though also perhaps harder work: the first magazine contains a list of tips on how to meet your goals and stay motivated).

This book is about the connections between these things. More specifically, it's about hackerspaces, and the hacking and making activities that go on within them, and their connection to broader developments in society. Culturing sourdough; hacking together software or bike-glitterball hybrids; embarking on a lifestyle of active and engaged leisure: these things look quite different on the surface. I want to argue, however, that they share some central commonalities. Something similar is going on when one chooses to join a hackerspace, gets involved in crafting, or dabbles in traditional skills like sourdough baking. Taken together, these kinds of activities can tell us something about the kinds of societies we live in, and the kinds of people we are asked to be.

The rise of hacking and making

Hackerspaces and the maker movement are a growing trend. Though many people haven't heard of them, as of the start of 2016, there were 1,233 active hackerspaces around the world, and more than 500 spaces in development. This is a global movement: these spaces are anywhere from Surprise, Arizona to Yangon, Myanmar.[1] They can be anything from tiny rented garages to vast former factories or shopfront locations, situated anywhere from inner cities to residential suburban tracts. They may be private members' clubs or open to anyone, anytime. They may be literally filled to the ceiling with stuff – electronics supplies, wood, books, defunct tools, test tubes and fume hoods – or almost empty apart from a couple of tables and chairs.

What they share is that they are physical spaces, operated collectively, where members can use equipment they might not be able to afford, or have space for, by themselves.[2] This equipment can be anything from 3D printers to industrial sewing machines or server systems. It is, essentially, anything that hackers and makers need to help them hack and make. Hacker and makerspaces therefore bring together people who are interested in hacking and making, and offer them support in doing so. The result, the stuff that is hacked and made, is pretty diverse. Hacker and makerspaces can help you learn to code, give you access to the tools you need to make your own furniture, provide lessons in electronics, or give you space to do some tabletop genetic engineering. British freedom of information campaigner Heather Brookes has called hackerspaces the 'digital-age equivalent of English Enlightenment coffee houses',[3] which suggests something rather intellectual and discursive: a place where ideas might be shared. Hacker and makerspaces house communities of people who, together, learn and share and make anything from apps to oscilloscopes.

For a long time hacking had strictly negative connotations. Even now, the term can make us think of the activities of Anonymous, the loosely organized collective which has taken down the websites of PayPal and Visa and agitated for social justice,[4] or of solitary, bearded geeks with poor social skills.[5] President Barack Obama at one stage dismissed ex-NSA contractor and whistleblower Edward Snowden as a '29 year old hacker'.[6] Hacking as a criminal activity – as breaking and entering on computers, networks and servers – remains the top entry in the Urban Dictionary's definition of the term.[7] This understanding of hacking is as something that is strictly digital. It's generally illicit, referring to practices known as cracking, or black-hat hacking, rather than white-hat hacking, which is 'ethical' hacking that harmlessly tests the resilience of particular networks.[8]

But the idea of hacking, and, relatedly, that of making, is currently being rediscovered as something positive, exciting and useful. As far back as 2005, the American Dialect Society announced that 'lifehack' was one of its words of the year (definition: 'to make one's day-to-day behaviors or activities more efficient'[9]). Today the website Lifehacker continues to offer tips and tricks to help deal with everyday life, from how to effectively de-seed a pomegranate to a guide to making your own keyboard. IKEA hacking involves the re-purposing of IKEA products into anything from vibrators to personalized kitchen cabinets.[10] A 2014 book frames urban exploration as 'place hacking'.[11] Computing also remains an important context for hacking. Take, for instance, the growth of hackathons, software hacking marathons which focus on contributing to a particular technology, or on a social issue or problem.[12] In the UK, a 'National Health Service Hack Day' is held several times a year, to help develop better healthcare technologies.[13] The trend to use technology to hack social problems[14] has reached such a pitch that there's now an annual 'Stupid Hackathon' satirizing it, at which participants attempt to develop projects with 'no value whatsoever'.[15]

Hacking has even entered the heart of the establishment. The Royal Institution of Great Britain's Christmas Lectures have been running since 1825 and were started by Michael Faraday. Presented in the Institution's lecture theatre, with its high-banked round of seats, wooden panelling, and stage from which Faraday himself once spoke, the annual lecture series aims to provide engaging science education to young people. Among others, Nobel Prize winners have given past lectures. It's a sign of the reinvention of hacking, then, that in 2014 the lectures took as their focus 'how to hack your home'. Over the course of three lectures, Professor Danielle George (an engineer, and the sixth woman in the history of the Christmas Lectures to present them) showed viewers how to unpick and reconfigure everyday household devices, from light bulbs to motors. As the Royal Institution's press release proclaimed, Professor George would:

> take three great British inventions – a light bulb, a telephone and a motor – and demonstrate how viewers can adapt, transform and 'hack' them to do extraordinary things. This is tinkering for [the] 21st century. Danielle, who grew up in Newcastle, said: '[…] I want young people to realise that they have the power to change the world from their bedroom, kitchen table or garden shed. If we all take control of the technology around us and think creatively, then solving some of the world's greatest challenges is only a small step away'.[16]

Hacking seems to be becoming mainstream. It's something you can do to household devices – phones and light bulbs – as a kind of twenty-first-century update of the tinkering your grandparents might have done in their garage. But it's also about 'changing the world' through invention and creativity, and taking control of the technologies that surround you. Professor George isn't thinking small: solutions to the world's greatest challenges, she says, can come about from young people hacking at their kitchen tables.

New tools and technologies

The rise of hacking and making is often presented as related to the rise of new kinds of technology. 3D printers, for instance, are increasingly accessible as consumer products, and allow you to print out digital files as physical objects in plastic or other materials (including sugar icing and pancake batter).[17] Some models are well under $1,000, and are evoking visions of a world where the stuff around us, from coffee makers to children's toys or the widgets that hold our furniture together, can be printed at home whenever we want.[18] 3D scanners, laser cutters (which use a computer-guided laser to cut materials), CNC mills (another cutting tool), and the software to support all of these are similarly dropping in price, or are available as open-source software or blueprints. This increasing accessibility, coupled with digital networks that can connect makers and hackers across the world, is prompting excitement about a new wave of making that could change both business and everyday life. The McKinsey Global Institute discussed new fabrication technologies in a 2012 report on 'manufacturing the future',[19] arguing that these technologies could revitalize manufacturing industries around the world. In 2008 the Californian think tank Institute for the Future suggested that all organizations, big or small, need to take the implications of the move towards making into account. This might mean, for instance, ensuring that your products or services are 'authentic': as 'cyberspace becomes a layer on top of the physical world', the report notes, 'a newfound appreciation emerges for authentic experiences, interactions, and products'.[20]

Chris Anderson's 2012 book *Makers: The New Industrial Revolution* encapsulates many of these arguments. Anderson is a tech journalist and entrepreneur, and his book heralds in no uncertain terms the coming of a 'new industrial revolution' through the activities of what he calls the 'Maker Movement'. This revolution, he argues, will emerge as the power of the web – the digital – is applied to the material world:

the physical products and stuff that surround us. Because 'making things has gone digital',[21] everything that the web has enabled – new forms of collaboration, easy sharing of designs, readily available desktop tools – can now be used to support physical production and entrepreneurial activities connected to such production. It's now easier than ever to make a product: anyone, Anderson suggests, can learn to use desktop digital tools to design a physical object, prototype it through 3D printing or other making tools, share and improve the design through online collaboration, and outsource larger-scale production to what he refers to, somewhat coyly, as 'low-cost labour centres' such as China.[22] Anderson's vision is of making as enabling new forms of business and entrepreneurship, helping to develop an economy in which many small-scale 'industrial artisans' earn their living through their passions. He illustrates this vision with existing success stories, such as the credit card processing solution Square, MakerBot Industries (the producers of low-cost consumer 3D printers), and his own company, 3D Robotics. Neil Gershenfeld of MIT's Center for Bits and Atoms similarly believes that the advent of 'personal fabrication' technologies can empower people around the world. His book, *Fab: The Coming Revolution on Your Desktop*, describes how bits (the digital) can be used to control atoms (the physical) so as to support entrepreneurship as well as to enable individuals to make the one-off, customizable technologies that they want in their lives (one example that he gives being a portable, private space for screaming, for use in public places).

Making, hacking and new fabrication technologies are not just prominent in policy reports and business books. They're also hitting the news. A widely reported 2013 story tells of how Californian Mick Ebeling, of Not Impossible Labs (a business which 'believes in technology for the sake of humanity'),[23] travelled to Sudan's Nuba Mountains to set up what he thinks is the world's first lab for printing prosthetic limbs and training local people to print, assemble and customize them. Inspired by a news story about a boy who had lost both arms in a bomb blast, Ebeling had mobilized an extensive community of tech businesses, scientists and inventors to crowdsource the design for the prosthetics. With support from industries such as Intel, Ebeling was able to set up the lab in South Sudan and to start printing and fitting prosthetic arms. By the time the story hit the media, the lab was printing a prosthetic a week,[24] and the South Sudanese boy, Daniel, who'd inspired the project had received a prosthetic arm and was able to feed himself for the first time in two years. All the designs, Ebeling promised, would be open-source and easily available. Anyone could access and then tweak, develop or customize them. Prosthetic limbs could be printed anywhere in the world, by anyone.

3D printers have also been used to produce more controversial devices. Cody R. Wilson, a University of Texas law student and entrepreneur, was also in the news in 2013: his company was attempting to design, and make freely available, plans for a 3D printable gun. There is now a large community of 'digital gunsmiths' devoted to developing printable, fully operational guns,[25] with multiple designs available, demonstration videos, and at least one arrest connected to ownership of 3D printed guns. The developments, Wired Magazine wrote, have 'left legislators and regulators in the dust'. There are plenty of other examples of makers and hackers becoming, however briefly, high-profile heroes or villains. In 2015 teenage maker Ahmed Mohamed shot to prominence when he was suspended from his Texas high school, and then arrested by police, after bringing a homemade digital clock to school: one of his teachers had thought it was a bomb.[26] The resulting social media furore included tweets of support for Mohamed from Facebook CEO Mark Zuckerberg, Google, and other Silicon Valley stars.[27] Despite writing off Edward Snowden as a mere hacker, President Obama has publicly driven forward an emphasis on making into US policy: 2014 saw the inauguration of a 'Nation of Makers' initiative and 2015 a national Week of Making.[28] The 'rise of the Maker Movement', a fact sheet on these initiatives notes, 'is a huge opportunity for the United States. [...] the democratization of the tools needed to design and prototype physical products can support entrepreneurship and a renaissance of American manufacturing'. Writing in early 2016, it seems that hardly a month goes by without another news story publicizing, celebrating or problematizing new hacker or makerspaces and the projects that go on within them.[29]

Experiencing hackerspaces

Sometimes this rhetoric, this intense excitement about the potential of making and hacking, can seem rather divorced from what actually goes on in hackerspaces. The times that I've come across 3D printers, in hackerspaces or elsewhere, they have almost exclusively been used to print what we might term cheap plastic crap: tchotchkes, slightly wonky though theoretically useful household organizers such as soap dispensers or pencil boxes, miniature figurines (Thingiverse, one of the sites that hosts ready-to-print open-source designs, has a whole collection called 'Gnomes'). People tell me the resolution – the fineness of the plastic 'lines' that are printed out – is improving in recent models. In 2014 I saw a shopfront display of the MakerBot Replicator-2, described by its manufacturer as the 'easiest, fastest, and most affordable tool for making professional quality models'.[30] It was surrounded, as an illustration of its capacities, by small plastic elephants and what I can only describe as decorative spiral shapes.

Despite any gaps between public discussion of the potential of hacking and making and what is actually being developed, it is clear that, for whatever reason, hacking is having a moment. Governments celebrate it, the media cover it – and, most importantly, hacker and makerspaces are proliferating. The number of hackerspaces has gone from around 30 worldwide in 2007 to almost 500 in 2011 and some 1,233 active spaces in 2016.[31] Something is happening here, something that is driving people to set up and participate in these kinds of spaces, and that is convincing businesses, policy makers and commentators to get excited about them. Professor George's 'Hack your Home' lecture series at the Royal Institution and Obama's 'Nation of Makers' initiative both illustrate that policy makers and educators are putting their money where their mouths are, and supporting hacking and making in financial and practical ways. Hacking, it seems, resonates with contemporary society in some important way. The ideas and practices that circulate within hacker and makerspaces are being picked up and magnified by the media, government and business because they are viewed as useful and timely – because, we might speculate, they somehow represent the zeitgeist, the spirit of the time.

To understand what a hackerspace is, nothing comes close to the experience of stepping into one, and being immersed in its noises, smells, textures and colours. Hackerspaces are, above all, physical spaces in which people spend time, either alone or (more often) with other people. As important as digital connectivity might be to the maker movement, online engagement is not what is seen as central to participation in a hacker or makerspace. This is hacker and author John Baichtal describing an (imaginary) visit to a hackerspace:

> You step through the doorway and into a noisy room full of people and equipment. Everywhere you look there are men and women doing interesting things. At one table, a couple of guys are hunched over a 3D printer that is outputting in plastic, layer by layer. As you watch, a sprocket begins to take form on the printer's build platform. In the wood shop a woman is milling hardwood for a suite of custom furniture she's designing, peering through her safety goggles at a table leg spinning in a lathe. Other members are playing around with a CNC machine, a computer-controlled milling machine that grinds away at a block of wood or metal, while others are soldering electronic components together. Still

more members are collaborating on some project or another, drawing up schematics on a white board.

The collaboration is the aspect of the space that strikes you the most. People are working and talking together. They're sharing information, learning about new things, asking questions, and discussing mutual areas of interest. They're building projects to fill a practical need or simply for the love of it.

This is a hackerspace.[32]

Baichtal describes some of the equipment hackerspaces often feature (3D printers, lathes, CNC routers, soldering stations) as well as the kind of projects people may be working on. But above all he emphasizes the social nature of the space. Hackers often work together on projects, and even when they don't, collaboration is still key: people share knowledge, help out if someone is stuck on a particularly tricky problem, ask what others are working on, or simply chat as they work. As Baichtal hints, projects can be a combination of the practical, the entrepreneurial and the purely pleasurable. One person may be building custom furniture as part of their business, while another hacks glitterball-bikes or open-source software simply because they can and want to.

Nothing replicates the experience of being in a hackerspace. But for some kind of digital approximation, one can spend time at hackerspaces.org, which operates as the key networking and knowledge-sharing tool for hackerspaces around the world. Its wiki, in particular, is both an important source of knowledge concerning the logistics and spirit of hackerspaces and itself mirrors the way in which many hacker and makerspaces are run. (It also includes a list of hackerspaces worldwide, so you can easily find out if there's a space near you and check out the hackerspace experience for yourself.) A quick browse through the site gives some sense of how this burgeoning movement is organized.

First, the site structure is bottom-up. There's no one in particular coordinating everything: it's not one person's pet project, and there's no leadership structure or hierarchy. The meat of hackerspaces.org is run as a wiki, so anyone can log in and contribute, and different people in the community take on different roles. (On the page that describes these roles, there's a plea relating to the Flickr group associated with the site: 'I have no clue who's behind that...would the real maintainer please stand up?'[33]). This openness and lack of fixed hierarchies is typical of hackerspaces generally. Many hackerspaces describe their organization as oriented around consensus, bottom-up decision making, and what gets called 'do-ocracy': the person who does something (rather than just talking or complaining about it) is right.

Second, this is a global movement. Hackerspaces.org maintains a map of hackerspace locations,[34] and though there are hot spots in North America and Europe, there are also hackerspaces registered in Indonesia, India, Iran and Ivory Coast (just to pick countries starting with an I). Historically, hackerspaces were a European phenomenon that were brought to the USA in the mid-2000s. They exploded in number towards the end of that decade (John Baichtal says that more than 500 were started over a period of three years[35]), and are now spreading around the world.[36] As previously noted, in early 2016 there are at least 1,233 active spaces, with over 500 more planned.[37]

Third, this is a reflective community. The hackerspaces.org wiki provides resources on anything and everything you might want to know about hackerspaces, including how you might get one started yourself. There's a set of 'design patterns' which can be applied to your nascent hackerspace organization, advice on what hardware you might want to invest in and what software can be used to keep track of membership dues, and a list of the key ways that hackerspaces and hackers communicate (from Internet Relay Chat – IRC – channels to the different email discussion lists that hackerspaces.org runs). There's also a section on 'Theory', which links to discussions on the nature and purposes of hackerspaces. Hackers and makers like to document what they're doing, and they're happy to share the knowledge they develop through their activities. Hacking isn't about being secretive, particularly not when it comes to sharing the knowledge that can help the maker movement grow.

Fourth, this is a diverse movement. Although there are some norms in how hackerspaces are organized and run (encapsulated by the design patterns and advice on funding structures), many of the spaces that are listed do not conform to these. In practice, all kinds of groups, with all kinds of affiliations, fly under the hackerspace banner. One hackerspace in Brazil, *LabHacker Câmara dos Deputados*, is located in the Brazilian Chamber of Deputies, and its Facebook page says that it is a government organization. Other spaces – like Noisebridge, in San Francisco, one of the earliest US hackerspaces – emphasize their counter-cultural and critical status. BioCurious, in California's Bay Area, focuses on DIY biotechnology. Some spaces double up as co-working offices, or as Fab Labs (fabrication laboratories), or are situated in libraries or museums. Hackerspaces might choose to call themselves makerspaces, community labs, factories or playgrounds. Just as is the case for the maker movement generally, the hackerspace label draws different places and organizations together. Diverse people, groups and practices are being caught up in this emerging network of communities.

Finally, these are spaces that do some pretty cool stuff. Photos on the hackerspaces.org wiki show darkened rooms filled with sofas and coloured lights, computer caves decorated with paper stars, and people soldering, welding, typing and just hanging out. The projects page lists everything from agricultural robots to a hackerspace-run global space programme and a Tardis console as shared projects currently under development. If nothing else, this whets your curiosity – but it also conveys a sense of excitement, of thinking big. If hackerspaces are going to send people to the stars (whether via a spacecraft or Dr Who's Tardis), then what *couldn't* they do?

Where the book is going

Hackerspaces are interesting places to visit, and to study. They're clearly a growing phenomenon. As of yet, however, we don't know much about precisely how they operate or how and why people participate in them. The research on which this book is based took this as its starting point. Why do people get involved in these spaces? How are they organized? In 2012, my colleague Dave and I visited hacker and makerspaces around the US to ask these kinds of questions, and the chapters that follow will give you an idea of the answers that we were given. Beyond this, however, hacking and making are interesting because they can tell us something about the ways in which particular societies are organized. It's not a coincidence that there's so much excitement about hacking and the maker movement at the moment, or that these developments are being featured in the media and supported by government funding. The starting point for this book is that by exploring hacker and makerspaces we can get some insight into what it means to be a citizen of contemporary North American and European societies. Understanding the rise of hacking and making can tell us something about why I might find myself culturing sourdough, why active leisure is promoted as a positive choice, and even what our governments expect of us as citizens.

The rest of this book takes hackerspaces, and hacking and making, as a starting point for thinking about these wider trends and developments. The next chapter discusses these trends, from the rise of crafting to the philosophy behind DIY. There's been a concerted move, I suggest, towards the kinds of active leisure exemplified by the *Guardian's* 'Do Something' campaign, and it's important that we view hacking and making within this wider context. Chapter 3 starts to focus more specifically on hacker and makerspaces by telling some of the histories of hacking. These include the stories that are told about the history of computer hacking: this is part of the background to the rise of hacker-spaces, and software hacking (whether black- or white-hat) forms part of the suite of activities hosted by hackerspaces. But overall this won't be a major theme, largely because this is a version of hacking that has been explicitly rejected by many of the people who run and participate in hackerspaces. Cracking, we were told, is the antithesis of genuine hacking. It's a destructive travesty of a creative, productive process. In telling the history of hacker and makerspaces it's therefore just as important to talk about DIY bio, MAKE magazine and the European counter-culture as MIT's Tech Model Railway Club or phreaking (for instance).

From chapter 4 onwards I dive directly into hacker and makerspaces and the conversations we had within them. Chapter 4 asks how hack-erspaces work, and examines the practicalities of how these spaces are initiated, run and imagined. Chapter 5 explores the kinds of practices that go on within them by discussing the idea of the 'hacker spirit', a composite of the characteristics that hackers and makers told us defined their activities. Chapter 6 asks how hacker and makerspaces *really* work, and finds that the answer is community. For many of those that we spoke to, the single defining feature of their hacker or maker-space was its unique sense of community. This, we were told, was what kept their space both operational and distinct from the world around them. Hacker and makerspaces offered an experience of committed, messy, mutualistic community, focused on doing and making things, that was not readily found elsewhere.

From chapter 7 I start to widen the lens again and to reflect on how hackerspaces and the maker movement relate to, and reflect, wider trends and developments. This involves writing with more critical distance from the often infectious enthusiasm of hackers and makers. Chapter 7, for instance, looks at the dark side of community by discuss-ing how some hacker and makerspaces have excluded particular indi-viduals or groups. Hacking's emphasis on 'do-ocracy' can, I suggest, result in rendering invisible the structural inequalities that make it easier for some to make and hack than others. Chapters 8 and 9 turn the focus onto the projects that are developed in hacker and makerspaces. A good project is a 'cool project', and I look at what it is that makes a project cool, from its novelty to whether it gives you 'bragging rights'. I also start to consider more explicitly the relation between hacking as a counter-cultural, subversive activity and the ways in which it is entering the mainstream and becoming commodified. Chapter 10 returns to the wider context of DIY, craft and sourdough baking to ask whether the maker movement is actually anything new. This chapter looks at some of the fancy footwork that is going on in defining the movement and the nature of hacking and making: they are simultaneously revolutionary and ancient; open and accessible and cloistered and elite; and counter-cultural and business-oriented. The final chapter continues this focus on tensions and faultlines that are emerging within hacking and making. In drawing together the arguments of the book I outline some of the key questions that are emerging in terms of what hacking is, who it is for, and what it will do in the world. I also return to the central question that animates the book as a whole: why are hacking and making viewed as so timely, so necessary to this particular socioeconomic moment? I argue that these activities do indeed capture something of the spirit of our times – but not for the reasons that many public commentators are suggesting.

The reader will find more details about the research that is the basis for these arguments in chapter 3, as well as a discussion of the different activities and terms that are being drawn together as the 'maker movement'. In brief, this tells you that the hackers and makers we spoke to tended to use 'hacking' and 'making', and 'hackerspace' and 'makerspace', synonymously. You will probably have noticed that I do the same. Hacking and making is extremely diverse, and some of the tensions that I discuss towards the end of the book do raise questions about the politics of terminology. But for the bulk of my discussion I follow the lead of those who welcomed us into their spaces, and told us about their practices, and use 'hackerspace' as a catch-all for the labs, spaces, places and playgrounds that support hacking and making.

2

Craft, DIY and Active Leisure

It Started With Stitch 'n' Bitch

It started with Stitch 'n' Bitch. Almost overnight, it seemed, it became normal to see people – usually women – knitting on buses, in coffee shops, even in university classes and seminars. This was about 15 years ago, when I was living in London, and it was new: throughout my teenage years knitting, sewing and crafting had been pretty much invisible. These weren't things that your parents did, they were things that your grandparents did – perhaps, and even then often unwillingly (both of my grandmothers hated domestic chores of any kind. I had a great aunt who was a prolific knitter, but she was regarded with a kind of awed fascination by the rest of the family, as weirdly skilled and dedicated). But suddenly, somewhere in the mid-2000s, knitting was something that young women, living in cities, did by choice. It was a fun, sociable activity: you could join a Stitch 'n' Bitch group, find patterns and community online, and read lively, feminist-inflected how-to guides such as Debbie Stoller's *Stitch 'n Bitch: The Knitter's Handbook*.[1] Friends admired each other's handmade scarves (featuring fashionably chunky yarn or technically impressive designs) and swapped patterns. The rise of cool crafting had begun.

This rise has only continued over the last decade. Skills and techniques that were previously viewed as outdated, unnecessary or time-consuming to the point of drudgery are being revived and celebrated.[2] It's not just knitting: sewing and embroidery are currently having a moment, as indicated by the popularity of television shows such as the BBC's Great British Sewing Bee, in which members of the public compete to be named the UK's best home sewer.[3] The *Guardian* newspaper's 'Do Something' campaign has featured furniture upholstery as a potential hobby, and describes growing interest in classes in it.[4]

Meanwhile, websites such as Etsy (the online retailer for 'all things handmade') and Folksy (focusing on modern British craft) simultaneously showcase the possibilities of crafting – encouraging visitors to invest in supplies and get creating on their own account – and enable enthusiastic amateurs to turn professional, selling their homemade ceramics or jewellery or notebooks.[5] The 'artisanal' and handmade are seen as commercially valuable, and thereby as worthy of premium prices – but also as politically and morally important for the maker and user (often the same person). There is talk of 'craftivism'.[6]

This interest in the handmade and creative is an important part of the context of hacking and making. In this chapter I want to introduce this wider context, outlining some of the trends and developments that are concurrent with recent interest in hackerspaces, making, and new fabrication technologies. The key argument I want to make, you will remember, is that hacking is on the increase because it resonates with wider developments in society. Here, then, I outline some of these developments, linking them together through their emphasis on what we might call *active leisure*. I also discuss the ways in which they have been analysed, and in doing so start to develop some tools for thinking about hacking and making. The key question I want to consider is: what, if anything, connects knitting, sourdough baking and blogging?

The New Domesticity

Faythe Levine, the author and filmmaker responsible for the *Handmade Nation* book and documentary (which chart the rise of DIY craft around the US through interviews with over 80 crafters and makers), is clear that crafting is on the increase. She wants to celebrate this: her book is written in a whirl of energy and excitement, telling of the support and encouragement she experienced as she took part in Renegade Craft Fairs, started a gallery, and 'found her people' (a phrase that is echoed by her interviewees) in the burgeoning indie craft movement. Her interviewees include glass artists and bookbinders and seamstresses and stuffed toy makers, but she suggests that, however diverse the practices these crafters engage in, the same kind of spirit connects them together; these, she says, are 'people who were taking their lives into their own hands and creating what they didn't find in their everyday lives'.[7] There was a similar eclecticism to an exhibition held at London's Victoria and Albert Museum in 2011, *Power of Making*, which was co-curated by the UK's Crafts Council. The exhibition – held in the UK's national gallery for the applied arts – featured arts and crafts classed as fine art[8] alongside pieces created by amateurs and enthusiasts, from ceramics to needlework to beaded QR codes and 3D printers. Just as in Levine's account, the exhibition catalogue celebrates the way that craft has moved into the mainstream. Making things, it says, is 'no longer marginalized'.[9] Given that a 2012 'State of the Craft Industry' report published by the Craft and Hobby Association suggested that almost half the US population had engaged in at least one type of crafting activity over the last year,[10] this certainly seems to be the case.

This growth in crafting at the level of the individual (alongside that of the fine arts) has been accentuated, or at least brought into focus, by the turbulent economic times we are living in. After the financial crises of the period 2007–12, and the continuing, tenuous recovery, thriftiness became not only necessary for many people but something of a statement – a sign of respect for straitened times. Cookbooks such as Delia Smith's *Frugal Food* (re-issued from the 1970s) or Jack Monroe's guide to feeding a family on £10 a week[11] show how to make the most of cheap ingredients and re-use scraps and leftovers. In the US, thrift stores such as Goodwill have boomed as customers became unwilling to pay retail prices.[12] Knowing how to take a skirt hem up or down, or preserve a glut of summer vegetables, is financially important as well as personally satisfying. More subtly, it has became hip to re-use and repair, rather than give up on your broken belongings and engage in another round of conspicuous consumption. The Repair Cafe movement, for instance, which started in the Netherlands but which now has locations all over Europe and North America, seeks to promote sustainability by encouraging people to share their knowledge and skills at meet-ups where you can receive help with mending your possessions.[13] In Copenhagen, the cafes are found in the young, hip districts of Nørrebro and Vesterbro, and are an opportunity to learn how to repair anything from clothes to coffee machines.

These developments are not homogeneous. Being interested in craft can look like anything from watching a TV show like the Great British Sewing Bee, choosing to 'make do and mend' your family's clothes, selling your handmade prints on Etsy, or participating in guerrilla knitting missions (where public spaces are 'graffiti-ed' with knitted accessories). One way of understanding the rise of these different activities is through what writer Emily Matchar calls the 'New Domesticity': the reinvention, and reclamation, of traditional practices of homemaking.[14] Here crafting is of a piece with related do-it-yourself activities, such as gardening, preserving, home baking and even home schooling. Young, educated professionals are increasingly turning to these traditions, Matchar argues – even to the extent of 'homesteading': trying to live off the land in an entirely self-sufficient manner – out of frustration with work lives that stifle their creativity and freedom and, to boot, offer less and less security. Young people are concerned about their work prospects, so they re-skill by learning craft techniques that they can use in a second business. They don't trust government education programmes, so they home-school their children. And they are worried about the food chain, and the way in which everyday products become pumped full of preservatives, so they shop at farmers markets, preserve their own home-grown produce, and bake their own bread.

Matchar is enthusiastic about many aspects of this New Domesticity. She wants to learn to knit, gets obsessed with homemaking blogs that feature aprons and jam recipes, and thinks people are right to be concerned about the power of large corporations. But she's not entirely convinced by the back-to-nature rhetoric of many of the people she interviews. She writes:

> So many of the values of New Domesticity are wonderful: an emphasis on family, a DIY spirit, a concern for the environment, an unwillingness to be beholden to corporations. But [...] there's also a dark side. An emphasis on DIY as a solution for social problems can disenfranchise those who don't have the time or money to DIY it. A privileging of individual rights over group goods can lead to serious problems, as we've seen with the antivaccination movement. An emphasis on what's 'natural' can be sexist and can disenfranchise men. A negative view of all work as a soul-killing rat race can demoralize ambitious workers and can lead to women's exclusion from potentially promising career paths.[15]

For Matchar, the rise of crafting, whether that's as a fun hobby (as with most Stitch 'n' Bitch-ers) or a viable career option, is very much tied to broader social anxieties about issues such as globalization, healthcare or commercial farming. The DIY mentality enables people to respond to these anxieties by becoming self-sufficient in different ways. Crafters and homesteaders can opt out of the unethical working practices much big business involves by making their own clothes or cleaning products. They can make goods, such as jewellery or kitchenware, that are personally designed for them rather than standardized and mass-produced. They can care for their children in the way they think best by rejecting mainstream childcare practices and education, and take control of their health by growing vegetables or keeping chickens or bees. As with 'craftivism' – the idea that crafting can and should be connected to action for social justice[16] – there is a perceived connection to political choices. Crafting becomes something more than just a hobby. Certainly, not everyone who bakes sourdough bread or does cross stitch or grows tomato plants on their balcony is fully signed up to a self-sufficient lifestyle, or even frames their activities in these terms. But at least some of them do, often in quite public fora – one of Matchar's key interests, for example, is in the influence of domestic bloggers (those homey lifestyle writers who publish their recipes alongside photos of their adorable children, rustic kitchens or homemade tableware).

Matchar's discussion of domestic bloggers – writers like the Pioneer Woman, Soule Mama or Ella Woodward – brings us to the web. The rise of crafting has been almost exactly concurrent with the rise of Web 2.0 – blogging, wikis and social media – and has been intertwined with it.[17] Matchar is clear that blogs, in particular, have been influential in the growth of the New Domesticity: they have enabled knowledge sharing (recipes, tips and tricks, tutorials), built community and 'sold' lifestyles (those adorable children, those gluten-free muffins...). This rise, which has taken place over the last decade and which has resulted in the current dominance of social media tools such as Facebook, Twitter and YouTube, is another important part of the wider context of contemporary making.

On the one hand this is because the near ubiquity of digital communication has created a generation of digital natives who are as at home in sociable online spaces as they are in cafes, bars and classrooms. Email, web fora and social media messaging are taken-for-granted communicative forms, which cannot be clearly distinguished from phone calls or face-to-face discussion. But there may also be something about Web 2.0 tools that specifically enables and supports creativity and collaboration. In his book *Making is Connecting*, David Gauntlett argues that, after a long period in which monolithic, homogeneous broadcast media have dominated, the web now offers new opportunities for people to express themselves through creative projects, to voice their views, and to connect and work with others. For Gauntlett, creativity is both universal and universally beneficial: people are happier, he writes, when they are 'doing or making things for themselves'.[18] Platforms such as YouTube provide a structure by which people can readily share their creations, and then share their comments and feedback on other people's work. Online creation is thus not an individualistic or self-indulgent enterprise. Instances of creativity – whether that is a knitting blog or your personal YouTube channel or the Star Wars Uncut Project, in which fans recreate fifteen-second segments of the *Star Wars* films[19] – are embedded in collaboration and community. They thereby enhance what is known as social capital: the resources gained from being part of communities and networks. Online creativity integrates individuals into communities and provides those communities with meaningful activity and a sense of shared purpose.[20]

The development of Web 2.0 platforms is therefore connected to the rise of crafting and making not only by virtue of the timing being the same. They are related because they both promote similar ways of engaging with the world – a mode that is creative, collaborative and active. The development of contemporary crafting communities has been dependent on online connections, which have enabled knowledge sharing but, more than this, have given crafters a new way to think about what they are doing. Their activities are now something that go beyond the individual (my great-aunt knitting for her family) to bring you into what one researcher refers to as a 'networked social' enterprise[21] (someone knitting for their family, sharing their patterns online, getting feedback, and telling the story of how their ungrateful great-niece never wears that scarf anyway). Community is both mirrored and produced in the online world. You know you are part of a community because you see it performed in the blogs you read and the social networks you are part of. Knitting and blogging and connecting are somehow all the same thing. Everyone is a creator. Everyone is a participant in something bigger than themselves.

In this respect Gauntlett's arguments are in line with others who have written about the emancipatory power of the internet. Clay Shirky's book *Here Comes Everybody* argues that the web is enabling powerful new forms of collective action; like Gauntlett, he suggests that, now, 'everyone is a media outlet', able to produce and curate their own content, from breaking news to travel advice.[22] Web-enabled networks mean that sharing, organizing and, ultimately, changing the world around you are possible in new ways. Not only is everyone now a creator – even a Facebook feed requires curation, as you select photos, think of witty posts and link to friends' videos[23] – but everyone is (or can be) an activist. It's easier to share information, organize with like-minded groups and individuals, and voice your opinions. The web, this line of thinking suggests, is enabling people to participate more, in new kinds of ways. It can support knowledge collation (Wikipedia), protest and collective action (the role of Twitter in the Arab Spring), and community support for those who might feel isolated (Mumsnet). It can empower individuals and build communities.

Serious leisure

The rise of New Domesticity activities, growth in crafting and thriftiness, and online creativity can all be seen as forms of 'serious leisure'. Robert Stebbins, the veteran sociologist who developed the notion that leisure activities can take very different forms and have very different meanings, distinguishes between casual leisure – 'relatively short-lived pleasurable activity requiring little or no special training to enjoy it' – and serious leisure, which involves the 'steady pursuit' of some activity which may, in and of itself, not be immediately satisfying.[24] Casual leisure might involve chatting with friends or watching a movie: it is, Stebbins says, instant gratification that allows one to effectively wind down from physically or intellectually arduous work. (One friend, Stebbins writes, works so hard that his leisure is simply 'Seinfeld and scotch'.) But serious leisure is more deeply meaningful. It is in itself a 'career', involving perseverance, challenges and frustrations, and the gradual accumulation of skills and abilities. Because of this, it is imbued with a richer meaning than casual leisure activities. It allows one to become part of a larger project, and to develop and enrich one's sense of self. One's identity becomes intertwined with the pursuit. Examples of serious leisure 'careers' can include volunteering at a museum or art gallery, dog breeding, becoming a committed marathoner, developing a stamp collection – or being devoted to some craft activity, like tapestry or carpentry.[25]

The notion of serious leisure nicely brings out the seriousness with which the current resurgence in crafting and making is being taken. These activities are exactly not about instant gratification, relaxation or pleasure without pain; rather, their satisfactions are more intangible, derived from overcoming challenges and accessing new personal and social worlds (one discovers oneself as one finds new communities). Stebbins notes that those who work '60 hour weeks' don't tend to need or want such forms of leisure: their identities and energies are entangled with, and directed towards, their professions. His view is that serious leisure activities aid those, like the beneficiaries of early retirement, who have plentiful free time on their hands. Matchar's argument, however, is that even those who have demanding professional careers are no longer finding meaning within them. Their leisure has to be serious, enabling them to form themselves as individual citizens who are part of larger, meaningful projects, because their experience is that their work is not.

Earlier on in this chapter I asked what connects activities like knitting, blogging and baking. One answer is that, as purposeful, long-term activities and interests, they are all forms of serious leisure. Another is that they all incorporate an emphasis on personal empowerment. Crafting, DIY, thriftiness and Web 2.0 are all depicted as tools for taking control of one's life, making choices for oneself rather than accepting what is given, and becoming independent of wider structures and forces (from governments to the tyranny of home decor magazines).

Faythe Levine, the author of *Handmade Nation*, is quite clear that her commitment to crafting comes from the opportunities it presents to seize control of her world. These opportunities are something she wants to see others have as well. She writes:

> For me, sewing, playing music, making art and films, and even writing this book are about having control over my life. I am making my own destiny with what I create, whether it is with the materials I pick, the colors I choose, or the words I write. [...] I hope this book educates, inspires, and provides guidance for others to join the handmade nation.[26]

'Making your own destiny' is a notion that might be applied to other activities. It hints at the frustrations with government and work that are powering the New Domesticity, the financial control that thriftiness and DIY entails, and the autonomy from multinational media producers that personal artistic production brings. It is about not accepting what the world at large has offered you, but actively seeking out what you want, on your own terms. Many of these ideas come together in the *Guardian* newspaper's 'Do Something' campaign mentioned in chapter 1. This monthly magazine, distributed as a part of the *Guardian*'s Saturday edition, offered a standing invitation to try something new and different. As the name suggests, the emphasis is on being active, rather than accepting that you are a passive consumer. Sure, watch movies, but why not start a film club to do so? Take a walk in the countryside – but do so in a way that forces you to talk to strangers. Don't just sleep – learn to lucid dream! At its launch, the campaign Manifesto explained that:

> In this and every issue of our monthly magazine, we invite you to try something new. This isn't a matter of over-ambitious life makeovers that promise a total fresh start, but then just make you feel worse when they fail. Nor need it entail spending money on exotic travel or expensive new hobbies. Instead, it's about the modest but concrete things you can do to broaden your horizons, learn new skills, or implement more beneficial habits.[27]

One iteration of the magazine featured articles on reader recommended walks in the UK countryside, tips on how to get the best from a visit to an art gallery, a guide to becoming a citizen scientist (helping research projects with data collection and analysis), and the resurgence of tea dances. Other editions have featured crafting activities such as knitting and carpentry, cheap home-baking ideas, and more tech-related projects such as learning to make art on your iPad.[28]

The campaign is not unusual. Many lifestyle magazines and services emphasize the power of gaining skills and taking control of your life. Just as with the other developments I've discussed, the campaign emphasizes the value, and accessibility, of everyday craftiness and creativity, and contains links to helpful online resources and communities. But what's particularly interesting about 'Do Something' is that it highlights that these developments as a whole, from making YouTube videos to growing your own food, are exactly about being active – about 'doing something'. The *Guardian* wants you, the reader, to 'try something new', and suggests that by doing so you can 'broaden your horizons, learn new skills, or implement more beneficial habits'. To make the point bluntly, the vision of you, the reader of the 'Do Something' magazine, is that you are not a consumer: you don't sit around on the sofa, reading, but instead actively and consciously go and do interesting things. You take care of yourself by deliberately seeking to broaden your horizons and experience new things; you want to learn, and to acquire new abilities and skills. You are not passive. You do things. To use Faythe Levine's language, you make your own destiny.

Scholars who have written about DIY have suggested that getting involved in DIY activities – whether that's fixing up your house or printing fanzines – comes down to a desire to take control of your life. 'Making your own destiny' by choosing to follow your creative passions, as Faythe Levine did, seems in line with this. Academic Kevin Wehr defines DIY as any project done independently of professionals,[29] a definition which certainly includes individuals' crafting, online creativity and lucid dreaming projects. Wehr argues that such DIY is an expression of a desire to avoid the control of impersonal systems, such as government or the market, and instead to be self-reliant in your needs or entertainment. This desire is heightened not only by necessity – many people get involved in DIY simply to save money – but because we live in an age when it's easy to feel powerless. The world, Wehr writes, feels 'increasingly unmanageable':[30] governments ignore us, our workplaces make decisions over our heads, and terrible, tragic things happen to us, our families and people on the other side of the world. By DIY-ing anything from our education to home decor or food supply, we seek to live our lives outside of the control of experts or bureaucracies, and to rely on our own knowledge and know-how. We 'take back' some agency. This is certainly Wehr's own experience. He writes about building a chicken coop for his yard, growing his own vegetables and repairing his car: 'I feel', he says, 'that if I know how things work, I have more control'.[31]

The irony is, of course, that these efforts to escape the power of markets and bureaucracies are themselves constantly being commodified – with the 'Do Something' campaign being a case in point. However laudable the campaign's aims, and however helpful its tips and suggestions, the *Guardian* is selling itself (boosting sales and circulation) by selling a particular version of its readers. It strokes our egos, entices us with potential lifestyle changes (I've definitely been seduced by visions of myself as a committed aqua-hiker, jam-maker, or successful internet dater), and turns us into ever more committed users of the services the *Guardian* provides. However counter-cultural the thinking behind DIY is, then, it is constantly being absorbed back into the market and turned into something that can be consumed. TV channels broadcast home renovation shows that allow us to passively consume the DIY vision without doing any of the work. Hobby stores sell products, from kits to tools to materials, designed for crafters and DIY-ers, often with marketing and branding targeted at this type of consumer. And online retailers such as Etsy allow people to purchase 'artisan' products, and thus buy into the lifestyle of the crafter, while simultaneously boosting capitalist markets (Etsy is a for-profit business). One scholar of DIY distinguishes between 'pro-active' and 're-active' forms of DIY, the latter involving 'activities mediated through the agency of kits, templates or patterns and involving the assembly of predetermined components', while the former emphasizes 'skilled manipulation of raw materials'.[32] Some forms of DIY, in other words, are more DIY than others. Some of us are quite happy for our apparently self-reliant and quirky hobbies to rely on consumer products.

It's not surprising that the figure of the active, engaged crafter or DIY-er is one that is ripe for commodification. There are many admirable features of the lifestyles I've discussed, including creativity, an eye to sustainability, and independence. Crafting and DIY are currently hip, but they're also associated with what might be viewed as the ideal citizen: a politically thoughtful, proactive and responsible individual. By 'doing something', whatever that might be, these citizens enhance social capital (as we saw in Gauntlett's account of Web 2.0 creativity), respond to environmental challenges (by fixing rather than buying) and take responsibility for their lives (by crafting and gardening their way towards self-reliance). These counter-cultural and alternative characteristics of the DIY-er are exactly what make them an attractive lifestyle to sell. What emerges, then, is a dance between commodification and resistance, as markets try to subsume counter-cultural self-reliance into their logics, and (some) DIY-ers resist that. These active pursuits can be understood as standing at the intersection between opting in and opting out, mainstream and counter-culture, and consumption and resistance. Their practice may go in one direction or the other – or indeed both.

The pleasures of making

However emancipatory people's experiences of crafting, DIY and other forms of serious leisure seem to be, then, there are good reasons not to take these practices at their face value. Even self-reliance can be com-modified and, perhaps, end up supporting the very structures – such as global capitalism – that it seems to subvert. But it's also worth asking whether these dynamics of consumption and resistance are all that's going on in the rise of crafting and creativity. Can we explain Stitch 'n' Bitch, or sourdough baking, or the Great British Sewing Bee, solely with reference to a desire for control, the commodification of the counter-culture, and personal self-actualization?

I am not sure that we can. There also seems to be a satisfaction and pleasure in the practice of craftwork, creativity and the hands-on in and of itself. As many authors have suggested, creating things with our hands is something that feels good to do. Philosopher-turned-motorcycle mechanic Matthew B. Crawford, for instance, has argued that we lose something fundamental to our satisfaction in life when we lose touch with the hands-on and become completely absorbed in 'knowledge worker' careers and passive, consumption-oriented leisure activities.[33] Crafting things – whether that is fixing a motor-bike or making your own clothes – has, Crawford argues, an intrinsic satisfaction derived from the process of learning we go through, the problems we overcome, and a sense of pride in our work. Similarly, Richard Sennett has celebrated the work of the 'craftsman' (sic) in a book that suggests that craftwork should be seen a template for living.[34] Craftwork allows us to feel the satisfaction of a job done carefully and well and anchors us in 'tangible reality'.[35] There is something special, Sennett suggests, about engagement with the material world. Such engagement unites 'the head and the hand' in a process that is funda-mentally and importantly human – part of our human condition.

What this suggests, then, is that among the many reasons more people are getting involved in crafts and DIY is quite simply that they *like* doing these things, and in particular that they like the engagement with the physical world that it entails. Kneading bread is satisfying. Making a stop-motion video feels fun. Working with yarn to make scarves or socks occupies your hands in a way that feels productive. Even when the material you are working with is recalcitrant, or resistant – when your solder won't melt or your fingers are stiff from crocheting – there is something joyful about (eventually) conquering it, fixing the problem and getting the material to behave as you want it to. It is therefore important to remember that the motivations and drivers behind these active leisure pursuits and DIY activities will inevitably be tied to the materials and practices that they involve, as well as to the desire to take back control or to be on-trend. Such activities involve pleasure, as well as resistance to consumption, thriftiness or simply being fashionable. Another way of putting this might be to say that these activities are always specific – always tied to particular combinations of people, materials and practices. Whatever is going on in crafts, or online creativity, or New Domesticity will always be related to the specific properties of the stuff that is being worked on. People take control of their lives through DIY in part *because* they enjoy building or painting, or through craft because they like the experience of knitting yarn, or through homesteading because they care deeply about the production, taste and preparation of food. Political concerns are mediated through the properties and experiences of particular materials.

One might say that these questions ultimately come down to the nature of democracy in our societies. DIY can be understood in terms of individuals attempting to regain some control over their lives within a chaotic and largely uncontrollable world. It might thus be seen as a process of *democratization* – a means by which democracy is enhanced as ordinary people reject the expertise and edicts of elites to make their own decisions about style, livelihood or leisure. From homeowners refusing to employ a professional painter-decorator in the first half of the twentieth century (a trend which drew ire from professional associations[36] because it threatened their expertise and thereby business) to today's crafting entrepreneurs who give up jobs in the 'system' – lawyers, civil servants or teachers – to become Etsy sellers, these active pursuits seem to offer an opportunity for citizens to become more powerful in a tangible and immediate way. DIY, the design scholar Paul Atkinson writes, has:

> acted as a democratizing agency. This has occurred in a number of ways: giving people independence and self-reliance, freedom from professional help, encouraging dissemination and adoption of modernist design principles, providing an opportunity to create more personal meaning in their own environments or self-identity, and opening up previously gendered or class-bound activities to all.[37]

In the context of design, DIY and crafting can free people from elite-mandated principles of 'good taste' or 'style'. It doesn't matter what the Royal College of Art, the Victoria and Albert Museum or the Museum of Modern Art thinks is good quality or currently on-trend: as a DIY-er, you can paint your living room purple, crochet gold-spangled bikinis, or craft furniture according to your own design. What matters is your personal taste and preferences. (Eventually the dictates may even start to flow in the opposite direction – witness, for instance, interest in 'street style' in the domain of fashion, or outsider art, where the work of ordinary people has become influential.) If you are active, if you do things and express your personality and your style and taste, then you have the opportunity to take on more power in a society that may still tend to follow the lead of a few powerful individuals or cliques.

It was these kinds of arguments that originally got me interested in hacking and making. Like any other elite pursuit, scientific and technological research can be a closed circle which is difficult for citizens to access, understand and participate in. Over the last century or so, the places that new technologies are developed – like university laboratories or industry workshops – have been closed to those without the right kind of credentials. Only a handful of people were able to try out nascent computing technologies (in the 1980s), or to access the tools needed for sequencing DNA (in the 1990s). Scientists have largely governed themselves, with little intervention from wider society. If DIY has enabled the democratization of design, allowing citizens to make their own decisions about 'taste' and to use its tools for their own purposes, the same thing certainly hasn't happened for science and technology. Even today the resources one requires to, say, get involved in cutting-edge biotech research are considerable: multiple university degrees, a position in research or industry, and a set of peer-approved publications, just for starters.

Hacking and making seem to change all this. The development of new fabrication technologies suggests that we are entering an age when scientific instrumentation, such as 3D printers or electron microscopes or the machines that sequence DNA, is within the reach of a much wider range of people.[38] Hacker and makerspaces offer people with no academic credentials or affiliations the opportunity to get up close and personal with technology and knowledge that is at the forefront of technoscientific development. If you want to ask particular research questions, build specific scientific instruments or make your own technologies – well, go ahead and do it. And, certainly, the history of DIY has highlighted the importance of technology in democratization. Access to tools, such as power drills, contributed to a rise in amateur home improvement,[39] and even today new kinds of paints and sealants are making it easier and easier for people with little skill or experience to carry out crafts and DIY.[40] Perhaps hacker and makerspaces are enabling the same kind of democratization of technology that has occurred in design through DIY and crafting. As we've seen, there is plenty of excitement about what could happen through such democratization, and about the potential that access to tools has for citizen-led manufacturing and innovation. If DIY is about citizens taking control of their lives, escaping the dictates of elites about everything from education to decor to food, then maybe new fabrication technologies will enable more people to take control of innovation, industry and science itself.

3

Histories of Hacking and Making
There Should be Diversity in the Hackerspace Movement, He Says

It's a Friday night, and I'm in a crowded bar in Vesterbro, one of the edgier districts in Copenhagen. There's a DJ, a queue at the bar, and plenty of elegant hipsters in black clothes – but, compared with the other bars on the same street, something slightly different is going on. I'm at an event called 'Bits and Beers' and, in addition to the packed bar, the venue I'm in boasts demos and mini-exhibitions of new tech products, a competition to guess the number of batteries in a clear plastic box, and a workshop with a 3D printer and laser cutter. In a room next door, presentations from start-ups are being given to an audience of techies, geeks and interested hackers.

I bump into Theis,[1] who's a member of a hackerspace nearby, and we chat about the event and the hackerspace movement as a whole. Looking around I'm struck by the focused hipness of this space: the sleek outfits, the benches with artfully placed cushions, the well-dressed entrepreneurs with the next big idea. It's a very different aesthetic to that of the hackerspace Theis belongs to, which is in a basement and is piled high with computer parts and machinery to the extent that picking your way through is a challenge if you're wearing a heavy coat. We get talking about recent government investment in hacker and makerspaces, and I ask Theis what he makes of this. (Some people have seen cooperation between hackerspaces and governments as hackerspaces selling out – an idea I'll come back to.) But Theis thinks it's fine. There should be diversity in the hackerspace movement, he says. There's a need for different kinds of spaces, from hip venues like this one to what he calls 'old school' hackerspaces like the one he's a member of. Growth (and funding) is good – in as many different forms as possible.

Theis' comment brings us to the sheer diversity of the maker movement, as well as to the way that it's seen, by participants, as ultimately interconnected. For Theis, the Bits and Beers event and his 'old school' hackerspace, with its small community and quirky feel, were part of the same trend, despite their very different look, feel and (perhaps) demographic. On the face of it, this is surprising. Not all hackerspaces look like Theis' basement hackerspace, or the snappy workshop at the Bits and Beers event. The spaces I've visited range from tiny converted garages in suburbia to hackerspaces in office buildings with hundreds of members. These differences are not just cosmetic, but also relate to terminology. The spaces where hacking and making take place don't all have the same relation to the idea of a hackerspace – some, for instance, call themselves makerspaces, choosing not to publicize the word hacker at all. Others view themselves as part of a movement in DIY biology rather than hacking more generally. Still others feel that they have more similarities with groups like community acrobatics or bike co-ops than other hackerspaces. Despite Theis' celebration of diversity, the question inevitably arises: is this really a coherent movement at all?

Although the notion of hacking has only hit the mainstream recently, there's a fairly well-established history of its development and meaning. This is told by Stephen Levy in his 1984 book *Hackers: Heroes of the Computer Revolution*.[2] Levy argues that the notion of hacking emerged out of MIT in the 1950s and 1960s, as students involved in the Tech Model Railway Club developed ever more complicated track systems, got into early computer programming, and executed practical jokes around campus.[3] This first generation of hackers was followed by two others: the hardware hackers of the 1970s, exemplified by the activities of the Homebrew Computer Club in San Francisco (many of whose members were instrumental in the early years of the personal computing industry, and in particular in the free software movement[4]), and the 'game hackers' of the 1980s, who developed software for early home computers, hacking them into something that was fun as well as useful. Levy argues that across these three generations there is a coherent 'hacker ethic' – a 'philosophy of sharing, openness, decentralization, and getting your hands on machines at any cost to improve the machines and to improve the world'.[5] Transparency and sharing are key – one of the features of Levy's summary of the hacker ethic is that all information should be free – as is the sense that hackers should be judged on their skills, not their backgrounds or education or positions in particular hierarchies. This approach, Levy suggests, can lead to ground-breaking creativity that can change the world. As the book's subtitle, *Heroes of the Computer Revolution*, suggests, Levy sees hackers, across these three generations, as the real force behind the computing revolution of the past forty-odd years.

Levy focuses on hacking in the context of computers, but notes in passing that the ideals he describes can be applied to other kinds of activities. (There are clear connections, for example, between the activities of the Homebrew Computer Club and Stewart Brand's *Whole Earth Catalog*, the 1970s product guide for independent living.[6] Historian of technology Fred Turner has argued that the ethos and community that emerged around the *Whole Earth Catalog* was in many ways instrumental in paving the way for the computing revolution.) But as the ethnographer of open-source coding Gabriella Coleman has suggested, Levy's account – with its focus on particular 'generations' and specific locations such as Boston and San Francisco – still tends to elide the diversity of hackers and hacking.[7] Coleman argues that the notion of the hacker ethic, as codified by Levy, has itself become influential in shaping hacking: once Levy wrote it down, it was widely discussed, shared and adopted by journalists, scholars and hackers themselves. As a code or ethic, it thus not only reflected the way in which the hackers Levy studied comported themselves, but ultimately *changed* it, through being used as an inspiration to many in the hacking community. Levy's book, Coleman writes, 'set into motion a heightened form of reflexivity among hackers'. In practice, there have always been multiple streams within hacking (not all of which subscribed to the ethic as Levy describes it), with multiple genealogies. As the significant amount of space devoted to the term in the *New Hacker's Dictionary* (an online collection of hacker slang[8]) suggests, many other definitions of hacking are also in circulation. Many of these lack Levy's emphasis on specific technologies, such as computing, and on open source as a key ideology. Take, for instance, the following definition of hacking, from the hacker St Jude (Judith Milhon):

> Hacking is the clever circumvention of imposed limits, whether imposed by your government, your IP server, your own personality, or the laws of physics.[9]

St Jude was a computer hacker – an associate of the Homebrew Computer Club and journalist of Silicon Valley digital culture – but her definition only tangentially points to computing. Rather, her notion of hacking is more general: it is about clever ways to defeat limitations, whether they are in ourselves, the systems we interact with, or the world at large. For many hackers, then, hacking is something that goes beyond Levy's definition of the hacker ethic. There may be a connection to computers, an ethos of openess, or a desire to improve the world, but these things are not essential. For hackers like St Jude, hacking is a whole life activity – something that transcends technologies or tools. Rather than an ethic (with its rather moralistic overtones), it's something more like a lifestyle, approach or spirit (an idea I'll come back to in chapter 5).

The rise of hackerspaces

Understanding the movement that has led to the rise in hacker and makerspaces is not as simple as looking for the spaces in which hacking seems to occur. Not only can 'hacking' mean anything from computer programming to managing the limits of your own personality, there are a number of different labels for hackerspaces or hackerspace-like groups: terms I've come across include hacklab, makerspace, DIY bio lab, Fab Lab, or (more formally, and by academics) 'community-based digital fabrication workshop'.[10] Of course, this terminology may not really matter to those using the space. Some of these apparently different kinds of spaces may in practice look pretty much the same: I've visited DIY bio labs that are filled with 3D printers as well as wet lab equipment, and hackerspaces that dabble in food hacking on the side. The differences are often not clear, and many hackers use at least some of these labels interchangeably. But, crucially, the history of these terms, and therefore the imagination of what happens inside the spaces that use them, is somewhat different.

Hackerspaces tend to be the spaces that have the most overt connection to computer hacking as an activity. The hacker ethic, as described by Levy, can be traced back to MIT in the 1950s and then on through the activities of the pioneers of the computing revolution; this history of hacking, then, is one that is tied very specifically to playing with, taking apart and hacking on computers. For at least some hackers and makers, hackerspaces are things that have grown out of computer hacking activities like the 2600 network and 'phreaking' (a technique to gain unauthorized access to long-distance telephone networks, which had its heyday in the 1960s and 1970s). Indeed, what is generally viewed as the very first hackerspace, the Chaos Computer Club in Germany, started (as its name suggests) as a small group focused on discussing computers and related technologies. Founded in the early 1980s, the Chaos Computer Club, or CCC, is still in existence. As well as having a membership in the thousands, and inspiring spin-offs around Europe, it runs a four-yearly Chaos Communication Camp (and a yearly Chaos Communication Congress) – a kind of Burning Man for hackers in the German countryside.

The CCC, and the other hackerspaces that emerged around Germany and the Netherlands in its wake throughout the 1980s and 1990s, viewed computer hacking as part of a very particular context. The CCC has been explicitly political, and concerned with issues such as freedom of information, since its earliest days (with many of its members working in the tradition of white-hat hackers, seeking to expose weaknesses in software systems or poke fun at over-bureaucratic systems[11]). For many in European hackerspaces this emphasis on politics is an essential part of hacking: these hackerspaces are anti-authoritarian, concerned with internet freedom, and (as in Levy's notion of the hacker ethic) committed to the free and open-source software movement.[12] In 2009, Johannes Grenzfurthner and Frank Apunkt Schneider, of the art-technology collective monochrom,[13] reflected on this history in an online essay called 'Hacking the Spaces':

> the first hackerspaces fit best into a countercultural topography consisting of squat houses, alternative cafes, farming cooperatives, collectively run businesses, communes, non-authoritarian childcare centres, and so on. All of these established a tight network for an alternative lifestyle within the heart of bourgeois darkness.... [But] without the political demarcation lines of a cold war society, hackerspaces changed sometimes without even noticing it. The political agenda was mushroomed by individual problems that techno nerds tried to solve in nice fearless atmospheres, non-aggressive states where the aggressiveness of the market was suspended; where one could discuss technical and creative problems and challenges politely with likeminded people. As such, the political approach faded away *en route* into tiny geeky workshop paradises.[14]

For Grenzfurthner and Apunkt Schneider, hackerspaces started off as something inherently counter-cultural. The technology was almost an afterthought: hackerspaces were a more technically minded iteration of squats, communes, cooperative businesses and other alternative venues. But historical changes over the last decades – the fall of the Berlin Wall, the rise of neoliberalism, the slow commodification of the counter-culture – have worked to change the tone of hackerspaces – for the worse, in Grenzfurthner and Apunkt Schneider's view. They've become apolitical, comfortable, inward-focused. They're 'tiny geeky workshop paradises' where people work on their own projects without reflecting (and acting) on the wider justices and injustices of the world around them.

Not everyone would agree with this history of the development of hackerspaces. For many North American hackers, European hackerspaces still remain very much focused on political action, retain-ing a whiff of anarchism and collectivism at the same time as Grenz-furthner and Apunkt Schneider despair at the complacency of those same European spaces.[15] The history that is generally told of hack-erspaces in North America and the rest of the world is much more recent.[16] This history can be dated very precisely, to 2007, when a group of 35 'Hackers on a Plane'[17] flew from DEF CON (an annual computer hackers convention in Las Vegas) straight to the CCC's Chaos Commu-nication Camp. What they saw – 'cool projects, beautiful art, wonderful crafts, creating community, serving community, helping each other, teaching, learning, sharing'[18] – inspired many of them to start their own hackerspaces around the US.

These early spaces, which include NYC Resistor in New York, Noise-bridge in San Francisco and HacDC in Washington DC, have now become famous in their own right. Hackers and makers talk about them with a sense of awe: they hear about them through personal connections or online sources and are inspired by them, or visit and never forget the experience. The success of these early US spaces, and the passion of those behind them, very quickly led to the explosion in hackerspaces around the US, and then the world, that has been so pronounced over the last five years. In some ways the fame of hack-erspaces like NYC Resistor has overtaken that of the CCC and other, earlier, European hackerspaces: many of the spaces that are currently starting up around Europe and beyond are more influenced by the culture of US hackerspaces than by their early German counterparts. In particular, they have an emphasis on hardware hacking alongside software and computer hacking (making the most of emerging fabrica-tion technologies such as affordable 3D printers), and they often have more of an apolitical, leisure-oriented culture of hacking and making (though of course both of these vary greatly from hackerspace to hack-erspace). In the current wave of hackerspaces, hacking is not necessar-ily restricted either to computer-related activities or to a libertarian, anti-authority, justice-oriented stance. Rather than being embedded in the counter-culture in the way that Grenzfurthner and Apunkt Sch-neider describe, they are, at their most basic level, 'simply workshops that are available for rent',[19] and can be used for whatever purpose a making-minded individual might wish.

From makerspaces to DIY bio

Makerspaces often have a similarly generous definition of what can go on inside them. It is, however, much harder to trace a specific history to makerspaces. There's no clearly defined origin story, as there is with 'Hackers on a Plane' for US hackerspaces, and the very openness of the term – making, after all, could imply all kinds of very different activities – means that it tends to be used as a label for a more diverse range of spaces, with a wider range of histories, than hackerspace. Though it's not a trademarked term, the notion of a 'makerspace' is often also implicitly associated with *MAKE* magazine and the suite of commercial enterprises related to it (including the online community makerspace.com). *MAKE* was started in 2005 by Dale Dougherty, who had previously been involved in tech publisher and mover and shaker O'Reilly Media (the business that popularized the term Web 2.0).[20] The magazine, Dougherty writes, was inspired by mid-twentieth-century publications 'like *Popular Mechanics*, which had the attitude, if it's fun, why not do it?'[21] It is, as its name suggests, all about making. It features instructions on how to make anything from bamboo hors d'oeuvre trays to handcrafted drones, alongside stories from inspiring makers, product reviews, and features and facts. The magazine led to Maker Faires (the first took place in the Bay Area in 2006), a now global phenomenon where everyone from garage tinkerers to budding entrepreneurs and established commercial operations set up stalls to showcase their wares – or, more accurately, what they have made, as the emphasis is on showing and telling rather than selling products. The 2011 Phoenix Maker Faire, which took place in a disused parcel of land in the city centre, featured exhibitors displaying everything from fire-breathing robots to lock-picking know-how and homemade wearable TVs; Dave, my colleague, had a stall demonstrating how to brew your own beer. More recently, MAKE has extended to include Maker Shed, an online store selling kits, components and tools, and a 2014 MakerCon, where, at a price, you could join speakers from government and industry to 'discuss the impact of the maker movement and making on education, the economy, and emerging markets'.[22]

MAKE, then, is widely considered to be the commercial wing of the hackerspace movement.[23] Unlike some aspects of old-school hacker culture, it is child-friendly, broadly accessible and business-oriented. (As well as exquisitely branded, its bright aesthetic and chunky font extends across all of its various aspects, and features a patriotic, occasionally star-spangled, red, white and blue palette.) Of course, and importantly, the vast majority of makerspaces have no connection with MAKE itself – indeed, some of the spaces we visited which called themselves makerspaces had far more in common with anarchic, messy hackerspaces like the CCC or San Francisco's Noisebridge. But there is inevitably some transfer between the activities of MAKE and the way in which people imagine makerspaces. Gui Cavalcanti, for instance, who founded the Boston makerspace Artisan's Asylum, draws a distinction between hackerspaces, which he sees as focusing on more techie, computing-oriented activities and as being marked by a tendency to collectivism and activism, and makerspaces, which he thinks are both more open and more professionalized. He explains makerspaces in the following terms (tellingly, he is writing on MAKE's blog):

> Makerspaces, to me, became associated with a drive to enable as many crafts to the most significant extent possible.... whichever crafts were represented in the space were represented with well-considered shop layouts, significant manufacturing infrastructure such as high-voltage electricity and ventilation, lots of supporting tools dedicated to each craft type, and appropriate tooling to accomplish a variety of projects. Each craft area could be used both by hobbyists and professional craftsmen alike, and the act of hosting multiple types of craft in the same space was the magnetic attractor to everyone involved. More often than not, the spaces were structured along the lines of traditional businesses (instead of democratic collectives), due to the significant expense and energy involved in maintaining multiple types of professional-grade craft areas and training new members to use the tools responsibly.[24]

For Cavalcanti, at least, a makerspace is rather more slick than a hackerspace – more business-like, featuring professional-quality equipment, and quite possibly run by dedicated staff. It's also more open. Makerspaces invite the participation of people interested in any kind of making, from woodwork to needlepoint to app development, and of those working at any level from the complete beginner to the small business owner. (He points out how offended a professional carpenter would be if their work was called a 'hack'. In the context of craftwork, the term doesn't necessarily have positive connotations.) Makerspaces, then, tend to have more generalized interests than hackerspaces, and to be more open to commercial structures and interests – both in terms of how they are run and in their membership.

This emphasis on commercial development – something which is present in some hackerspaces, but which doesn't tend to be promoted in quite the same way – brings us to some other important brand names which situate themselves within the maker movement. The first of these is TechShop. The first TechShop opened in 2006, and the business now has some ten locations across the US: it is, its CEO says, the 'first, largest and most popular makerspace'.[25] TechShops are huge (all of the locations are over 15,000 square feet[26]), they are professional (Mark Hatch, the CEO, lists fifty-six different pieces of equipment, from '30 or more design computers' to a quilting machine, that he sees as 'a good start' for a makerspace[27]), and they are loud and explicit cheerleaders for the maker movement (Hatch has written a maker movement manifesto[28]). But TechShop is also squarely a business, and one intent on expansion, while many other makerspaces operate as non-profits, or aim just to scrape by. Though its branding talks about the opportunity to 'come and build your dreams',[29] and Hatch, in his *Maker Movement Manifesto*, writes that the 'best hope for improving the world is us',[30] the company also touts for investors and aims to become the first international, billion-dollar makerspace.[31] Hatch and others like him (such as Chris Anderson, the ex-Wired editor who argues that making will bring the next industrial revolution[32]) are clearly excited about the opportunities that new fabrication technologies present, and in particular the merging of ideas, digital technology and physical making that locations like TechShop enable. They think that a new wave of innovation is emerging, and that this could change the world for the better. Unlike many hackerspaces in the European hackerspace movement, though, the fundamental frame these opportunities are imagined in is that of commercialization and entrepreneurship. 'Changing the world' will be done by creating new products – like Square, the mobile payment technology, or the DODOcase (hip bookbound cases for Apple products), both of which were developed using TechShop facilities. As Hatch writes, 'the distribution and diffusion of easy-to-use, powerful, and cheap access to the right tools are critical to the success of every industrialized economy'.[33]

Fab Lab is another term that essentially refers to a franchise. Fab Labs are associated with the Fab Foundation, a not-for-profit organization that emerged from Neil Gershenfeld's MIT Center for Bits and Atoms. The Center – which researches 'how to turn data into things, and things into data'[34] – is often viewed as having triggered early excitement about the maker movement, thanks in part to Gershenfeld's 2005 book *Fab: The Coming Revolution on your Desktop – From Personal Computers to Personal Fabrication*.[35] The Fab Foundation is its public wing, which supports an international network of Fab Labs which align with its vision. Affiliated Fab Labs are open to the public, support the Fab Lab Charter, contain a standardized set of tools and equipment (including a laser cutter, a milling machine, and an electronics workbench), and collaborate and partner with other labs in the network.[36] Unlike many hacker and makerspaces, Fab Labs also have an explicitly educational mission. They are often attached to universities or schools, and the Fab Foundation also produces formal educational resources for science, engineering and maths teachers. Fab Labs are a global movement: there are now some 200 affiliated labs worldwide from Afghanistan to Burkina Faso.[37]

Hacklab, on the other hand, is a term that is rarely used outside of Europe (though there are a number of hacker and makerspaces that use the language of both hacking and labs in their names – there is a Hacker Lab in California and a HackLab in Toronto, for instance). The researcher and hacker Maxigas distinguishes between hacklabs and hackerspaces, arguing that they have somewhat different histories (with hacklabs peaking in the period 1995–2005). Maxigas traces hacklabs to a mostly Southern European movement of squatting and media activism, in which secure communication became important in supporting and protecting grassroots activism; hacklabs, he writes, 'tended to focus on the adoption of computer networks and media technologies for political uses, spreading access to [the] dispossessed and championing folk creativity'.[38] As the use of the language of 'hacklabs' in the names of contemporary North American hacker and makerspaces suggests, the term seems to have lost its historical meaning, and with it its connotations of political activism and rebellion.

Finally, DIY bio also represents something of a parallel strand of development in the rise of hacking and making. Some hackerspaces incoroporate biohacking into their activities: they might have a wet lab room or bench within the main hackerspace, where members can hack on food or carry out DIY bio experiments. But biohacking also has its own history and a (rising) number of spaces dedicated to it. It's perfectly possible – indeed, perhaps the norm – to use a biohacking lab and work on DIY bio projects without ever really coming into contact with the other kinds of technologies and projects that are part of the hacker and makerspace movement more generally (such as 3D printing, electronics, software hacking). While amateur biology has a long history,[39] DIY bio emerged in its current form in the mid-2000s (sometimes under the moniker of 'garage biology'), at the intersection between personal genomics, the rise of big data and online participation, and the development of more accessible biotechnological tools and techniques. Perhaps inevitably, this emergence was focused in the Bay Area and in Boston, both historical hotbeds of hacker culture. As with the hacker and maker movement more generally, technology has played a key role in the emergence of DIY bio. The development of low-cost, open-source hardware has meant that relatively high-tech activities can now be carried out in an everyday kitchen. (One example is the OpenPCR. PCR machines are a common, but expensive, piece of equipment used in biotechnology; the OpenPCR is sold as a kit for under $600,[40] with the designs – the physical and digital blueprints – available for free.) DIY bio is also particularly well networked, such that designs for DIY equipment are readily shared through the global diybio.org website and discussion list. Community labs and groups emerged in the wake of these online discussions, with some twenty-five currently listed for North America. DIY bio is thus somewhat more centralized than the hackerspace movement as a whole, and perhaps rather less diverse. Its participants, researcher Alessandro Delfanti writes, belong to one of three different groups: 'young biologists, such as graduate or even undergraduate students; computer scientists and geeks who want to tinker with biology; and bioartists interested in applying the critical approach of DIY to biology'.[41]

This centralized approach means that DIY bio activities do not always necessarily intersect with the wider hackerspace movement. Instead – and despite a widely shared desire to open up biotechnology to those outside academia or big pharma – biohacking spaces often have formal or informal connections to universities and private companies. Users of DIY bio spaces may have backgrounds in studying or working in biotech, but use these spaces to pursue side projects, develop their own spin-offs free of university intellectual property (IP) regulations, or, if they are students, get access to hands-on research. DIY bio is viewed as citizen science: there is suspicion of the limiting effects of institutional bureaucracy, the crushing weight of the requirements of commercial biotech, and the cramped nature of contemporary scientific funding. It is thus about escaping the limitations of institutionalized biology, alongside educating the wider public in its tools and techniques. But it also has well-established links to government and regulators, particularly in the US, where a good relationship with the FBI has ensured that some of the early DIY bio spaces (such as GenSpace in New York) have survived and flourished. Finally, DIY biologists are often committed to open-source innovation, and to entrepreneurial activities (an interest in many biohacking spaces, though not a universal one) that utilize models of open IP or copyleft licenses.

Making a movement

The maker movement thus captures a set of very different kinds of groups and organizations, right through from anarchistic collectives to education-oriented communities like the Fab Foundation and the business-mindedness of TechShop. (And this doesn't even start to include more informal or one-off groups and events – like the Bits and Beers networking event I started off this chapter with, or the co-working space, complete with digital fabrication workshop, it was hosted in.[42]) It's also a movement in transition, with new kinds of spaces emerging as hackers and makers diversify and specialize their activities. One newer type of space, which I'll return to in chapter 7, is that of the feminist hackerspace – spaces which have emerged out of critique of the kinds of cultures promoted in other hacker and makerspaces.[43] It's worth asking, then, if there is any coherence between these different kinds of spaces at all. Is this really a single movement?

I think the answer is yes, for two reasons. The first is the technology: all of these different kinds of spaces, and interest in 'making' as a whole (particularly as articulated by people like Mark Hatch and Chris Anderson), are being formed around excitement about new, accessible fabrication technologies. Even DIY bio, with its re-purposing of kitchen equipment and emphasis on low-tech high-tech, makes use of easy-to-build kits for lab technologies (like PCR machines) created using laser cutters. Making physical stuff using digital technologies and networks is becoming easier – and, perhaps more importantly, the very idea of that ease is generating excitement. Not everyone in a hacker or makerspace actually has access to a 3D printer, laser cutter or milling machine, or needs it for their activities. But pretty much everyone is excited about the fact that these technologies are becoming more and more accessible, and thinks that they could change their experience of the world.

The second reason is the language. With a few exceptions (Fab Labs, in my experience, operate as a slightly separate community), hackers and makers use a shared language that very often fails to distinguish between the different spaces that make up the maker movement. This isn't just about shared concepts of the nature of hacking itself; rather, it's about slippages between the terminology of hacker, maker and lab spaces. It's not always clear, in other words, whether you're standing in a hackerspace, a makerspace, a community workshop, or something else entirely: the answer might depend on which of the people in the space you happen to ask. For many users of making-oriented spaces, the differences between hacker and makerspace are academic at best.

One example is TechShop. This is, as we've seen, a chain that situates itself firmly as a makerspace and which is even a very particular type of makerspace, one that is a commercial enterprise. For some people (including some of the hackers and makers we interviewed), TechShop is actually the antithesis of a hackerspace. But it's still found on the hackerspaces.org global map of hackerspaces around the world, and other people – including, again, some that we interviewed – would call it a hackerspace without thinking twice about it. In practice, the distinctions between different kinds of spaces, and their particular genealogies, are not as pronounced as they might appear from the outline I've just given. Few hackers and makers care much about these histories, or indeed about scholarship on the nature of hacking itself. (One hacker we spoke to told us it simply didn't matter whether her space called themselves a hacker or makerspace. 'It's the same thing, you know', she would tell people who quibbled over the name.) Most hackers don't worry about definitions, or where the practice they're engaged in has come from; instead, they take their local instantiation of a hacker or makerspace more or less for granted, and use it according to the terms of reference it provides.

Our research

Which brings us to the voices of hackers and makers themselves. This chapter has focused on what we might call the authorized history of hacking: the rise of hackerspaces, and related organizations, as told by the leaders of the movement (the hackers on a plane, Mark Hatch, the European hacker provocateurs Grenzfurthner and Apunkt Schneider) and historians and scholars of it (Stephen Levy, Gabriella Coleman, Maxigas). By and large, the rest of this book moves away from the accounts of these leaders and trailblazers to explore how the users of hacker and makerspaces understand and carry out hacking and making. Rather than authorized histories or grand visions, it looks at what we might call the *mundane practices* of hackerspace involvement.

As I've mentioned, one reason I got interested in hacking and making was that I'm interested in the different ways that non-scientists make use of science and technology. When I heard about hackerspaces, I was intrigued, not least because they seemed to provide an example of laypeople – non-scientists – accessing new technology on their own terms. I was interested, then, in how people were using hacker and makerspaces. What was it that drew people to these spaces? Was this an example of technology being 'democratized'? Working with a colleague, Dave Conz, I started to visit hackerspaces around the US and to carry out interviews with the people who used them. We were primarily curious about 'normal' users of hacker and makerspaces – not the stars, or the entrepreneurs, or the high-profile founders. Though we spoke to some people who had, or were setting up, hackerspaces, in most cases this was because they were at that stage pretty much the only members of that space. Our focus was therefore on how hacking is part of everyday life for users of hackerspaces, and less on the visions that drive key figures in the hackerspace movement. We wanted to understand the mundane practices that comprise hackerspace involvement, rather than the (perhaps) more lofty rhetoric of the movement as a whole.

In the end we spent time (throughout 2012) in four regions across the US: our home location of Phoenix, Arizona; the Bay Area in California; Boston; and New York. We visited 12 different hackerspaces and carried out more than 30 interviews (some of which were with groups of people). At the same time we followed hackerspace-related debates via email lists (in particular hackerspaces.org's Discuss email list, which has been an essential resource) and as they popped up in the mainstream media. We were given tours of hackerspaces and had their equipment demonstrated to us. We watched as hackers worked on projects or had organizational meetings. We asked questions about how hackerspaces were run and how users had got to hear about them and why they worked on the projects that they did and how they communicated and shared knowledge. We tried, in other words, to understand what happens in hacker and makerspaces and what these activities meant to those participating in them.

This book is the result of this research. Before talking about what we found, though, there are a couple of important things to emphasize about the limits of the research on which the book is based. Firstly, and importantly, this was a highly geographically bounded study. Our interviews and visits were confined to the US (though I've since spent time more informally in hackerspaces around Europe). Though the movement as a whole is an international one, it's inflected in different ways in different places. European hackerspaces, as I've said, tend to be more overtly political than those in the US.[44] Academic Denisa Kera has studied hackerspaces in Singapore and Indonesia; based on her accounts, these spaces are often more grounded in local cultures and needs than those in other parts of the world.[45] Although I draw on public discussion of hackerspaces from around the world, then, the interview data I present focuses on the US context. It's not clear how much the experiences and practices of hackers and makers might differ in other countries and regions.

One of the interesting things about hacker and makerspaces is how material they are. Hacking is often described as a deeply physical, hands-on process; for some hackers, it's exactly that which makes it special. While we asked those we interviewed about this aspect of hackerspace involvement – about people's projects, the materials they worked with and where hackerspaces sourced their materials and their tools – this takes us to a second limitation. This is primarily a study of how people *talk about* hacking and making. It focuses on how people answered our questions about their practices, and on the discussions about hacker and makerspaces that circulate in the public sphere. It can't capture all of the pleasures and pains, many of them hard or impossible to articulate in words, of actually hacking on stuff.

Finally, there's the obvious limitation of any research on a rapidly developing technology or movement: the developments have a tendency to leave you behind. Our interviews were carried out in 2012; I'm writing in 2016; who knows when you are reading this. The aim of the book is to provide a snapshot of a particular moment – one in which, I'll argue, hackers and makers came to embody wider social values and changes. But the movement around hacking and making is not static. For the latest word on hacking straight from the horse's mouth, I encourage you to visit hackerspaces.org, find a hacker or makerspace, and experience what is going on right now for yourself.

4

How Do Hackerspaces Work?

Hacker and Makerspaces Can Look, Feel and Smell Quite Different

The thing I remember most from my first visit to a hackerspace was the smell of burning rubber the 3D printers gave off. The space had two printers – one hacked together from scratch, a second one built from a kit – and both had been in action that evening. Someone was printing some kind of plastic sprocket, a part for something else they were making, and I remember its warmth as it came out of the printer, and the satisfaction of snapping it free from the plastic scaffolding around it. I also remember crowding around the space's laser cutter for a demo and noticing our feet clustered around it, far over the yellow line that was taped on the floor to show the correct place to stand.

Visiting another space, in a different city, what stuck me was how dark it was. Though it was on the second or third floor, the windows were mostly blocked up, and there was little natural daylight. But it didn't feel gloomy. Instead, there were lamps and blinking screens and lots of curtains and sofas. The overall impression was a kind of cosy nest of technology: there were shelves of boxes with wires and cables spilling out of them, sewing machines, and, mounted on one wall, something that looked a lot like a magnetic resonance imaging machine. (Annoyingly, I forgot to ask what this was. An actual MRI scanner? A mock-up? Or something else entirely?) A lot of the colours were bright – reds, oranges, tattered browns – and this added to the sense of warmth, even in a big ex-factory on a cool day.

The largest space we visited was tens of thousands of square feet, and comprised several large halls connected together. Some were devoted to workshop space, and held wooden benches, plastic bins for waste, wall-mounted racks of tools (saws, hammers, spirit levels), and a multitude of presses, grinders, cutters and saws. Vast industrial metal shelving units lined the corridors, piled high with thick slabs of wood and boxes with more materials in. The space was high and echoey, all hard surfaces and harsh sounds; it was another former factory, and had metal beams in its ceiling, some metres up. In its more populated areas there were whiteboards with equations on, homebrewing set-ups, and a bike in the process of being turned into something else. Even on a quiet afternoon, the sound of drilling bounced around the space.

Hacker and makerspaces can look, feel and smell quite different to each other. In one place you'll remember the scent of melting plastic, in another the chewed-up smell of children's toys and nappies. Some are all bright lights and white walls, while others don't contain anything approaching white (though there may be many shades of grimy grey). But there are commonalities. They tend to have the same set of tools and technologies: 3D printers, laser cutters, CNC routers, saws, computer servers and electronics tools (such as soldering irons and meters) are all common. There's a shared language and imagination of hacking and making. And, despite how different the aesthetics and dimensions of hackerspaces can be, there are similarities in how they are run. Hacker and makerspaces are organizations. They don't just happen, but are initiated and managed, often in rather similar ways. This chapter asks how this takes place. How do hacker and makerspaces work?

There are quite a lot of resources available for anyone who wants to start and run a hackerspace. There are a set of 'design patterns'[1] which originated at a Chaos Computer Congress and give advice on everything from how many people you need to start a hackerspace to how to resolve conflicts and why you need comfy chairs. The founder of one of the early US hackerspaces, Eric Michaud, has written a blog series on starting a hackerspace,[2] and John Baichtal, in his book *Hack This*, has a whole section on developing your own hackerspace.[3] Rather than repeating this, this chapter looks at how this kind of advice is used in practice by hackers and makers on the ground. It focuses on what we were told about the origins and organization of the hacker and makerspaces we visited, and the kinds of norms and attitudes that hackers saw as important in this. It explores the work that goes into making and maintaining a hacker or makerspace – the processes that are the 'behind the scenes' of cosy hackerspace caves or echoey ex-factories.

Origin stories

How do hackerspaces start? One of the first spaces we visited, in Arizona, was relatively well established. It was some three years old at the time we visited, and Yan, whom we interviewed there, was one of its founder members. For him, the hackerspace first started to emerge into reality when he visited DEF CON (the hacking conference that also led to the Hackers on a Plane trip) for the first time:

> So actually I went to my first DEF CON in like, I want to say '08 or '07, and I went with one of my peers from college, a fellow alumni. [...] I met some people from Phoenix and we exchanged cards or whatever. And we got back and we were like, That was really awesome. How come there's nothing like that in Phoenix? Because literally the other techies I knew in Phoenix were my coworkers in the IT department and some friends from college, that's about it. So we're like, Why are they here in Vegas when we meet them there and not back home where we all live? What's going on? We need to start something. Do some kind of meet-up or something.

When he got back to Phoenix, Yan started hunting around for something similar to the DEF CON experience. He went to a local meeting associated with 2600, the hacker magazine, but found it full of 'noobs' who just wanted to hack wifi; that, he said, was not what he was after. What he had loved about DEF CON was the mix of technologies – there had been a hardware-hacking village as well as all the software-related stuff – and the sense of meritocracy and openness. The 2600 group seemed a little childish in comparison (a 'bunch of nerds', he told us, 'sitting in a coffee shop and saying, "Oh, look, I'm hacking the wifi"'). But, fortuitously, he met a couple of people who did seem more interesting at the first meeting he attended.

> And they were like, Hey, we want to start up a hackerspace. And I'm like, I don't know what that is, but it sounds cool. And so I was like, Yeah, give me the details. And so that's how it started. We were going to meet up at the Police Lodge in two weeks, come and bring your ideas because we want to make this thing a reality. So it was an exciting meeting.

That meeting – held in a backroom of a local police fraternity – became the first of a series. Yan was thrilled: in contrast to the 2600 meeting, which he thought was a bit 'meh', the first meeting of what became the hackerspace was full of 'eager people who wanted to make stuff'. A core group of six to ten people would get together, work on some small, portable projects they would bring along, and discuss the possibilities for a more permanent space. But after a while Yan got frustrated. It was clear, he said, that the hackerspace was having 'trouble getting off the ground'. It was great to be meeting, but having a borrowed, temporary space where you had to clean everything up at the end of the evening simply wasn't very productive. He knew of a local co-working space; maybe the hackerspace could move in there?

This is what ended up happening. The co-working space offered them some room – 'two workbenches and a soldering bench', said Yan, but still something they could use around the clock and which they could run classes from. The core group built up a community, something that itself was a challenge: Yan and the other founder members fought hard to persuade people that this was their project and their responsibility, as well as that of the 'leaders'. The group applied for non-profit status and eventually found a space of their own. By the time we visited them they'd been in this new space – an old shop on the city's Main Street – for nine months and were solvent enough to have acquired a swathe of equipment, from a homemade 3D printer known as a 'fakerbot' to a laser cutter shipped from China. The space felt comfortably lived-in, full of people and tools and books and comfy chairs and discarded pizza boxes. Part of the reason the hackerspace chose the Main Street location, Yan told us, was that they wanted to be close to 'food and places people wanted to be'. Membership was growing, they'd received some press coverage, and when we asked Yan where he thought the space would be in five years' time he was ebullient enough to say that, based on their past growth, 'it could be anything'.

The hackerspace that Clare was involved in setting up was at a much earlier stage in its development when we visited. We happened to be in town on the evening of the event that inaugurated their physical space, and went along for the party (along with visiting hackers and makers from all over the city). Not that the space was empty: housed in a garage in a residential neighbourhood in New York City, it already had brightly painted walls, piles of boxes and half-finished projects, and a set of the obligatory beat-up sofas. Clare had been in New York for a year or so, and had been a member of a hackerspace in Alabama before she moved. 'I always knew', she told us, 'I wanted to start one up here.'

> Because there's so much space and it's cheap space too. So in January I made a post on Reddit just saying, this is an idea I have. You can see it's worked in these other places. Would it work here? And we got – how many showed up to the first meeting? Fifteen or twenty to the first meeting, which was at the bar that's below our apartment. And then we started having meetings and ten people were coming regularly. And then we had I think twelve people actually make monthly dues, like start paying in April.

We were speaking in June, just a few months after her tentative enquiry on Reddit. As well as finding themselves a permanent space and beginning to set themselves up as an official organization – they were still discussing, Clare said, whether to become a for-profit or not-for-profit entity – the group had completed a number of projects. They had built a fire-breathing dragon for a local parade, run classes on composting and brewing (using their apartments and yards as locations for these), and acquired an old piano which they were planning to fix up with LEDs and a plexiglass cover. Clare herself was an artist and was planning on installing a darkroom in the space; she also used the sewing machines the space had and was hoping, eventually, to get some woodworking equipment into it. She was thrilled but a little overwhelmed by the number of people who had come to their first open evening, not least because she didn't want to attract too much attention from their neighbours (good neighbours are key to a successful hackerspace. The hackerspace Design Patterns note that you don't want neighbours who are too 'picky'[4]). And, like Yan, she was thinking big. She saw hackerspaces as an essential public service, something that everyone should be able to access:

> People say, there's already hackerspaces elsewhere, why would you put one [here]? Hackerspaces are like libraries. You don't have one for New York City, you have branches everywhere. And ideally there should be a hackerspace on every block. Just a place for people to go share ideas, share space, share tools and resources. People in New York, in a tiny New York apartment, can't have a band saw and a table saw and a drill press and stuff, so you have these people pooling resources, and pooling skills even.... I want classes here. Free classes here. I want to provide a lot of classes to the community, just how to set up an operating system. How to set up this, this or that.

Just as the Arizonan hackerspace Yan was part of had made a conscious decision to set up on Main Street, close to restaurants and take-aways and other services, Clare was highly attuned to their local community. Part of the reason she thought it was important to have hackerspace 'branches' around the city was that each neighbourhood had its own feel and its own needs. 'We want to help', she said, and you could only help if you knew your community well enough to understand what its schools and parks and residents needed. That was one reason the dragon the hackerspace had built for a local parade had been a good project: it got people out of the space and involved in local events.

Clare and Yan's accounts of how their hackerspaces got up and running were typical. In most of the spaces we visited a community had emerged before a physical space. That community might have developed through personal connections and friendships, through social media and meet-ups, or, as in Clare's case, through a specific search for others interested in hackerspaces. Once a core group had coalesced it woud meet informally, in bars or each other's homes or in a borrowed space (like the Police Lodge for the Arizona space), and start the process of becoming a hackerspace: members would look for a physical space, work out how they were going to organize (how would they make decisions, and was there a need for a leadership structure?), and perhaps think about registering as a non-profit organization. In many cases there was a core, committed group of a few people who were particularly instrumental in pushing the idea into reality – perhaps someone, like Clare, who had had experience of being in a hackerspace already, or who had visited one of the early US spaces and been inspired. After that, spaces would tend to grow rapidly and to receive attention from local media – and indeed from social scientists. One hackerspace I visited told me I was their third anthropologist that year.

'Do-ocracy'

Once set up, there are inevitably organizational issues that hacker and makerspaces have to grapple with. Using the Design Patterns, prior experience from other spaces, or just trial and error, those at the heart of hackerspaces (such as Yan and Clare) have to figure out how to make things run – how to pay the bills, keep the space clean(ish), and find new members, for instance. There can be tensions here, because it is key to the ethos of hackerspaces that their governance – the running of the space – isn't really organized at all. It just happens, sometimes effectively, sometimes not. The assumption within many hacker and makerspaces is that they should be run from the bottom up. Leaders, managers and organizers are viewed with suspicion unless they are steeped in the culture and needs of the general hackerspace membership.

This bottom-up organization can be semi-formalized through the notion of 'do-ocracy'. This is famously enshrined in the constitution of Noisebridge, one of the first US hackerspaces, which espouses the notion of do-ocracy alongside its one rule ('be excellent to each other'[5]) and which was often mentioned to us as the source of this model. Many other hackerspaces use some version of it. Do-ocracy is different from democracy, or consensus, or meritocracy. Essentially, it prioritizes the actions of people who turn up and contribute. 'If people are arguing about something [in the hackerspace]', one Boston-based hacker told us, 'and one person just does it, it's done. At least it's done.'

Of course, anything that one person does – whether that's painting the walls pink, donating a new piece of equipment, or installing a webcam – can be undone by someone else. While initiative is seen as important, it's clear that shared decisions and not pissing other members off are also prioritized. So if you really, really want the hackerspace to have pink walls, it's generally considered good practice to ask around and see what other people think before you start painting. If a majority would prefer sea-green, then that might be a better direction to go in. Discussion, negotiation and (to some extent) compromise are therefore also seen as key alongside the more assertive practice of do-ocracy. What is never okay is to not participate in the discussion or the painting and then to complain, after the event, that you actually wanted the walls to be yellow. Explaining how his hackerspace worked, Yan said it was simple, and involved 'community governance': 'The person who is doing it is right. The person who is bitching is wrong. If you don't like it, wait until he is done doing or help him, and then do it yourself.'

Simple, ad-hoc solutions to potentially contentious issues were therefore celebrated as the ideal. One hackerspace had a webcam installed in it which transmitted live to the web: none of the members objected, but a few non-members had visited and found it 'kind of rude' that their image was being streamed without their consent. A discussion emerged within the hackerspace. Should they get rid of the webcam? Could they find some other solution? 'While they were talking', said Ulrik, the hacker who told us the story, 'someone went downstairs and used the laser cutter and made a sign' telling visitors to the space that there was a webcam present, and that they were therefore being recorded. 'Once there was a sign', he said, 'everyone lost interest in having an issue with it and we just moved on.' Similarly, someone else told us about complaints building up about the degree of mess in their space. Eventually one of the members circulated a message: cleaning was happening the following Saturday, they would bring beer, anyone available should come and help. People showed up, did the cleaning, drank the beer – and the issue was dealt with. Maintenance of hacker and makerspaces was therefore viewed as a combination of grassroots activity (the do-ocracy idea) and community discussion. Equity was key. Assuming you, as a member, had met the all-important criteria of participation and activity (turning up and contributing), the hackerspace should be 'a space for all the members equally'.

Bottom-up organization is thus about avoiding structures. The hackerspace shouldn't be defined, or governed, through some kind of rigid set of rules or a fixed and specific mission statement or a tight governance structure. It was always emergent, and as such could be anything its members wanted: if you wanted a knitting area in the space, rather than 3D printers, you needed to make that happen. 'Community governance' meant that ideally, and with perhaps a few prods on issues like tidying up, the hackerspace should more or less run itself. It should, as one hacker told us, be 'natural and democratic'.

This was the ideal. In practice, all of the spaces we visited had some kind of formal leadership structure; often they had a board of directors, with positions such as President, Secretary and Treasurer. This was at times a cause of frustration and annoyance: several people that we spoke to said they'd rather have a completely open, perhaps even anarchic, structure. The result was that in many ways hackerspace governance could look, at least on the surface, 'just like any kind of corporate governance' (as one biohacker noted).

One reason for this was that many of the spaces we visited were registered as non-profit organizations, a legal status which required them to have a board of directors.[6] Once those individuals were named on the paperwork – either because they were the founder members or because they'd been voted into the positions – they often found it hard to share responsibility for the space in the way that they wanted. Decisions might need to be made quickly, particularly in the early stages of a hacker or makerspace, or someone might need to have the final say on a financial decision. Often, we were told, it was simply easier for the rest of the membership to sit back a little, and let the 'officials' bear the brunt of hackerspace administration. Thus, although all of the spaces we visited promoted some kind of grassroots involvement in managing and leading the hackerspace, in practice the degree of responsibility the board ended up taking varied. In some makerspaces (which tended towards more professionalized structures), this leadership team was rather separate from the main membership, taking decisions on behalf of it, while a number of hackerspaces also had boards that met separately and were the main decision-making power. (For Gui Cavalcanti, the founder of the Artisan's Asylum makerspace, hackerspaces are distinguished by their use of 'collectivism, and radical democratic process as a method for making decisions', while makerspaces are more like 'traditional businesses'[7] in their professionalism and use of paid staff.) Other boards, however, met only once or twice a year (particularly in more established hackerspaces), and aimed for decisions to be made collaboratively, in weekly or fortnightly meetings which all members could attend.

Such meetings are another semi-institution of hackerspace organization. They feature, for instance, in the hackerspace Design Patterns, which suggests:

Problem: You want to resolve internal conflicts, exercise democratic decision-making, and discuss recent issues and future plans.

Implementation: Have a regular meeting with possibly all members. Have an agenda and set goals. Make people commit themselves to tasks. Write down minutes of the meeting and post them on a mailing list and/or Wiki.[8]

The spaces we visited tended to have between one and four meetings a month (traditionally, and arbitrarily, on a Tuesday evening[9]) – times when the focus was on members discussing any issues that might have arisen, projects being worked on, or activities that were planned. Though they weren't always as formal as the design patterns suggest ('having an agenda' and 'setting goals' doesn't always come easily), they were generally minuted, led by some of the leadership team, and included votes on decisions to be taken: what tools to purchase, whether to get involved in a local Maker Faire, whether to fund materials for a shared project. They were also used more pragmatically than the emphasis on 'democratic decision-making' in the design patterns might suggest. Ulrik (who told us about the webcam controversy solved through do-ocracy) noted that he didn't think 'people come here to take part in the meeting. That's the night that you're likely to find the most people here'. In Ulrik's hackerspace, at least, the weekly business meeting was simply the best time to get advice, find people to collaborate with, or just hang out with fellow hackers – as well as being a formal opportunity to participate in the organizational life of the hackerspace.

Becoming a member

If this weekly, biweekly or monthly meeting offers an opportunity to see your fellow hackers, what goes on the rest of the time? As we saw from Yan and Clare's descriptions of how their spaces got set up, having a permanent space is a priority for hacker and makerspaces. Even though many groups started meeting informally, in bars or cafes or each other's homes, they were generally working towards getting their own space. A key part of users' definition of a hackerspace is thus exactly that it is a *physical* space, rather than – or as well as – a digital or floating community. Plenty of hackers like to hack at 2am, or straight after a night shift, or all weekend; ideally, then, spaces granted 24-hour access to their members. Of course, some periods remained more popular than others. Part of the pleasure of using the space, for many hackers and makers, was sharing it with others; it therefore made sense to visit at times when you knew others were going to be there.

How open to the wider public hackerspaces were, and saw themselves as being, could vary from space to space. Twenty-four-hour access was generally limited to members, and regulated through keys or door codes to which only certain people were given access. However, many hackers emphasized how open they were to the community that surrounded them, and that the hackerspace aimed to welcome anyone at any time – to be 'accessible to everyone'. On the other hand, a few hackerspaces operated more like private members clubs, into which you had to be invited. This is Tiah, who ran a women-only hackerspace (the need for which I'll return to in chapter 7), talking about this contrast:

> The other [hackerspaces] that I know of are like more hidden from the outside, where there's codes and alarms and everything to get in. And the idea is to sort of have a little space where they can hide out and do their work individually, not necessarily be community-facing the way we are. So we got this place because it has a storefront. It's on the street. There's foot traffic. And there's a studio-like space. It's welcoming. It feels welcoming.

For Tiah, a hackerspace being 'hidden from the outside' wasn't a good thing. While such privacy might in some ways be nice, in that it provides a place where you can 'hide out' and work on your projects, her aim was to be 'welcoming' and 'community-facing'. For her, at least, a hackerspace should be highly permeable to the outside world: it should welcome in passers-by, or at least be visible to them.

However public – or not – the everyday life of the hackerspace was, hackers almost always saw themselves as having some role in broader outreach to the community that surrounded them.[10] More than this, they tended to view such outreach as an essential part of their activities. It was taken for granted that it was important to draw other people into the experience of hacking – those we spoke to talked about wanting to 'grow the community' and 'further the causes of hackerspaces'. Some hackerspaces had, alongside their members' meetings, specific 'public evenings' where anyone could drop in for a tour of the space or to work on their own projects. Some allowed anyone into the space, at any time, as long as there were members present. Almost all ran events, training sessions and workshops where non-members might get an introduction to a particular technology or become certified to use a piece of equipment (some makerspaces, in particular, required you to have such certification before you were allowed to use their heavier machinery – wood lathes and the like). Some spaces we visited operated with an '18 and over' policy, or limited access for non-members.

Hacker and makerspaces might therefore use workshops and classes, funded by donations, or through a set fee, or at the teacher's discretion, to provide training for young people or to otherwise reach groups who normally didn't use the space.

More importantly, these public workshops and activities were seen as a kind of gateway drug into hacking. Hackers and makers were often very aware that public knowledge about hacking and hackerspaces was low, and that many people didn't know what they were missing out on. Some of those that we spoke to had first stumbled across the hackerspace through participating in a course or workshop: once they had visited the space and tried out some of the activities available, they were hooked. Kev, a hacker in an Arizona hackerspace, told us that their workshops and classes offered an easy way into getting involved in the space, giving 'people who maybe are scared to come in or don't have a reason to come in' an incentive to overcoming any fear or awkwardness and getting through the door to 'learn Arduino,[11] learn how to use the metal shop, do the glass fusion stuff'. The workshops thus operated as an accessible first step into hacking and making – a way into a culture which, however much hackerspaces aimed to be open and welcoming, could be experienced as intimidating.

Once someone knew about the hackerspace, liked what went on there, and wanted to become a member, what happened next? Even the most open hackerspaces operated a membership system, to raise funds, if nothing else. Becoming a member generally meant that you committed to paying a certain sum every month, the amount of which might vary depending on your employment status or the type of membership you wanted. A basic membership might cost $50, with a key for 24-hour access to the hackerspace, for instance, while the $100 membership might give you a storage locker where you could leave tools and materials you were working on. Some larger spaces also rented out booths or desks which self-employed members could work from. Being a member would also generally mean that you could vote in members' meetings and run for election on the board – formally have some say, in other words, in how the space was governed and run.

Membership was thus never simply seen as a financial transaction. Spaces tended to vet potential members quite carefully – most explicitly in the spaces which emphasized their private status, but also in those which saw themselves as more open. Applicants were expected to have expressed interest in the space already, for instance by attending public evenings or classes. They often knew existing members, who could vouch for their trustworthiness. Personality and temperament – being 'a little crazy but not too crazy' – was seen as key: an essential question was whether existing members were comfortable hanging out and sharing a space (and operating machinery) alongside this person. Nick, who was part of one of the more private hackerspaces that we visited, talked about this process as a period of 'stalking':

> We invite members. Typically, it might be a friend that someone knows who's of like mind. People who attend our regular [public] meeting nights, we sort of look – I mean, we get to know them. They get to know us really. [...] So when a member identifies someone that they think would be a good fit, we put them in the stalker notebook. And that's pretty much like it sounds. They put a general word out to the group, Hey, there's this person I think that might be a good fit. This is what they do. I know them or met them or they show up on craft night consistently. And in some cases they're a member of another hackerspace that moved here. That's also a way that we find people that are interesting.

This formalized period of 'stalking' was fairly unusual. More common was an implicit attempt to understand whether potential members were a 'good fit' for the space, and to check that they would align with the community of the hackerspace. Nick's space also operated a strict policy of allowing any existing member to veto a potential member; anyone, in other words, could say that they didn't feel comfortable with that person becoming a member and the membership process was stopped there. This, Nick told us, ensured a community in which everybody liked and trusted one another – where people were comfortable with everyone else to the extent that 'you can give your apartment keys to them'. Other spaces tended to have less explicit blackballing systems, but still operated a membership process in which new members were voted in (or not). The emphasis was thus on relationships. Did the potential member seem to have the right attitude to the space? Did they do crazy stuff that might have hurt other people (like using equipment wrongly)? Did they get angry, or get on badly with others in the space? Ultimately, the key question was: did other hackers and makers want to share the space with them?[12]

There was thus a strong sense that membership of a hacker or makerspace was a privilege that shouldn't be taken for granted. It wasn't always that easy to get in, and it was also a privilege that might be revoked if the hackerspace felt that was necessary. There were times, our interviewees told us, when it had been or might be necessary to discipline or throw out members. This could be a vexed issue within a do-ocracy. How should the decision that somebody had crossed the line, and needed to be excluded, be made within an open, grassroots-run space?

Hacker and makerspaces generally tried to keep rules and bureaucracy to a minimum. Though not all were as streamlined as Noisebridge, with its single rule of 'be excellent to each other', we came across very few formal regulations, and those that existed tended to relate to safety (you need to have taken an introductory class before you use the wood shop, don't bring food into the wet lab, no members under 18 because of insurance issues). Brian, in a recently opened space in the New York area, told us that they didn't have formal rules, but the general gist of what was expected was: 'Please don't sleep here, and please don't make this your 9 to 5. And beyond that, respecting each other.' When memberships were revoked, this was often framed as being about 'a bad fit' rather than breaking particular regulations: people had issues with anger, behaved inappropriately towards others in the space, or consistently did things that hurt themselves or others or equipment. From what we were told, such interventions were made relatively rarely, and many spaces had not needed to do anything so drastic. Nor were these sudden decisions. If a member was behaving in a way that concerned other members, this triggered a process of mediation and discussion. Would they change their behaviour? Why not? And, finally, did the hackerspace community agree that that person should be thrown out? Though, occasionally, boards had stepped in to overrule community decisions – or at least to make a decision after prolonged debate – the ideal was that such questions, as with other important issues within the space, should be decided communally.

Online, offline

All of this highlights how central the physical space of the hacker or makerspace is, and how important face-to-face interactions are within it. Classes and workshops, meetings and discussion, and the use of machinery and tools all rely on having a space where people can meet and equipment be installed. But hacker and makerspaces also operate through parallel virtual environments. They have websites, Facebook pages and sometimes Twitter feeds. More importantly, they have wikis, which often contain the most important information about the space (when it's open to the public, how to become a member, what projects members are working on, how the space is set up and governed), email lists, and IRC (internet relay chat) channels (through which users can send instant messages). Several spaces we visited had LED screens through which IRC messages would scroll (such as, when we visited, 'in the space talking to Sarah about hacking').

But the beating heart of online hackerspace communication has to be the email list. Individual spaces often have several, focusing on different aspects of hackerspace life: groups for particular projects or technologies, for instance, or for organizational issues (finances, particular events). But there is almost always one central list for general discussion, where people can post questions, requests, complaints or news: 'we need a team to fix the 3D printer'; 'BBQ at the space tomorrow night!'; 'Wifi module free to a good home'; 'Please clean up after yourself in the wood shop'; 'Arduino class next month'; or, more ominously, 'disagreement in the space'.

The 'discuss' email list therefore acts as a continuation of the interactions that take place within hacker and makerspaces. Many of the people we interviewed told us that issues to be voted on at members' meetings were often debated on the email list beforehand, in order to save time at the meetings; similarly, a request for help with a particular tool or problem on the mailing list could easily segue into further suggestions and assistance at the space. Indeed, for many hackers and makers there wasn't a clear distinction between these forms of communication: as Fee, a hacker in Boston, told us, 'people will be in the space and someone will say, oh, you know, this was just put on the mailing list and then people will talk about it and then email back'. At the same time the email list is, for many spaces, also a format that can bring to the fore disagreement, debate and what often gets called 'drama'. Influenced by online hacking culture more generally (which, as Gabriella Coleman points out, often has an 'abrasive and elitist tone'[13]), and by geeks who have engaged in 'years of flamewars on the Net'[14] (this quote is from the Design Patterns), email communication can be curtly judgemental if not full-on aggressive. As Noisebridge's Wiki notes, of their discuss list: 'It can [...] get a little heated and in-jokey sometimes, but don't fear – the space itself is friendly'.[15]

Hacker and makerspace email lists can be heavily trafficked, with five or ten or fifteen messages a day depending on the space and on what topics are being discussed. They are also notoriously full of 'lurkers' – people who might have visited the space once or twice, or who were members but then moved away, or who are interested in it but don't want to commit – so that the lists can be far larger than actual hackerspace membership (some relatively small spaces we visited had email lists that numbered in the hundreds). Nevertheless, discuss email lists allow a tight community to emerge which intersects in some way with the physical community present in the space. That sense of community tends to be focused on the hackerspace itself, rather than on hacking and making more generally or on broader networks of hacker or makerspaces. Few people that we spoke to, for instance, were members of general email lists (like the hackerspaces.org discussion lists), had strong connections with multiple hackerspaces, or knew about activities or groups that sought to network hacker and makerspace together. One hacker, Lynn, told us that while some people might want US hackerspaces 'under one flag', 'most hackerspaces don't see an upside to doing that'.

For those who were interested, there were (and are) attempts to network and coordinate North American hackerspaces. Hackerspaces. org is obviously a key resource, and several people we interviewed talked about using this to identify hackerspaces in a city or location they were planning on visiting, so that they could meet local hackers. Space Federation and School Factory are two interlinked programmes which aim, respectively, to support the founding and development of hacker and makerspaces and to transform education more generally.[16] Few people we spoke to had heard of these efforts (perhaps because we didn't visit cities where they were particularly active; both are associated with the makerspace Bucketworks in Milwaukee). *MAKE* magazine and its associated activities were occasionally mentioned as providing a network of resources about hacking and making more generally. There is also a hackerspace passport, an idea developed by the founder of Noisebridge and a physical version of which can be bought for a few dollars.[17] The idea is that hackerspaces around the world develop their own stamps, so that travelling hackers can get their passports stamped and have a record of their visits and connections.[18] For us, the hackerspace passport highlighted the different ways in which hacker and makerspaces are and are not connected, and the differing networks they are part of. Some people we spoke to had never heard of the passport, and instead emphasized their connections to other kinds of communities; some had heard of it (they thought) but didn't think their space had a stamp for it – and one space sold us a passport and stamped it straightaway. The message to take is that the *local* community, rather than a wider national or international network, is central to most users' experiences of hackerspaces. While those we spoke to were certainly interested in other hackerspaces, might take the opportunity to visit spaces in different cities or countries, and were often interested, in the abstract, in the idea of some kind of network or federation, connections between hackerspaces in practice tended to be sporadic, personal and informal. It was the organization and maintenance of their local space, rather than a broader movement around hacking and making, that was the focus of hackers' and makers' interests and activities.

How do hacker and makerspaces work? What we've seen is that they function through a tangle of concepts and tools, from email lists to do-ocracy and non-profit organizational status and the legal structures required by this. There are practical issues, certainly, such as the need for a physical space and having the ability to set up a wiki. But more than anything it is people who are important in making hacker and makerspaces function, and in defining what they are. A hacker or makerspace is not a particular kind of physical environment, an organizational structure, or even a group devoted to hacking; rather, any given hackerspace is the sum of its members and their particular interests. This is why so much care and attention is devoted to the process of allowing people to become members of a hackerspace. Once in, any single individual can change the character and aims of the space through their involvement. Hacker and makerspaces shouldn't be seen as a service, or as something whose nature is defined by a core leadership or central ethos. Rather, these spaces need to be owned (financially and emotionally) by those who participate in them, and to take shape according to their interests and passions. Dan, who was involved in a San Francisco hackerspace, told us that:

> there's so many different flavors [of hacker and makerspaces], and each one's going to be whatever its group of members make of it. And we could easily, a year from now, have a different group of primary members that make this completely different. It doesn't have to be any one thing. Our mission statement pretty much says as generically as you can, we like to work on things and teach people about things. And kind of with a focus on electronics and building and stuff like that. But there's nothing, you know, really driving in one path or another. It's really what people make of it. And again, if you've got the gumption to follow through on an idea, that's what we are right then.

The notions of do-ocracy and discussion that were seen as central to hackerspace governance support this sense that, as Dan says, a hackerspace is 'whatever its group of members make of it'. Nothing is fixed: members are invited to make of the space what they will. Having the 'gumption to follow through on an idea' – being active and getting on with things in the way that do-ocracy promotes – is rewarded by seeing your idea realized, and perhaps become influential, within the hackerspace environment. We met Clare earlier in the chapter, and heard how she had gone about prompting the setting up of the brand new hackerspace of which she was part. Clare also told us that hackerspaces should be like libraries, with one on every block, or at least for every community. A hackerspace, then, like a library, reflects its membership and the community it is in. It is something which can be meaningful to different kinds of people, in different kinds of ways. It is what it is, not by virtue of its lineage or its label (Clare told us she found the distinction between hacker and makerspaces meaningless), but by the people it is made up of.

5

The Hacker Spirit
I'm a Big Advocate for this Sort of Lifestyle and Culture

When we started talking to people in hackerspaces, one of the first things we were told was that the word 'hacking' came from an Old English word that meant to make furniture with an axe. Kev – who told us about this etymology – liked the rough and ready feel of this: it fitted with his understanding of what hackerspaces should be like. Kev pointed us to the hacker and open source advocate Eric Scott Raymond's *New Hacker's Dictionary,*[1] which does, indeed, suggest that this was the first sense of the word 'hacker'[2] ('originally, someone who makes furniture with an axe'). But the *Dictionary* also contains 17 other words or phrases incorporating some variant of 'hack', many of which themselves have multiple definitions. Depending on context and tone, hacking can be used to denote anything from being annoyed (hacked off), a process of focused work on a particular object (such as software code: you might hack on a particular program), a quick and dirty fix (something's been hacked up), or a generic greeting (hack, hack). Clearly, the verb 'to hack' contains a lot of nuance.

A key argument of this book is that hacking and making are somehow of the moment – that their growth, and their celebration by governments, the media and business, are in part because of their relation with wider trends in our societies. But this raises the thorny question of what hacking *is*, exactly. (Thorny exactly because of those 17 plus definitions, in one online source alone. Which should one choose?) If we are to relate the growth of hacker and makerspaces to other developments, then we need a clearer sense of what their users believe they are engaged in. What is it that defines, and unites, the activities that go on in hackerspaces? What is hacking?

We've already seen a few answers to this question. In chapter 3 I talked about some of the histories of hackerspaces, and the ways in which hacking has been written about. Writing from the context of computing, author Stephen Levy sees hacking as a 'philosophy of sharing, openness, decentralization, and getting your hands on machines at any cost to improve the machines and to improve the world'.[3] Others – like computer hacker St Jude – view hacking in more general terms, as an approach to overcoming the limitations of the world around you. In practice, there are probably as many definitions of hacking as there are hackers. So this chapter focuses on how the users of hacker and makerspaces talk about the practices they are engaged in. What does hacking mean to hackers and makers?

The hacker spirit

When Dave and I first started visiting hackerspaces, we thought we were primarily going to hear about the activities that went on within them – the stuff that got built, the techniques that were learnt and shared, and the interests that people had. It was these that we imagined as the main focus of those who used hackerspaces, and we expected to spend a lot of time talking about particular projects, technologies and tools. Our initial intuition was that people got involved in hackerspaces so that they could make or do particular things more easily.

This is certainly the case, and we did spend a lot of time talking about different kinds of projects (discussions that I'll come back to in chapter 8). But it quickly became apparent that those we spoke to didn't see hacking as being a discrete, bounded set of activities. It wasn't about programming, or using a CNC router effectively, or making a particular kind of technological object. It wasn't even about the kind of ideals that Levy describes in *Hackers: Heroes of the Computer Revolution*. Some people cared passionately that information should be free, or that everyone should be able to access tools such as computers, but many others weren't even aware that these commitments were part of the pre-history of hacking. Instead our interviewees told us two important things. They said that they were part of a hackerspace because they were hungry for a particular kind of community, and they said that this community was marked by a commitment to a particular kind of lifestyle. To them, hacking wasn't about doing things. It was about being someone.[4]

It was in this way that we started to develop an understanding of hacking as a mindset, or spirit, or ethos. Hacking, people told us, wasn't really about having technical skills or an interest in technology or turning up at a hackerspace once or twice a week. It was an approach you took to your whole life. This, of course, is also suggested by St Jude's definition of hacking. It's an approach to overcoming limits, wherever you experience them.

Some people used the notion of a hacker lifestyle to describe this spirit. Here's an extract from one of the conversations we had about what this lifestyle meant in practice – I'm talking to Kip, who was one of the key figures in a student-run hackerspace.

> Kip: I'm one of the officers at the club. I'm the vice president, right now, of it. So I'm a big advocate for this sort of lifestyle and culture.
> Sarah: It's interesting that you use the word lifestyle.
> Kip: Lifestyle, yeah.
> Sarah: Talk a little bit about what that's like?
> Kip: So you think of the hacker or maker, depending on how you want to describe it, lifestyle – it's just sort of people who really want to understand the world around them. They walk down the street and don't take things for granted as much. They stare at everything and they think, Oh, how does that traffic light work, and if I were to take that apart what would I find in it, and I wonder if I could make it better. It's a constant thing like that.

This is towards the beginning of our conversation, and Kip has started talking by telling us about his involvement in hacker culture: he's an advocate, he finishes off by saying, of this 'sort of lifestyle and culture'. (Like many others we spoke to, he doesn't distinguish between hacking and making; it's all the same 'hacker or maker… lifestyle'.) The idea of advocacy already starts to suggest that this is something important, which goes beyond a particular set of activities – one advocates for things that are important, or meaningful, or worthy. He explains that this lifestyle is a 'constant' attitude or approach, one where you're fundamentally interested in understanding the stuff around you. Hackers stare at everything; they walk around and notice and want to take things apart. Kip went on to describe a hacker friend who wouldn't let themselves buy a Roomba, a robot vacuum cleaner, because they knew they'd end up dissecting it and putting it out of action. Hackers are always switched on, always interested.

If being a hacker is not about being a member of a hackerspace, or participating in particular activities, but instead about having a particular approach to life, then the next question is what exactly characterizes this approach. Kip has already suggested that the desire to understand is an important part of this, and, relatedly, a desire to experiment and to improve (hackers think: 'I wonder if I could make it better'). What emerged as we talked to more and more hackers and makers was a kind of constellation of attributes that were seen as related to hacking but which bled through into people's whole lives; together, they can be taken to represent a kind of 'hacker spirit'. I'll outline these characteristics in the sections that follow.

Making things

For many people we spoke to, an integral part of being a hacker was having the desire to create or make. It didn't really matter what it was you were producing; instead, the expectation was that you would follow your own interests and passions to make original and interesting stuff. This interest in being *generative* was seen as something that bound hackers together. You might make software or you might make giant walking robots or you might make new organisms or you might make sculptural art – but basically you were someone who was interested in 'making new cool things' and 'being your own creator' (to quote two people we spoke to). You were creative rather than destructive.

Let's go back to Kip's experiences to see what that could mean in practice. Kip's interests, as a hacker, were primarily focused around electronics and programming (he described one of the projects he was working on as a kind of 'home-brewed server system'). But he told us about a time when he met a member of another hackerspace on a bus; they got talking, and were delighted to realize they were part of the same community. Kip was fascinated by this woman's hacking activities, which were totally different to his: she made mechanical walkers which required hardly any electronics but did involve quite complicated pneumatics. The final products, Kip said, looked like giant spiders, only with six legs rather than eight. For Kip, even though the materials and methods and products they engaged with were completely different, the woman on the bus was pretty much the same as him. They were both into 'building cool things' – and they therefore had lots in common, and lots to talk about. In fact, the differences in what she did to his own interests only made it more interesting for Kip, who found it incredible that something like that – so mechanical and structural – could be built by an amateur.

Kip and the woman on the bus had a moment of recognition when they met and realized they were both hackers. That recognition was related to making stuff, whether servers or mechanical walkers. That, we were told repeatedly, is what hackers do.[5]

Doing things

Creation is important in hackerspaces. But so is a more general sense of activity – a mode in which people get on with stuff, do rather than talk, and act as proactive participants in what's going on around them (characteristics familiar from the notion of do-ocracy discussed in the previous chapter). Often these two things – making and doing – were conflated in our interviewees' discussions of hacking. Hackerspaces, we were told, were places for people who have a desire to 'make or do'.

The ability to do stuff was actually seen as pretty unusual. This, for instance, is Yan, a member of an Arizona hackerspace, talking about how people in their space operate.

> We action. And what separates us from so many other people in the world is we're not sitting there having a conference, having a focus group, getting approval from the executives, raising the funding with car washes. We're like, what can we do right now to make this thing a reality, even if it's small, even if it's shitty, make the first step, get the ball rolling, see what happens. If it needs to be approved, get it approved. Do the bare minimum. I'm the king of doing the bare minimum.

Talking was viewed as the enemy of making stuff happen. As Yan suggests, too much time is wasted looking for a perfect solution (and holding focus groups to try and understand what that might be). Hackers shouldn't let themselves get overwhelmed by getting approval from authorities, or having a plan for every step of a process. *Action* is what counts, however small-scale and messy and imperfect. Just get something going, and see what happens.

Again, this attitude was understood as applying to one's life generally rather than only to involvement in a hackerspace. It was certainly a mark of how hackerspaces were meant to run: too much bureaucracy and discussion was seen as diminishing the spirit of hackerdom. But it was also relevant to learning (try something out rather than waiting for authorization or accreditation!), projects (don't just have a great idea – do it), business (take a commission, and see what happens), and personal life (don't sit at home – get out and do something). The spirit of doing things was seen as a spirit of experimentation and of freedom. As we were told: don't ask, just do. Done is better than good.

Understanding how things work

In Kip's description of the hacker lifestyle, he emphasized that hackers are people who want to understand the world around them. Many other people we spoke to expressed something similar: hacking, they told us, was about not being content with the 'black boxes' that surround us, whether those are our phones, cars, computer software or food. Hackers are interested in how these things work and are made. As Kip said, even when walking down the street, surrounded by the mundane technology of traffic lights, cars and road systems, hackers see a mystery and want to solve it.

For some hackers this was expressed as a sense of alienation and frustration with the world around them – the sense that most people had lost touch with the realities of creation and production. Kim, for instance, was involved in running a makerspace that incorporated a wide range of activities, from software development to work with textiles and food. 'It's good', she told us, 'to understand how things are made', because too many people think that milk or furniture or kimchi just 'come from the store'. As a hacker you become engaged with the realities of how such products are created and can therefore understand their value. You lose your disconnection from the stuff around you, the alienation that the majority of people experience (and which mechanic-philosopher Matthew Crawford has argued is one of the profound frustrations of our time[6]). Others took seriously the dictum that you didn't really own something unless you had taken it apart and put it back together again: 'you don't want it', one student hacker told us, 'unless you hack it'. Many people were uneasy with the increasingly closed systems that surround us. 'Magical black boxes', such as iPhones or closed source software or webcams or car engines, which are designed to be un-openable and un-alterable (outside of certain delimited options) were at worst an insult to how we are expected to engage with our technologies – and at best a satisying challenge for hackers to overcome.

Making things work better (for you)

Understanding was also seen as tied to improving. If you could understand a system – whether that was a computer or a robot vacuum cleaner or a mobile phone or a piece of furniture – you could not only put it back together in working order (probably), but tweak and alter it so that it worked a little better. Specifically, you could make it work better for *you*, and for your personal needs and situation. This is what Clare had to say about hacking:

> To me, the term hacking is you're wanting to find out how something works and maybe make it better; or to change it in some way that just makes it more useful to you – maybe not even make it better – but it's more useful to you, whether that be garments, or taking apart your computer, whether that be making software to better interface, whatever, fixing up the old piano, that's what hacking is. It's not nefarious, it's not, I'm going to steal your credit cards. It's taking things and making things better and finding out how they work.

Hacking therefore enables people to better control the world around them, making it fit to their needs and desires rather than having to put up with out-of-tune pianos, ill-fitting clothes or awkward software interfaces (to use Clare's examples). As with the emphasis on doing stuff, this is about taking responsibility – actively 'taking charge of your daily life', as someone else told us. This wasn't only about straightforward improvement, though many people were interested in getting the stuff around them to work better. Making things work better for you might also mean adapting them to your quirks or sense of fun or personal aesthetic. Having LEDs integrated into your clothes or magnets fitted under your skin might make the world feel more satisfying for you, and is therefore hacking just as much as developing or improving open-source software is.

Creativity and passion

So hackers make, do, understand and tweak. But the hacker lifestyle, or spirit, as it was presented to us, also involved something more intangible than this set of concrete activities. It was marked by a particular *style* of approaching these things – a disposition, as much as a to-do list. Hackers, hacking and hackerspaces, we were told, were marked by creativity, passion and drive. Hackers cared about what they were doing. They did things because they wanted to, not out of duty or because they were told to. And strange, exciting things could happen when they came together, because their different passions could multiply and go in new directions.

This was perhaps most apparent in some of the really big hacker and makerspaces we visited, where there was scope for very different activities to co-exist in the same space. Katharine, for example, is a member of a makerspace which incorporates wood, machine, welding and fabric shops, and houses anyone from professional jewellers to amateur brewers and bike hackers. She came across the space almost by accident (she was interviewing its founder for an article she was writing), but was immediately hooked on two things in particular: the driven, self-motivated nature of the people there, and the crazy and invigorating mix of activities present. Anything that combined robotics and woodworking, she said, had to be good. She likened the creativity that developed when these different techniques and characters were together in the same space to that which emerges, perforce, when you open the fridge to make dinner and find watermelon, bourbon and turkey. 'There's all sorts of things', she told, us 'that you can do with that that are probably off the beaten track but worth going to find'.[7]

Even when they weren't combining robotics and woodwork (or turkey and watermelon), others also saw the process of hacking as fundamentally creative. Tweaking and making things work better for you means that you have to think in new ways about what objects or technologies can do, hacking them away from their original purpose or design into something new, different and perhaps surprising. Getting on with things – just doing something – requires you to innovate and make do with the materials to hand. Many hackers were also interested in the intersection between what has traditionally been understood as technology – computers, robots, biotech – and what's been understood as art (sculpture, painting, video art, music). Indeed, at times they found it hard to distinguish between these as different fields of activity. Making and creating are intrinsically creative, whatever it is that you happen to be working on, and for whatever purpose.

Learning by doing

If hacking is about innovation and creation, it almost inevitably involves learning. Hackers saw learning new things as fundamental to their activities, not least because they were often guided by their ideas – wanting to integrate technology into their body, or produce art with microbes, or fix the hackerspace's 3D printer – rather than by their knowledge of a particular domain. The people we spoke to therefore only rarely presented themselves as specialists with no interest in activities outside of their personal area of expertise; instead, they tended to pick up different skills (electronics, welding, working with 3D printing software) as and when they were needed for a particular project. If lack of knowledge and experience is no barrier, and if it's important to get on with things and try something out, then you will certainly end up learning quite a lot, including through your failures and mistakes.

This learning process was viewed as something that had to be hands-on and active. If you wanted to learn to weld, you didn't prepare by reading books about welding or going to a college class on it. True knowledge – we were told – is only ever experiential. This, for instance, is Orla, who is involved in a DIY bio-oriented space, talking about what she thinks attracts people to the group.

> I think it's not enough to read an article in a newspaper or a book. There's a difference to the theoretical self-education that you could give yourself to being part of the community and just being among people. And you know, it's almost like cooking. Somebody can tell you, 'This is the recipe. Go and do it.' Or you can look how your mother and grandmother did it. And when it says a pinch of sugar, you understand what it means to make that cake as good as you want it to be.

Head knowledge, gained through reading or lectures or formal education, is never enough. Orla draws a comparison with cooking: in this respect, making cakes is similar to being in the lab and culturing bacteria in that you will never really learn without trying something out for yourself (and engaging with others who already know a technique, whether 'your mother and grandmother' or other hackers in the lab). This ethos wasn't only a personal commitment – the belief that you could learn enough, on the hoof, to meet the needs of your projects and interests – but an approach to teaching as well as to learning. Everyone was expected to make an effort, and to get their hands dirty by trying out tools and techniques that might be outside of their comfort zone. (One Arizona hacker gleefully told us about getting a roomful of teenage girls angle-grinding and welding the first time they visited the space.) It was only through actually doing things, for yourself, that knowledge would 'stick' and become useful to you.

Sharing knowledge

Once you had learnt something, though – once you had become expert in 3D printing or developed a neat programming trick or knew how to use an industrial sewing machine – that knowledge wasn't just yours. A key aspect of the spirit of being a hacker, as people described it to us, was that knowledge was always shared. Your expertise should be available to other people – and, in return, you were part of a community where you could also access knowledge and know-how whenever you needed it.

This was expressed in a number of different ways. For some people, it meant a commitment to the idea of open source (whether that was software, hardware or design). Some of the hackers we spoke to were involved in developing free or open-source software (FOSS) – non-proprietary programs that are collaboratively developed and improved. Others shared or used designs for open hardware, such as the OpenPCR (the low-cost biotech equipment kit and blueprints mentioned in chapter 3). Many others made their own designs for software, 3D printed objects or laser cut patterns available on online repositories such as Thingiverse or YouMagine. Though it was by no means a universal sentiment, some hackers were clear that use and development of open-source products was integral, to them, to being a hacker.[8]

But most people saw their knowledge sharing as taking place on a smaller scale, one that focused on the hackerspace itself. To them there was simply an expectation that you would be generous with your time, knowledge and expertise: if someone had a question you knew the answer to, or was struggling with a technique you'd mastered, or was stuck on something you'd spent a lot of time working on, then there was really no question about the fact that you would do your best to help them out. In the spirit of doing things, there was an expectation that anyone struggling had already made an effort to get their stuff to work. Simply coming with a question and expecting someone else to make the effort for you was not seen as acceptable. But hackerspaces were seen as an environment where you could turn up and learn from other people's experience. If you didn't know anything about electronics, but wanted to build a wall-mounted shelf unit constructed as a lighthouse, with working lights (as one person we spoke to did), you could confidently arrive at a hackerspace and find someone who was willing to give you some tips. (Again, you would be shown *how* to do something – not have it done for you.) This sense of sharing was one of the key themes of our interviewees' discussions of what it meant to be a hacker, as well as one of the great pleasures, they said, of hacking. Hackers, we were told, learnt for themselves, learnt from others, and shared what they knew.

Community

This emphasis on sharing and on learning from others starts to hint at another important aspect of the hacker lifestyle. Contrary to the image of the solitary computer hacker hunched over a laptop in their bedroom, the hackers we spoke to were clear that a sense of community was essential to their activities. It was great to make cool stuff, they said, but it was much better, and more productive, to make cool stuff together.

This community was seen as operating at a number of levels. On the one hand, many people felt part of something that was almost like a fraternity, or family, that was spread across the globe. I've already talked about Kip's delight when he met another hacker on the bus – his sense of recognition, even though his fellow hacker was part of a different hackerspace, and worked on different kinds of projects. Someone else described the sense of 'camaraderie and brotherhood' they encountered as they met other hackers, however different those people might be. Some hackers made a habit of visiting other hackerspaces as they travelled, or even organized specific trips to couchsurf hackerspaces around the world. It was great, one woman told us, to know that she would be warmly welcomed at any hackerspace she happened to visit.

But this community was also important at the local level. Just as sharing knowledge requires the (physical or digital) presence of other people, hackers were understood as best working in relationship with one another. People liked connecting with one another. They liked rubbing shoulders with people who cared passionately about very different things to them – biohacking and textiles, mechanical walkers and server systems – but who were still, somehow, part of the same community because they shared the same spirit. They liked sharing knowledge and meeting people with different experiences and passions. In fact, community was a word that we heard time after time as we talked to people about hacker and makerspaces. Being a hacker, it seems, involves an association with at least some of the different characteristics I've described – a commitment to making things, being active and passionate, acquiring hands-on knowledge – but, perhaps more than anything, it connects you to a group of other people with a sense of shared purpose and identity. 'The community', we were told, 'is what matters'.

'Anyone can hack'

Different people that we spoke to emphasized different features of this hacker lifestyle. Generally, however, it seems that there's a shared sense of hacking as being about doing, making, understanding, tweaking, learning and sharing, and about doing these things enthusiastically, creatively and communally. Taken together, these features give some sense of what it means to live as a hacker or maker. This identity is not about particular skills, projects or memberships (you're not necessarily a hacker or maker just because you pay dues to a hackerspace). Rather, it's a lifestyle where one is constantly thinking, questioning, unpicking, improving, creating and sharing. It's about being active, resisting the taken-for-granted assumptions the world around us presses on us (iPhones can't be tampered with, it's not possible to open doors via a magnet under your skin, you need decades of education to get access to cutting-edge biotechnology).

But if hackers and makers would recognize these ideas, then so would many others. The hacker spirit, as I've outlined it, is curiously non-specific. Unlike Stephen Levy's account of the hacker ethic, it doesn't involve a commitment to information being free or computers being a fundamental right. There's no particular emphasis on technical elitism or the need for expertise before you can be accepted as a member of the hacking community (in contrast to the computer hackers that Gabriella Coleman writes about).[9] This openness implies an obvious question. Is anyone who has the attributes of the hacker spirit a hacker?

Many of the people we spoke to would say yes. If hacking is a lifestyle, something which affects every part of your life and which can be applied to anything from university coursework to cooking, then it's something which is radically open. Anyone can hack, and anyone can be a hacker. More than this, everyone *should* be a hacker. Taking this approach to life was seen as healthy. It empowered people, and enabled them to get more out of their lives.[10]

So, for instance, many of the hackers that we talked to argued that hacking – as it was experienced within hacker and makerspaces, in any case – was accessible to pretty much anyone. You didn't need a degree in science, or to be a professional, or a 'stereotypical math person', or to have been into electronics since you were a child. You could join a biohacking space without knowing how to hold a pipette. Similarly, pretty much any kind of activity you wanted to hack on was fine. The hackerspaces we visited hosted anything from electronics to food preparation to woodwork to mural-painting: the important thing was that people brought their passions and ideas and worked on them. The sense that we got was that everyone had a bit of the hacker in them somewhere. Yan, the Arizonan hacker who talked about the value of action and getting the 'bare minimum' done, said that he thought that anyone who bought region-locked DVDs and circumvented the restrictions on them was a hacker. Someone else, Kim, noted that many of the activities currently being hosted by makerspaces, such as canning or sewing or making your own cloth or wool, were already done by people all over the world without the 'maker' label being applied to them.

Taking up the hacker lifestyle is therefore an option open to everybody. Many people were also explicit about the links between what goes on in hackerspaces and what they saw as very similar practices, such as DIY generally – practices which might involve aspects of the hacker spirit, such as creativity, doing things and tweaking your environment to be better for you, but which took place outside the hackerspace. Hacking was viewed as continuous with other parts of hackers' lives, like growing their own food or doing their own plumbing. Several people told us about growing up in households where their parents or grandparents were tinkerers, or where self-reliance had been an important principle. This was an important framework, they suggested, for their own induction into hacking. Somehow, these activities were the same. There wasn't necessarily a clear distinction between fixing your air-conditioning system when it broke, knowing how to change the oil in your car, growing and preparing your own food, and hacking open-source software to make it work better for you. (Though of course not everyone we spoke to did those things. Hackers could also be pretty single-mindedly focused on their particular passions and projects.)

It's easy to understand why DIY, self-reliance and hacking were seen as similar. If hacking is about a particular kind of lifestyle, one which emphasizes learning by doing, getting on with things and tweaking tools and devices to suit your needs, then it's certainly one that is lived out in other DIY activities. Both DIY and hacking help you to take control of the world around you (whether your technologies or your food supply). And both hacking and DIY were viewed as countercultural in that they provided a way to bypass commercialism and consumption, enabling self-reliance and signalling an approach to life that was active rather than passive. Here's Kate, a hackerspace member from Arizona, drawing a contrast between her lifestyle and that of her flatmate:

> I have a roommate who watches Netflix 24/7, and it drives me insane. I watch three episodes of something and it's like, Okay, it's time to do something. Should I take pictures? Should I microscope? Should I make this circuit? Should I machine stuff? Should I go to the lab and then there's 10,000 more things to do? Oh, my gosh, what will I do with my free time before I'm forced to go to bed and get up and work in the morning? Whereas, she's just like, I just want to watch TV and that's all I want to do, and then I want to go to bed and life is good. And I just don't find content in that.

Kate's point is that she is *active* in her pleasures. She has '10,000 more things to do' and is constantly moving between them: photography, machining stuff, working on stuff at the hackerspace she is a member of. She is not content to passively consume TV as her flatmate does. For her, hacking is just one part of a life that involves doing things, and she sees little difference between her work at the hackerspace and other activities like photography. In fact, her comment could be used as a summary of the hacker lifestyle generally, and its connections with wider activities such as DIY, active hobbies and crafts. 'It's time', she says, 'to do something'.

The contrast Kate draws between herself and her flatmate draws attention to one final important aspect of the hacker lifestyle: it's a choice. Being a hacker is something that is available to everyone, and something – we were told – that is incredibly exciting and valuable. But while hackers and makers were happy to point out the similarities between themselves and DIY-ers, unlockers of regional DVDs or home gardeners, they were also clear that the label couldn't be extended indefinitely. Ultimately – and, again, like Kate's flatmate – not everyone chooses to take up this lifestyle. They prefer a life of passivity.

Not everyone who visits a hacker or makerspace, for instance, has it in them to actually take up the hacker lifestyle. Some, we were told, were the 'wrong people', or 'not our people', in some way (phrasing which resonates with the language of members needing to be 'a good fit', discussed in the previous chapter). Often this was linked to an attitude of passivity and consumption. Our interviewees told stories of visitors to hackerspaces who weren't prepared to step up and get involved (or who did 'crazy stuff' like using equipment in a dangerous way). This is Kate talking about some of the experiences they've had with visitors to the space.

> People are stealing things, because they come in and they're like, Hey, what is this place? Oh, you guys can build stuff for me? And then it's like, No. And then they take the money jar and run. That's happened. But we also see people in here that just don't get it. It's like, Oh, you guys can build things for me? They get the idea that we build things for people. No, you come in here and you work on your project. Oh, what kind of projects can I benefit from? That's not how it works. So you waste time and then the people won't leave.

The hackerspace that Kate is involved in is located in the centre of town and has a big shop window; it's therefore very easy, if you're downtown, to stumble across it. But this can attract, she says, the wrong kind of people – firstly people who are out and out thieves, who grab the money jar and run, but then also people who just 'don't get it'. These are people who see the hackerspace as a *service*. They can only understand the making environment as something that they pay someone to do for them, whether by building stuff ('you guys can build stuff for me?') or from which they'll benefit in the manner of a shareholder. They're not prepared to do, only to have things done for them – and that, Kate says, is simply 'not how it works'. These encounters are frustrating, Kate says at another point, because the hackers in the space 'could have been working'. It's always more useful to be doing things.

Hacking is a lifestyle that is available to anybody, and which can be expressed through other activities – but many people just aren't interested in the attributes that comprise it. They don't understand their own agency, or the possibilities they have. They want to be passive, not active. Such people are the wrong people for hacker and makerspaces. As Kate told us, they actually 'don't want to be in a hackerspace. They're not interested in hacking and they just want to look around and waste their time.'

6

How Do Hackerspaces Really Work?

They Don't Have a Sense of Community that You Find in a Hackerspace

Given the breadth of the hacker spirit – its ready application to different kinds of people or activity – it's not surprising that the hackers and makers we spoke to were generally happy to see parallels between themselves and other kinds of collectives and organizations. For the most part, hacker and makerspaces were viewed as not very different from any other group of people. They functioned in similar ways, and spoke to the same needs and desires, as other organizations or activities in the cultures around them, from bartering collectives to cooperatively run businesses.

This sense of continuity with other groups made it all the more striking when hackers and makers told us that something was definitely not hacking or a hackerspace. In these cases talk of continuity and similarity came to an abrupt stop. A line was drawn in the sand: this thing, or group, or activity just wasn't about hacking, but something else entirely.

This happened, for example, when some people talked about TechShop. Dan was very clear that the TechShop located not far from their hackerspace was simply 'not a hackerspace'. It was:

> membership tool access. But they don't have a sense of community that you find in a hackerspace. [...] It's a business. That's the big line right there, is they're for profit. They're a business. They have a service they sell.

TechShop, Dan said, was a great resource: he was happy that they were there, and many of their members used it occasionally. But they were different to a hackerspace in two key ways: they were about making money and they lacked a 'sense of community'. It was the latter, in particular, that we were told again and again. Community is what makes hackerspaces special, and it's that which sets them apart.

We've already started to see this emphasis on community as central to hacking and making. Community, sharing and learning from one another are key aspects of the hacker spirit. In terms of organization, hacker and makerspaces rely on bottom-up engagement from members: any space is therefore shaped by the community of people who comprise it. It's this notion of community that I want to explore further in this chapter. What exactly are the characteristics of hackerspace community? What do people get out of it that they don't find elsewhere? The creation of community seems to be the hidden motor that drives hacker and makerspaces, and is a key aspect of what is making them expand and multiply. If the organizational ideals and governance mechanisms I described in chapter 4 describe how hackerspaces work, then community helps us understand *why* they do so.

Experiencing community

As we carried out our interviews we would ask people why they used their hacker or makerspace. How had they got involved in their space, and what was it that kept them there? At least as an initial response, we got a lot of different answers. Those we spoke to often emphasized the diversity in users of their space and in their motivations for participating. Hacker and makerspaces, we were told, might be used as a place to run your start-up, a cheap event space, a place to learn a specific skill, or as a 'community centre' or 'clubhouse'. The possibility of accessing tools or resources was a key theme. Many hackers in urban centres didn't have space for their own workshop or 'didn't want to be soldering with their nine-month-old running around', as one hacker, Brian, put it. Others might have the space but simply couldn't afford to install their own shop. Hackers also told us stories of university professors pointing their students in the direction of the hackerspace as a place to develop their own projects, or of being initially drawn to the space by the chance to try out the 3D printer or laser cutter.

But accessing tools was not the whole story – and in many cases, it was almost an aside. Some people that we spoke to did, in fact, have well-equipped workshops at home or at their workplaces; better, in a few cases, than the tools the hackerspaces featured. So the equipment was certainly not the only or the primary draw. What we were told was that though access to tools may have been the initial appeal, hackerspace users often found something much more than that once they became involved in the space. Though they might have come for the 3D printer, they ended up staying because of a certain kind of face-to-face community.

It was this unique sense of community that made hacker and maker-spaces special, and which drove users' involvement in them. The quote below, for instance, is Nick talking about what he valued about the hackerspace he was part of. We had asked him why he had joined: of course, he said, a big part of it was the resources the hackerspace made available to him. He lived in Manhattan and didn't have the space (or sympathetic enough neighbours) to have his own workshop. But more importantly, he said, he liked spending time with people who had the same attitude to life that he had:

> [i]t's hard to relate to other people who don't see the production of origi-nal things as a priority in their life because they have their eight-hour a day job, and that's what they consider their productive outlet. And then anything outside of that is meant to be relaxing and consuming time. I think that's a big part of it. There is a strong sense of camaraderie that comes with being in this community and you want that. And you want to be able to build bonds with people, and maintain them. And so joining hackerspaces is a way to do that that facilitates meeting those people, meeting more people like that, and having a sense of continuity because now you're a part of something and you're held to it. You can go to our open nights if you're not a member. But as a member you feel this con-nection that draws you back to it even if you're not currently engaged in producing something.

Nick values 'the production of original things', and wants to be part of a community which has similar priorities. This, he suggests, is rather unusual. He thus frames his involvement in the hackerspace as related to a contrast between creative, active production, and mainstream culture, which focuses on passive consumption. What he's hungry for, as a member of the hackerspace, is 'camaraderie', 'community', 'con-nection' – ultimately, 'bonds with people' who understand the world as he does. For Nick, and many others, the hackerspace was a place where one could feel at home, not only in terms of the setting – with its tools and comfortable environment – but because of the people around you. It was this that enabled you to feel 'part of something' to which you were committed, and which was thus a 'connection that draws you back'. Other people similarly spoke of their space and its community as a 'family', as providing a 'sense of respect', of 'banding together' or a 'third place' for community outside work and home. Again and again we were told some variant of: 'the community is integral'.

What does this community involve? One important feature was an emphasis on mutuality. *Sharing* was a key theme, whether that was of knowledge, resources, responsibilities or space. Just as the hacker spirit includes the sense that knowledge or skills, once gained, are there to be shared with others, hackers and makers spoke of the hackerspace community as one which was open, mutual and held resources in common. Anything from the hackerspace's tools to raw materials like wood or electronics supplies or the food in the fridge could, up to a point, be seen as available for use by hackerspace members.

This wasn't only about sharing resources – making the most of the tools you couldn't afford to have at home, the donated materials or the homemade cookies someone left in the kitchen. Hackers were also clear that the chores and responsibilities of the space should be shared. You should leave the space in a better condition than you found it in. Share your knowledge and your time if someone needs your help. If you're excited enough about a project, and you share that excitement, others will get involved. Share your designs, your blueprints, your programming, your ideas, in the hackerspace and beyond.

This sense of mutuality and generosity was at times experienced as something almost overwhelming. It was, people told us, something that was radically different to the way in which the outside world functioned, and accounted for much of the 'specialness' of being part of a hacker or makerspace. This is one hacker, Keira, talking about this unusual sense of generosity (the 'walls are short' because, in this makerspace, users rent small booths separated only by short walls, rather than being in full cubicles):

> But this is what I have found so unbelievably special about this community, and again, I think it's because the walls are short, we all have eyeball view of everyone, we all – we all come here and it's like not what I can do for myself, but what can I do for the [space], what can I do for the people.

This community, Keira says, is marked by a kind of altruism – a commitment to the good of the group above what 'I can do for myself'. In plain sight of each other, it's impossible to forget that you are there alongside others and part of the same enterprise. You are interested in looking after the space, improving it and maintaining it, even above your own interests. At a later point Keira's fellow hacker Willow, who was interviewed at the same time, explains that they 'all want to guard this thing'. It was this kind of atmosphere of dedication and openness that explained – people told us – the relatively few issues spaces had had with theft or misuse of equipment. The maintenance and running of spaces depended on volunteer labour, and members were, for the most part, happy to contribute their time and energy. Why would they then spoil the deep trust and sense of mutuality that had built up by selfishly removing resources from the community, or destroying tools that others would get pleasure from using?

Hackers and makers also got *inspiration* from each other through participating in the hackerspace community. Rather than the space housing a collection of individuals, those we spoke to saw others within the community of the hackerspace as deeply relevant to their own projects and activities. You might, for example, collaborate on a shared project, having met new people with complementary interests through the space, or use the hackerspace community as a resource when you were stuck or needed a new skill set or had questions about something. The community was a constant source of surprise and inspiration. 'I love to see', said one biohacker, 'what people are doing and how they're doing it.' Just being around other hackers could excite you and give you new ideas and inspire your own projects and plans. Such inspiration could also be helpful in other aspects of your life: some hackers talked about using what they had picked up in hackerspaces in their professional lives, or in their classwork, if they were students. Nina, for instance, is a member of a student-run hackerspace. Her experience of that space had, she told us, been transformative, both in terms of 'being able to really rely on yourself' and with regard to her studies:

> It's amazing to see somebody's perspective on a thing. Like Charlie, who's the current secretary, loves math. And just listening to him talk about math, you can tell he loves it. And if you can see things through that perspective, it's so much easier to be up doing homework until 2 in the morning on something that usually would be very dry. Just having people around you that are passionate about the things that you're learning is such an encouragement.

As described in the previous chapter, being passionate and creative – being excited about hacking and making and its potential – is a key part of the hacker spirit. This excitement is fired by being part of a hacker or makerspace community: as Nina's experience shows, being around people who are passionate about something can make you excited about it as well. Enthusiasm is infectious; even, in Nina's case, for math. The community that exists within hacker and makerspaces is therefore one which offers inspiration and excitement to its members. It multiplies creativity and the generation of ideas.

Hacker and makerspace communities also involved the simple opportunity to meet like-minded people in a social setting. Involvement wasn't all high-minded projects or learning new skills: it was also a chance to *socialize*, to have fun, to relax, make new friends and partners. Put simply, the hackerspace was a chance to meet new people. For many of those that we spoke to, the opportunity to participate in a community – to be with people who were interesting and like you in some way, and to commit to this group of people – was a key reason for their participation in hacker and makerspaces. When we talked to hackers and makers about the pleasures of hackerspace community, one theme that kept popping up was the dispersed nature of contemporary society. You could be living next door to all sorts of interesting people, we were told, but you might never know it. Hacker and makerspaces were thus a convenient way of drawing these interesting people together so they could find each another. Ulrik, for instance, told us that he didn't really work on projects in the hackerspace he was a part of, as he was more interested in 'the social aspect of the space…just kind of seeing different people and interacting with everybody'. Lynn saw her space as a 'community centre'. Its specific activities – technical courses, public events, the use of its workshops – were less important to her than building strong relationships between its members.

The desire to meet new people, to socialize through one's hacker or makerspace, intersected with a general desire for community that was oriented around face-to-face interaction and *physical spaces* and objects. Hackerspaces could provide a real-world space where people could get together and 'forge connections', and it was this, some people told us, that there was a particular hunger for. As one hacker, Keith, explained, this was about the difference between playing 'Words with Friends' on your phone and coming to the hackerspace for a games evening. Getting out, being with people, interacting face to face: these things made the experience totally different, even if the actual gameplay, what you were doing, was not dissimilar. Hackerspaces similiarly represented an opportunity to rediscover the material world, and to hack on physical objects, in a space shared with others with the same interests. The community found in hacker and makerspaces thus related to a shared desire to better understand, and manipulate, the stuff around us. This was often seen as a sign of the times, and a product of a more general exhaustion with the digital, to the extent that some people related this emphasis on physical interactions to the rapid growth that the hackerspace movement is undergoing. The cultural tide is turning away from the digital, it was argued, and towards the 'magic' of building and making and creating physical things.[1] This is Brian, a member of a New York hackerspace, explaining this appeal:

There's something magical about something that you can actually hold in your hand and interact with in real life. It's – I think it's part of why you see hackerspaces popping up all over the place. Because what people do is they're developing something virtually and they're – we have a need to hold things and to get that tactile pleasure of putting things together. So I think it's very interesting to, like, see how the – sort of how the interest and the number of hackerspaces tracks the shift to knowledge and information work.

We had been talking about the presence of IT start-ups in the building Brian's hackerspace is located in and in the neighbourhood at large; it's an area, Brian noted, that is big on entrepreneurship and software start-ups. But he doesn't think that this emphasis on software and the purely digital will last, exactly because there is something 'magical' about physical objects. His sense is that hackerspaces are 'popping up all over the place' in part because so many people now do 'knowledge and information work' and there is a correlating hunger for the 'tactile pleasure of putting things together'. Others similarly talked about the rise of hackerspaces, and their own use of them, as being related to an exhaustion with digital life. According to these accounts, the hacker and maker movement is growing because it represents a solution to a widespread problem: the networked, immaterial nature of both our personal and professional lives. The community one finds in hacker and makerspaces is powerful exactly because it combines face-to-face interactions between people who share a frustration with this immateriality with the opportunity to get your hands dirty making physical stuff.

Community and social capital

The sense of community that powers hacker and makerspaces is therefore one that mirrors and reinforces the hacker spirit. This community is mutualistic and sharing, inspirational, and enables new connections between like-minded people. It is focused on the physical environment of the hackerspace. At its most fundamental, it allows individuals to find a deep sense of connection to others around them, and a feeling of commonality. For Nick, for instance – whom I quoted at the start of the chapter – this community was premised on having the same interests in creating and hacking, and about being someone who actively creates rather than merely consumes. Essentially, this commonality is about having the hacker spirit, and emphasizing its characteristics of doing, making, understanding, tweaking, learning and sharing in your life.

It is clear that this experience of community was deeply meaning-ful to many of the hackers and makers to whom we spoke. Getting involved in their space had enabled them to 'find their people', begin new stages in their lives, or get fresh inspiration in their creative activi-ties. Such community could be impossible to find elsewhere. Nick told us about a friend who lived out in the country, in upstate New York: she had masses of land and a fully equipped workshop, including a laser cutter. She had all the tools and equipment and space she could possibly need. Why would she bother driving somewhere to hack on stuff, Nick asked, rhetorically, when she could just walk out to her garage? In practice, she was desperate to find a 'traditional hackerspace community'. She wanted to be part of a group of others who thought the same way, and who would inspire her. Of course that made sense, Nick said. For him the hackerspace was a big part of his life even when he wasn't focused on a particular project or didn't feel like hacking on something; maybe he would come there because he didn't feel like being alone, or just wanted to be around others to check out their proj-ects. People told us about meeting partners, friends, housemates and business collaborators through their hacker and makerspaces. They would 'babysit each other's servers and each other's kids' or give one another work when they needed it. Beyond these practical aspects, hacker and makerspaces could offer a sense of belonging that could be transformative. It was for this reason that some of those we spoke to simply didn't see spaces like TechShop in the same category as their hacker or makerspace. If the community wasn't there, then it wasn't at all the same animal.

How to explain and understand this? Clearly what people are getting from participation in hacker and makerspaces goes far beyond access to tools, or even the opportunity to meet others with similar interests. One concept that might help us understand the power of the community that people find in hackerspaces is that of *social capital*. This was popularized by the political scientist Robert Putnam, who rose to prominence with his thesis that the US is now 'bowling alone'. Writing in the early 2000s and focusing on the US context, Putnam was concerned that connections between people were weakening. He described a decline in membership of organizations and associations – such as local bowling leagues – over the last decades and argued that, as Americans became more individualistic and private, social capital was being lost. Social capital is a 'conceptual cousin' of community.[2] It is a kind of resource, one which encompasses a person's networks and communities: as Putnam notes, your 'extended family represents a form of social capital, as do your Sunday school class, the regulars who play poker on your commuter train, your college roommates, the civic organizations to which you belong'.[3] (His examples give a pretty good sense of the kinds of networks Putnam himself is part of.) Some people have lots of social capital and exist in multiple networks and communities. Others have very little. They bowl with the same couple of friends rather than in a league, don't attend religious meetings or other collective gatherings, and focus on private rather than civic life. They have few opportunities to meet new people, or extended networks on which they can call when they hit new or challenging situations in their lives.

Putnam is clear that social capital has benefits both for individuals and for society at large. There are personal benefits to having a lot of social capital: one can use extended networks to find jobs and career opportunities, to access economic or political clout, or engage in collective projects or activities that bring meaning to your life. Social capital also feels good. Connections can ward off loneliness, bring a sense of purpose and enable us to feel part of something bigger than ourselves. But there are also public goods attached to societies with high levels of social capital. Putnam views involvement in different kinds of associations and connections as important because he sees these as shoring up democracy. Though networks and ties may have different purposes – a political party seeking to create an equitable society, a religious group that meets to pray, a hackerspace where people build technical projects together – all of them, however apparently frivolous, have a role to play in enhancing 'civic engagement and social connectedness'.[4] Social capital enables trust, and thereby trust-based societies. 'Dense social ties', Putnam writes, 'facilitate gossip and other valuable ways of cultivating reputation – an essential foundation for trust in a complex society.'[5]

Much has been written about social capital in contemporary societies, and the extent to which it is or is not actually declining. In a sense this doesn't really matter to the discussion here. The larger point is that social capital, in the shape of membership of associations and communities, is something that people may be hungry for. It has important emotional and psychological benefits. Put simply, connecting makes us feel good. According to the hackers and makers we spoke to, connecting through face-to-face interactions, focused around shared passions and commitments, makes us feel especially good. And these kinds of connections are not necessarily that easy to access these days. The urban centres we visited tended to be populated by people who may live far away from their families, who are not as likely to be part of religious communities as they would have been 50 years ago, and who probably don't 'play poker on [their] commuter train' (to use Putnam's example). Putnam is exercised by things like the growth of fast food, and, relatedly, increasingly brief, personality-free encounters in public spaces, as opposed to using a local diner or bar where one knows all the regulars. If he's right, and many people are struggling to develop meaningful social ties in contemporary life, then hacker and makerspaces offer one solution. The community that those we spoke to had found in these spaces offers social capital in spades: engagement in a shared enterprise, opportunities to make new connections and extend one's networks, mutual support and encouragement. We might speculate, then, that the community of hacker and makerspaces is experienced as so special, even life-changing, exactly because such community is not readily found elsewhere in the dispersed, transient, digitized lives of their users. In this respect hackerspaces are operating as what Ray Oldenburg has called 'third places': social spaces, which are not one's home or workplace, where people can 'relax in good company and do so on a regular basis'.[6] They offer an experience of communal life that goes beyond the priorities of work or family to provide entry to a form of mutualistic public life.

The centrality of community to the functioning and meaning of hacker and makerspaces highlights how differently these spaces are being imagined in different contexts. Making cheerleaders such as Mark Hatch or Chris Anderson are excited about the accessibility of new technology and the potential for innovation. The maker movement is important, they suggest, because of its potential to disrupt and rejuvenate (US) innovation, entrepreneurship and business. Public discussion of hacker and makerspaces has often taken a similar line: they are viewed as seedbeds for entrepreneurship and economic growth, providing the skills of the future. Some of those we spoke to were also passionate about these possibilities – but for many others, they were at best a side issue. Our interviewees generally couldn't care less whether they were hacking on high-tech stuff, like biotechnology, or 3D printers, or mobile apps, or low-tech things, like beer or furniture. As we've seen, being a hacker wasn't framed as about your use of technology, new or otherwise; rather, it's about your lifestyle and your place in a particular community. Contrary to talk focusing on 'bits to atoms' or 'transformative tools', it's not about accessing new technology, but relationships. Close, face-to-face community as a defining feature of hackerspaces therefore suggests something surprising: the growth of hacking and making is only partly about technology and its increasing accessibility. For many that we spoke to, ideas like access to tools, democratization of science and technology, or disruptive innovation were not part of their experience of hacking and making. What was more important was accessing community.

Community, then, is central to the hacker and makerspace experience – and indeed to being a hacker or maker more generally. But it's also important to note that this community wasn't experienced unproblematically. At best, it was seen as something rather fragile, to be protected and worked at. At worst, a strong community could act to exclude, intimidate or distract.

I'll discuss the potentially exclusionary character of hacker and makerspaces in more detail in the next chapter. In the rest of this chapter I want to look at how community was crafted and negotiated in the spaces we visited, and in particular how this related to how these spaces were governed. Hacker and makerspaces, as I've argued, *are* their communities. The model of governance they follow relies on a bottom-up, engaged community, which shapes the space through their interests. Do-ocracy and discussion assume that users are constantly working for the space and for each other. What does this creation and management of community look like in practice?

'What's that in the fridge?'

Yan was proud of the hackerspace he was part of. We've heard him tell the story of how it originated (in chapter 4), and when we met him, some years on from those first meetings, he continued to be satisfied with its growth. It was, he told us, famous as a space that *worked*: it had a great community, a nice location, good equipment. People came from all over the world to visit. He was particularly pleased given that they had local 'competitors' who had tried to copy them, but on a more commercial basis. One ex-member had set up his own, TechShop-like makerspace (which quickly failed: membership was widely seen as too expensive), while a local co-working franchise was setting up a hardware section to try and emulate – Yan said – the hackerspace's success. But these places were 'dead and lifeless', more like a 'museum of tools' than a vibrant, active community. They were chasing money and trying to copy a vision that wasn't their own. They were examples of the 'McDonald-ization' of hackerspaces.

Yan was clear that these spaces deserved to fail. They didn't have a genuine sense of community in the way that his own hackerspace did, and because of this they were 'museums' – places that were full of nice tools that no one used, and which were about consumption (buying a service) rather than creation. But he (and other members in his space) was also upfront about the challenges of developing a community that functioned well. Their success hadn't come easily: he and the other founders had, he told us, 'forced people to be grassroots'. They had been clear that the space only got what its members really wanted, when they wanted it enough to act to make it happen. Yan's hackerspace didn't exist as a service – something that provided tools or expertise or even the use of a physical space to people – and it was this that distinguished it from their imitators. It could only be what its members wanted it to be.

This notion of 'forcing people to be grassroots' represents a central tension in the creation of hacker and makerspace communities. People told us, over and over, that community was key to being a hacker or maker, and that genuine community was bottom-up.[7] At the same time, it was clear that this ideal of community – where everyone is active, committed, and fair – was often difficult to realize in practice. Hacker and makerspaces often struggled to self-organize in the way that their users, at least theoretically, believed they should. Yan's space had, by and large, managed to force its members to act in a 'grassroots' way, taking ownership of what they wanted from the hackerspace – but (one might reflect) if you're forcing people to take ownership, is that really a bottom-up development?

The balance between hackerspace members being active or passive is therefore a fine one. The sense we got was often of a continual struggle to encourage all members to step up, rather than letting the space slip back into the hierarchical structures that are more common in the world around it. Here's Winni, for instance, talking about a crisis moment in the hackerspace she was part of. Things had been stagnating, she said, but everyone seemed to be waiting for someone else to fix the problem:

> You've probably noticed this about hackerspaces. It's not like a power pyramid. It's all of the members are – the idea is it's a space for all the members equally. [...] I was like we don't have – there are a lot of things we're unsure about and we don't have policies. We should get together and talk about the problems we have. Like all the members who are active, we should get together and talk about the problems we have and how to change it and how to make it better, how we should go forward in the future. [...] So we had a meta-meeting and everyone had opinions and ideas and everyone was suddenly like a contributor.

The fundamental thing about a hackerspace, Winni says, is that it is not 'a power pyramid...it's a space for all the members equally'. Again, this emphasizes the grassroots nature of the space – the fact that it has to be what its members demand of it. Her experience had been that stagnation in the space, and unwillingness for this grassroots nature to be lived out, was overcome by discussion amongst members. Just having a conversation made it clear that everyone had 'opinions and ideas', and, having expressed those opinions and ideas, people became more active contributors to the space. That one discussion, Winni told us, triggered a new sense of ownership of the space and with it a greater sense of responsibility. At that moment, at least, the space was operating according to its implicit ideals. Its organization was centred around active participation, discussion and a lack of hierarchies.

Meeting these ideals was a long-running issue. Winni's hackerspace had, like many others, a small elected board (the members of which were called 'officers') which was, at least in theory, a nominal position. She'd served on this for two years; ideally, she told us, she would have stepped down after a year but there hadn't been anyone to replace her. Winni was committed to what she saw as a 'hacker culture' of shared responsibilities and ownership, which she saw as empowering people to do what they wanted without worrying too much about what was allowed or not allowed. So she found the difference that the label 'leader', once applied to her, made to other members' perceptions of her, and of their own responsibilities, disorienting:

> I think people were very afraid to do things just on their own, like taking the initiative, and something I totally didn't expect, because I had never been in a leadership position before, is that once you become a leader, people just look to you to do things, look to you for permission. I'm just like no, you can do it, you can do anything that you want to do, you can paint the walls, you can like make something. If you have a project, tell me and I'll find money for you. But everyone was kind of waiting for the officers to make rules or for permission. There wasn't any sense that this space was also theirs.

In practice, other members were often 'afraid' to get involved: far from the space being a functioning do-ocracy, people felt they had to ask permission before decorating the space or starting a project. Everyone was waiting, Winni said, 'for the officers to make rules'. The problem was exactly one of ownership. Members didn't seem to realize that the hackerspace didn't belong to the officers, but to everyone that was involved – and therefore that they had both rights and responsibilities with regard to the running of the space.

The 'meta-meeting' that Winni called in order to talk about the space's direction seemed to help. After that, she said, people became more active and committed, and the space was in some sense rejuvenated. Others that we spoke to (in other spaces) were more pessimistic, and perhaps more cynical. Several people thought that these challenges were an example of the counter-cultural nature of hacker and makerspaces, and the ways in which mainstream culture was leaking into these. People were just too accustomed – we were told – to structures and authority and hierarchies. It was too easy for them to be passive and to expect to be told what to do. Kev, for instance, was a founder member of one hackerspace we visited, and had sat on its board throughout its early stages. 'Communities want to be taken care of', he told us, glumly. Because a central group had been active in setting up the hackerspace, and then became its first board, the expectation had been that they were somehow the ones in charge. People would ask Kev what to do when a particular material ran out in the woodshop, or what was going on with the workshops the space ran. I don't know, Kev would say. I'm not in charge here. He and the other board members 'were fighting like really, really, really, really, really, really hard, to the point of being annoying, that we're not top-down and we're not going to do it for you'. But it was hard to get the message across, and Kev could see it getting harder as they got more 'mainstream'. The people who came in off the street, or from their public advertising, didn't always have the 'hacker spirit', he told us, of self-reliance and independence.

A community's expectation of being 'taken care of', to use Kev's words, was often expressed through a lack of engagement with the needs of the space. Problems could emerge in terms of getting things done. The trash doesn't get taken out. The space is never cleaned. (Or the fridge. 'What's that in the fridge?' one hacker asked, rehearsing a typical argument that might take place in their hackerspace. 'Some of that has probably mutated'.) Projects fold as users lose interest. Tools or machinery aren't maintained as well as they should be. More seriously – as in Winni's experience – it might be that no one is prepared to step up to a leadership role, or to take on boring but essential administrative tasks (web maintenance, financial accounting, fundraising).

Most people treated these inefficiencies as annoying but inevitable, and as relatively easily solved by tirades on the mailing list or by particular individuals stepping up (to organize a cleaning day, for instance). Again, the problem was seen as one of ownership. When 'it's everyone's responsibility, sometimes it becomes no one's responsibility', said Kip, talking about the challenges of keeping their space 'clean and alive'. On the other hand, there could also be a tendency to let action get derailed by discussion, and for hackerspace admin to become overly convoluted in an attempt to satisfy everyone's needs.

In these cases, hackerspace members were ignoring the 'doing things' aspect of the hacker spirit, and becoming too caught up in talking about how those things should ideally (and eventually) be done. Lynn was particularly scathing about this. She was, she told us, more interested in 'horse-trading' than 'bike-shedding':

> Bike shedding means [...] like you're building a bike shed and the entire discussion of the bike shed gets completely derailed by what color it should be painted. And people are completely obsessed about it and the bike shed does not get built. But the perfect bike shed gets discussed by committee. And horse trading is like – so everybody is bike shedding. You find the people who seem to have a clue. You get off the mailing list in a private conversation with them. And you work together.

Horse-trading might not be in the spirit of consensus, where discussion is meant to continue until a shared, mutually satisfactory decision is reached. But it is certainly in keeping with a hacker ethos of getting things done, however imperfectly. Similarly, other hackers told us stories where taking action trumped – and ended – long, contentious and unsatisfactory discussions. Turning up and doing something was always seen as better than discussing a situation *ad infinitum* on the mailing list – just as everyone was grateful to the person who publicly pointed out that the contents of the fridge were mutating and organized a clear-out.

There was a further tension related to the challenges of building and managing community in hacker and makerspaces. This was a fear, expressed by a few of our interviewees, that the strength of hackerspace communities might actually overwhelm the hacking and making that went on there. As we've seen, some people were keen to view their spaces as 'community centres', and saw socializing as a primary reason for participating in them. At the same time, others were concerned that hacker and makerspaces exactly *shouldn't* become community centres or clubhouses. In line with the hacker emphasis on doing not talking, some worried that hackerspaces were in danger of becoming cool places to hang out, and that this could end up distracting from their central purpose of enabling hacking. Yan, the Arizonan hacker we've met previously, told us that it was important to understand 'you can't be everything to everybody'.

> So we kind of took that to mean, we're not a community center. [This hackerspace] is not a place for yoga. It's not a place for karate. It's not necessarily even a place for music, much as we would like it to be. It's kind of the place for the physical creation for things.

In Yan's space, this had meant reluctantly turning down social activities they could have done as a hackerspace. They would have loved to have more music in the space; someone had suggested a Star Trek marathon. But these things, they decided, were too focused on consumption and not enough on creating and making. They too easily led to a dynamic where members simply absorbed what was on a screen – a slippery slope on which the emphasis on creation was eventually lost. Yan and others we spoke to in this space acknowledged that this seemed strict, and perhaps overly exclusive. But they also actively feared having a space which people primarily used to hang out in and 'look cool'. 'We don't want to be a social space', Yan told us, 'because talking is not doing'.

A working hackerspace community is therefore fragile. It's easy to wax lyrical about the power of mutualistic, sharing, committed community; maintaining that sense of community in practice, and ensuring that everyone is actively seeking to do so, is more difficult. When things go wrong, members become passive and disengaged, and a harried leadership becomes burnt out. Those we spoke to recognized this. As well as devoting time to the challenges of encouraging activity and agency in hacker and makerspace communities, our interviewees talked about the need to protect the right feeling of community in their spaces. This was, for instance, one reason that the decision to make someone a member was seen as an important step, and one which the wider hackerspace community should be involved in. The wrong person could throw the balance of the space off completely, or shift it into a totally different direction. Hackers and makers also told us about working hard to keep discussion on the email list friendly, or ensuring that their space felt 'cosy' and welcoming. 'Drama' was avoided at all costs, and people sought to 'live and let live' in the face of minor annoyances. Where disagreements and tensions did occur, they were seen as something that could make the community stronger by encouraging participation. Negotiation and compromise could strengthen community by highlighting that 'no one's in charge' and that the hackerspace was a collaborative enterprise rather than the provision of a service.

But understanding community as central to hacking and making – as perhaps the defining feature of hacker and makerspaces – can also lead to tensions. Are hackerspaces community centres, whose primary purpose is to allow digital natives to access social capital? Those we spoke to were divided on this question. There were, as we've seen, concerns that these spaces were becoming the coffee shops and cafes of the 2010s: hip places to be seen hanging out with your laptop. This related to fears that hackerspaces could become too mainstream. Would the counter-cultural values of the hacker spirit be lost if hacker and makerspaces became too social?

Community also has a darker side. Putnam's work on social capital makes it clear that many close-knit groups provide community by excluding other people. A sense of belonging, of having found one's 'people', can come at the cost of openness and inclusivity. It's this issue, the extent to which hacker and makerspaces exclude certain kinds of people, that I focus on in the next chapter.

7

Exclusion
Whatever It Is Females Like to Talk About

Back in the first chapter I introduced hackerspaces using a quote from the hacker and writer John Baichtal. Baichtal was trying to encapsulate the experience of walking into a hackerspace for the first time. You would see all kinds of different 'interesting things', Baichtal wrote, from 3D printers to people soldering electronics and someone making their own furniture. Most of all you would get a sense of people working together, enjoying each other's company and actively collaborating on projects. Baichtal's imagined visit to a hackerspace ended by saying:

> The collaboration is the aspect of the space that strikes you the most. People are working and talking together. They're sharing information, learning about new things, asking questions, and discussing mutual areas of interest. They're building projects to fill a practical need or simply for the love of it.[1]

As we've seen, it's not just Baichtal who sees this kind of community as an integral part of hacker and makerspaces. Those we interviewed told us that relating to other people in the right way is a central aspect of the hacker lifestyle. Hackers, we were told, don't operate alone, they learn and teach as a part of a community. This sounds great. Who wouldn't want to get involved in this kind of friendly, collaborative environment?

But what happens if you visit a hackerspace and have a different kind of experience? What if you walk in and notice that everyone there looks different to you, or find that no one talks to you? What if you find that other hackers make assumptions about you and your interests based on your gender, or what you look like, or your sexuality? What if you're a woman, and when you walk in you're immediately pointed to the sewing bench, when what you really want is to do some coding?

So far I've focused on what we might call the aspirational version of hackerspace community, the one that hackers and makers (mostly) told us about and were passionately excited to be a part of. But this is not the whole story. Experiences of feeling out of place, alienated or excluded – experiences like those in the paragraph above – are not uncommon. This, for instance, is one of the founders of a women-only hackerspace writing about why they felt it was necessary to start their space. (Look out for the 'e-textiles' reference – this refers to a notorious discussion on the hackerspaces.org discuss list, where one contributor suggested that the way to boost women's participation in hackerspaces was to do more activities like e-textiles or 'whatever it is females like to talk about'.[2])

> Women go to hackerspaces because they sound amazing – full of equipment and materials to make things, people, and idealism about knowledge-sharing, open source and free culture and tech, like a fabulous grownup playground for learning and making. You get there and it's all that.
> But maybe it's also kind of dirty and cluttered and there's no toilet paper, and there is some creepy guy who won't stop talking to you about how he wants to teach you things that you already know, while he backs you into a corner. There's that level of harassment. Then there's a lot of behavior that's at a more 'e-textiles' level, that's irritating, annoying, where we have pressure to prove ourselves or our authenticity, where our knowledge and capacities are undermined.[3]

The writer, Liz Henry, points out that women are interested in hackerspaces for the same reason as men: they sound awesome, full of opportunities to learn and make and do. But very often they don't get treated in the same way that male visitors do. They may be patronized, harassed or simply made to feel that they don't belong. This – rather than a critical lack of e-textiles – is why those who identify as women or as gender-queer may not bother to invest in traditional hackerspaces. As another woman who leads a hackerspace, Georgia Guthrie, writes on the MAKE blog, it's lazy and incorrect to assume that hackerspaces tend to be dominated by men because women just aren't that much into hacking.[4] The problem isn't with women – it's with the culture of many hacker and makerspaces.

This chapter looks at these kinds of exclusions, and others. It complicates the emphasis on community that has run throughout the previous chapters. The picture that is presented as hacker and makerspace users talk about hacking is often an idyllic one, in which hacking is an activity that is open to all, regardless of race, age, gender, sexuality or ability. Many of those we spoke to had found their involvement in hackerspaces transformative: suddenly, they were part of a group that embraced them and which shared their interests. But there could also be ambivalence about this community. Some users continued to feel excluded, or to be anxious they weren't the 'right fit' for the space, or suffered from what is known as impostor syndrome: the sense of 'feeling a fraud', or of not being good enough to participate in a particular job or community, that some people may experience.[5] Two spaces we visited were set up specifically to be oriented around women or minority groups, in response to the sense that – however much rhetoric there was about openness – hackerspaces were not always places where those who weren't white, highly educated men in their twenties or thirties could feel comfortable. These issues of inclusion and exclusion were also obvious as we visited different spaces. The hackers and makers we met were friendly, excited to have visitors, and eager to talk about their interests – but there were plenty of instances when I was the only woman present. One of the very few surveys of hackerspace users that has been carried out, conducted in 2011, found that 90 per cent of those who responded were male; a similar percentage had some university-level education. The mean age was 31 years.[6] While we didn't collect data on the demographics of the hackerspaces we visited, it was clear that many did not reflect the make-up of the wider communities they were located within. At the very least, this complicates the stories of empowerment – technology to the people! – that some public accounts of hacking and making have emphasized. It also raises questions. Why do hackerspaces work so well for some people – providing the community they crave – but seem to exclude others from that same experience of community?

Empowerment and exclusion

Many hackers and makers found it hard to talk about these issues. Some of our interviewees, at least, were uncomfortable reflecting too hard on the composition of their hackerspace. They simply didn't understand, often, how the space or the behaviours of those in it could be construed as unwelcoming or intimidating. Sometimes there was a sense that those from under-represented groups – women, queer people, people of colour – needed to step up and get involved in demographically skewed hackerspaces in order to change the culture themselves. It was also clear, however, that many of those that we spoke to had had an experience of hacker and makerspaces that was the exact opposite of exclusion. Many of our interviewees told stories of personal empower-ment through access to hackerspaces; not only this, but empowerment, in the form of renewed self-reliance and personal agency, was seen as a key part of the hacker spirit.[7] 'The hacker lifestyle', student hacker Kip told us, 'has a lot to do with both tinkering and sharing knowledge, empowering other people, so they can learn freely.' The world tends to close off scientific and technical knowledge, creating barriers around it so that it cannot be accessed without a PhD and '20 years of experience', said Katie. Hackerspaces gave normal people access to anything from biotechnology to high-powered microscopes or space travel (perhaps, eventually...).

This emphasis on the emancipatory potential of hacker and mak-erspaces was heightened by the stories we heard about changed lives and transformative effects. Some people we spoke to were enthusias-tic but relaxed about their involvement in their hackerspace, seeing it as a fun hobby or means of getting to know new people. Others were quite clear that their lives had been transformed. They were new, better people because they had found their hacker or makerspace. One woman had a young family and a partner with a potentially terminal illness; involvement in her hackerspace gave her 'energy to deal with the rest of my life'. Another maker talked about regaining confidence after a lifetime of being labelled as having 'special educational needs'. Someone else now saw their hackerspace as their family and their home. Quite aside from any personal effects, many people believed that hacking and making could change the world for the better. Lynn quoted Archimedes to us: 'Give me a lever and a place to stand and I can move the world.' The hackerspace, she said, was 'the first lever I've found with handholds available that really does move the world, and for the better, I believe, so I don't plan to let go of it'. Almost everyone we spoke to was passionate about the potential of hackerspaces to help individuals as well as society at large. 'It's as if', one biohacker told us, 'fire had just been invented.'

So it is perhaps not surprising that there was some cognitive dis-sonance around the extent to which hackerspaces are empowering for everyone, not just certain groups of people. Many of those we spoke to had had such positive experiences, and were so excited about the maker movement, that they found it hard to see how those positive experiences might not be shared by everyone who visited a hacker-space. At the same time, ambivalence did creep in around the edges of some of our conversations. We met with hackers and makers for, at most, a few hours, generally within the space they were part of. The context of our interviews didn't encourage especially critical accounts or much acknowledgement of any problems within the community that, ultimately, interviewees were committed to and enthusiastic about. But it was still clear that some hackers and makers were aware of, and perhaps had experienced, exclusion, prejudice and the general weirdness of being part of a community where you are – for instance – the only woman, or person of colour, or queer, or old person, or person with no higher education or with a disability.

Sometimes this was expressed through concerns about cliques or cliquey-ness within hacker and makerspaces. Many of those we spoke to had concerns that their spaces could be too tightly knit as a community, to the extent that they had lost their openness and became intimidating or exclusive. David, for instance, told us that he had initially found it hard to get involved in his hackerspace because, when he visited, it seemed that everyone there knew each other, and that he was intruding on a 'group of friends'. Others recognized that visiting their hackerspace could be intimidating, leaving the visitor feeling like they didn't belong. Someone else told the story of being pushed out of a project as more expert hackers got involved in it: he 'stood back' as this group made the project happen. So much expertise and so many cool projects could, at times, be experienced as intimidating and even unwelcoming.

The conversation we had with Keira and Willow was indicative of some of these dynamics. Both were passionately enthusiastic about the makerspace they were part of. Keira ran her business, making jewellery, from the space, and saw it as a revival of the radical creative spirit she remembered from the 1970s. Willow was part of a bike co-op group, a subsection of the makerspace, which she said had changed her life. 'We can't explain it', said Keira, to Willow's agreement, 'but it's almost like a second lease of life.'

At the same time, as our conversation progressed, it became clear that both continued to feel ambivalent and somewhat insecure about their participation in that particular makerspace community. Willow, in fact, had been hesitant about joining. She had been to an early meeting promoting the space, before they had found their current location, and been underwhelmed:

> I listened to them talk about it, and I looked around the room and I said, well, that's nice; I don't think I have time for that, because it sounded like it was a lot of money, it sounded like it was sort of the kind of thing that white middle-class dudes with tech jobs do, you know, and I haven't succeeded in it yet but I keep thinking that, you know, I want to do something useful.

As it happened, Willow herself worked in the tech business; she already spent too much of her time (she told us) surrounded by white middle-class dudes. Why would she want to devote her time and energy to something that seemed to be more of the same and which cost a lot of money to boot? She was more interested in finding a way to 'do something useful', and the makerspace initially seemed self-indulgent. It was only later, when she became part of the space via her bike co-op, that she saw its potential for something more powerful. At the same time, it remained easy for her – and for Keira – to feel like she didn't belong. A year or so earlier the makerspace had been located in a smaller, colder, smellier room: 'I could live with it', Willow said, but she didn't like it. It felt like 'a boy's space'. Keira agreed: even though she didn't smoke, she used to go outside with people taking a cigarette break just to get away from the smell and the mess. Even now, when the space was bigger and cosier and cleaner, it was possible to get over-whelmed. There was so much going on, and so many people who were so expert at so many different things, that your own interests and skills could seem unimportant and negligible. Everyone seemed so confident and in control, Keira explained, telling a story about a crisis she had had one day when everything she was working on was going wrong and she just felt 'like an idiot'. It turned out that other people were having 'melt-downs' as well, but this wasn't immediately apparent to her. The culture of the space seemed to promote confidence and to encourage hiding the insecurities members were feeling. Maybe, Keira concluded, they needed a 'mentoring programme' to help people fit in.

Willow and Keira felt that they'd overcome their insecurities about being part of their makerspace. They were now more concerned that the space was able to be welcoming to anyone who might come in and feel 'I don't know enough, I'm not big enough, I don't fit in here'. Many of the concerns hackers and makers had about their spaces were similarly expressed not through people's own stories, but through reflections on what other people might think or experience as they visited. Members of several spaces told us they were concerned about being too cliquey, or about the 'intimidation' that Keira and Willow referred to. This is Karl talking about his space (a student-run hackerspace which he had previously been president of) and the effect it could have on visitors:

> Sometimes people just come in and see people – they're new; they don't know anyone. They've come to this space that they've been told is awesome and see all these kind of like older people working on projects they couldn't dream up. Like, hmm. And they just stand there and don't talk to anyone and everyone is working on projects and doesn't notice they're there. And they're like, oh, god, I should leave and they leave.

Karl was clear that this was a problem, and one that affected women disproportionately. Earlier in our conversation he had explained that the leadership of the space was concerned both that membership numbers were stagnating and that the gender balance was unequal (they had, he estimated, seventy men and twenty-five women as members – actually much better than the eight or nine to one ratio that some spaces told us about). Part of the reason for this, he suggested, was 'sex-biased intimidation, but also just general intimidation'. In other words, in his experience, *everyone* was freaked out by the general level of activity and awesomeness, but women were even more so. (Though the space also had, he noted, some pretty intimidating women members.) They were trying to implement a new strategy to address this effect, primarily involving taking 'a way different attitude'. They would also run introductory classes every other week and make an effort to be friendly to visitors; 'as soon as someone comes in', Karl said, 'we're going to immediately drop everything and say hi and show them around and stuff like that.'

Others were perhaps less reflective about how the dynamics of their space might affect its membership. Some people seemed to take for granted that they had only had a few women members, for example, because there was simply a lack of interest from women in what they were doing (shades of the e-textiles discussion). One very new space had eight male members and one female; this was, those we spoke to there said, 'very weird', but they had few ideas about what to do about it. Our interview there was with a group of its members, and a conversation developed around this question. One in five of those working in engineering and computer science is a woman, one person pointed out: why do hackerspaces tend to have an even worse ratio than this? 'People decide to go to a hackerspace or not based on personal interest', someone else said. 'If the gender gap is even wider, it's purely interest driven.'

The rise of feminist hackerspaces

Here it's worth returning to wider discussions of hackerspace demographics and in particular to the arguments and discussions that have led to the setting up of women-centred hackerspaces.[8] It is exactly the assumption that those under-represented in hackerspaces are not there simply because they are not interested that can be so enraging: this was, in fact, the trigger for the firestorm around the 'e-textiles' message on the hackerspaces.org discussion list. In a long thread, several people (generally men) argued that their hacker or makerspace was open to anybody, that the onus was on women to step up and get involved, but that maybe hackerspaces should promote activities that 'females like to talk about'[9] – like e-textiles. But this, others responded, totally misses the point. It essentializes women as uniformly interested in (and only competent at) particular, 'softer' technologies, rather than things like coding, metalwork or electronics; it ignores the real reasons that women may not want to hang out in hackerspaces (like harassment); and it promotes an idea of meritocracy (everyone can just step up and get involved) that ignores the power dynamics of wider society (stepping up might be much more costly for certain groups than others). To focus on interest – saying 'our space is open to everyone, they just have to be interested in what we do' – renders the culture of hackerspaces (and the societies they are situated in) invisible.

Liz Henry, whom I quoted at the start of the chapter, makes this point particularly clearly. Reading that hackerspaces.org thread, she writes, 'brought our alienation to a head'. What she saw was that '[g]uys kept saying that women don't come to hackerspaces and aren't hackers'. But:

> If we aren't at hackerspaces, it isn't because we don't make things, don't code, or aren't technical enough. It's because men act like the space is theirs. Women face harassment ranging from assault to much milder, but more constant, come-ons and innuendos. Our geek cred is constantly challenged or belittled.... That's what we fight at tech conferences too.[10]

Henry is suggesting that the culture of hackerspaces can in some ways be an extension of tech culture more generally – a culture that is known for its 'brogrammers', macho posturing and at times poisonous lack of diversity.[11] Writing on the website geekfeminism.org – a hub for discussion of diversity issues in technology and geek culture more generally – two computer science students wrote about attending a hackathon in 2014. A hackathon is an event focused on computer hacking, and often on tightening up a particular piece of open-source software; we met the concept briefly in chapter 1, when I mentioned the NHS Hack Day. There were 1,200 hackers present, only a handful of whom were women; more to the point, it was an environment, the students argued, 'that unconsciously shuts women out...We felt like we did not belong'.[12] Full of bragging and aggression, the event even smelt male: most of the hackers, the students wrote, seemed to have an aversion to washing over the course of the weekend, something which made the event even more uncomfortable for them. Their impostor syndrome – the sense that you don't belong somewhere, that your talents or skills are nowhere near good enough[13] – came out in full force. They felt intimidated and overwhelmed.[14]

None of the hackers or makers that we talked to told us about such extreme experiences. Indeed, other than those involved in the spaces which were specifically developed for women and minorities, these dynamics seemed to be invisible to many of our interviewees – something that is in itself rather telling. But it's clear that hackerspaces (and tech culture generally) do tend to have a problem with diversity, and that the cultures that are promoted – even through small things such as an emphasis on 'bragging rights', assumptions about what kinds of people are interested in what kinds of hacking, or a simple lack of awareness that the world contains people who are different to you – can be profoundly off-putting to some individuals and groups. One or two spaces that we visited were actively trying to address this, in different ways: they might have a 'no creep' policy, make a concerted effort to be friendly to everyone (as in Karl's hackerspace, discussed above), or control their membership to ensure that female members were comfortable with new recruits (through a blackballing system, for example). But it is, ultimately, hard work being the only woman, or queer, or person of colour, in any community, or even one out of the only two, or three, or four. However much goodwill there is in a mainstream hackerspace, and however thoughtful efforts to address problematic tech cultures are, it is exhausting and isolating to be what some activists call the 'unicorn': the exotic representative of a different gender, or culture, or sexuality, who has nevertheless managed to find their way into hacking.[15] The researcher and hacker Sophie Toupin notes that:

> When feminist and anti-oppression politics are not explicitly part of the ethos of a space whether virtual or physical, the burden of education will often be placed upon the people who are living these oppressions. The burden of educating about white supremacy will be placed upon indigenous or people of colour, while the burden of educating about gender analysis will be put upon women and queers.[16]

In other words, once again, changing the culture becomes *your* responsibility. For Toupin, this is asking too much. As Liz Henry and others have also argued, she suggests that there is a need for safe, feminist hackerspaces, where those who don't 'identify with the dominant hacker culture' can make and create without constant harassment or feeling excluded. Toupin argues that feminist hackerspaces can welcome in those who don't feel comfortable in mainstream hackerspaces, allow women hackers to work on their projects without harassment or unwanted and patronizing assistance, and act as spaces for community building and consciousness raising. Here, then, we return to the notion of community. If most hacker and makerspaces offer a form of community that can actually be experienced as exclusionary, can more focused, targeted spaces create something that is more genuinely empowering?

Crafting community

When we spoke to hackers and makers for this research, we told them that we would anonymize both individuals and the spaces themselves when we wrote up our study (as, indeed, I have done throughout). Some people were not convinced that this was possible: after all, they said, 'each space is unique', and any description of a particular hacker-space might render it recognizable to those in the know. Those involved in spaces which sought to specifically support women and/or minorities were particularly convinced of this. After all, their spaces had been set up in direct opposition to the bulk of hackerspaces: if all spaces are unique, surely theirs were even more so.[17] Surely there are simply so few of these specialized hackerspaces that any discussion of them would make it obvious, to other hackers, who we were talking about?

Perhaps. But it is striking that such spaces are on the rise. It's no longer the case that there is only one women-centred hackerspace, or two. There's The Attic, Double Union, Mothership Hacker Moms, LOL Space, Hacker Gals, and Spanning Tree, as well as other groups that have now closed their doors or which exist as a meet-up within a larger hacker or makerspace. And that's just in the US. Europe has Mz Baltazar's Laboratory (in Vienna) and MzTEK (in London), amongst others. Several of these are very new, or in development – but just as hacker and makerspaces generally contine to grow, so do those more focused iterations of them. There's clearly a hunger for 'safer spaces' for hacking and making.

We spoke to people involved in two of these spaces. One limited membership to those who identified as women; the other was led by, and sought to specifically encourage the participation of, people of colour, as well as women, queer and trans people, and anyone else who might not feel comfortable in traditional hackerspaces. Each therefore focused on a slightly different community; in addition, though both were relatively new, the neighbourhoods they were located in and the activities they provided were quite different, with one more tech-focused – in the form of coding rather than making and crafts – than the other. Despite these differences – further evidence that 'each space is unique' – there were some key similarities in how and why they were set up, similarities that also resonate with the public discussion of feminist hackerspaces described above.

First, both spaces had emerged out of particular personal experiences and passions. The former were generally bad experiences with mainstream hackerspaces, coupled with a desire to make some kind of difference to society or to the world. People spoke about visiting hackerspaces and being the only woman or person of colour present; they wanted, they told us, to create a different kind of hackerspace, one where this wouldn't be the case. One woman, Tiah, had a family member who was involved in a hackerspace, and had found out about the hackerspace movement through them. She'd been inspired by the way in which this space had been able to 'shake up the social structure [in the local region], influence the culture', and she wanted to develop something similiar for the community of which she was a part. Kim, who was instrumental in setting up the space focused on diversity, had been struck by the ways in which the maker movement resonated with traditional crafts and skills: canning, sewing, crafts (the same kinds of activities that Emily Matcham charts as part of the New Domesticity). She wanted to ensure that this resonance – the reinvention and marketing, she pointed out, of very old activities – was used to drive social justice. For her, she said, the maker movement:

> is about marketing. Marketing these things in a new way that gives them more value. So for example, [around here] we have a lot of people, most of them women, many of them Asian women, working in sweatshops making, you know, various textiles, cloth, clothes, whatever, and they get paid usually by piecework. It's like a few cents per thing that they make. And then you have these makers who are like doing this at home and selling things for a lot more and making a lot more money. And so the thought was, well, the thing that's missing here is that the access to the marketing – the things like Etsy and just the knowledge of how to do this – is missing from people who have the skills and are being really poorly paid for their work.

Her makerspace, she told us, therefore tried to do something rather different to most others. Rather than supporting the hobby projects or entrepreneurship of those relatively *new* to making – the refugees from banking and IT and management consultancy that we often met in other hacker and makerspaces – it instead sought to empower those whose making generally didn't have the edgy 'maker' label applied to it. The space, she said, was for skill sharing; skills like sewing and weaving and carpentry, certainly, but also things like how to set up an Etsy shop or start your own business. It also supported the learning and sharing of computing skills, not only to help in this kind of entrepreneurship but because those involved in the makerspace were interested in addressing the 'deficit of people of colour and women in...fields' such as programming.

Both spaces were therefore driven by a sense of a wider purpose than was commonly the case in the setting up of other hacker and makerspaces. They had an explicit focus on changing society for the better: though this was present in other spaces, it tended to take a back seat to having a good time through hacking and making. But this didn't mean that community within these spaces wasn't seen as important. In fact – and this is the second thing they had in common – there was a much more overt emphasis on the need to consciously construct a particular kind of culture and community. For some hackers in other spaces, community was just something that emerged, or that they found, fully formed, as they joined a hackerspace. It might be life-changing, but it wasn't particularly designed. Hackers and makers in these women- and diversity-oriented spaces, however, were explicitly aware of it as something that had to be worked at, even crafted.[18]

This was expressed in a couple of ways. Tiah, for instance, talked about the importance of the location and feel of the hackerspace itself. They had a shopfront location, which she thought was ideal: they didn't want to be hidden away in some industrial district, but part of the local community and visible to it. Initially the group behind the space had been negotiating with another local hackerspace about co-locating with them. What turned out to be the deciding factor was the space itself: this, Tiah said, 'just didn't work for us'. Like a lot of other hackerspaces, it seemed:

> kind of warehousey and kind of cold feeling, mismatched furniture. We want our place to look like Anthropologie,[19] like the space equivalent of a beige computer. So it has to have this you know like a homier feel to it. I mean, for kids, because they're here, it can't be just like cement floors. And for just, you know, a women's sensibility, it just has to be cuter.

Having children in the space was essential to this group (providing childcare was a priority so that full-time parents could participate fully). On a practical level, this meant that 'cement floors' and other hazards were out of the question, but the aesthetics of the environment were also important. What Tiah and others involved wanted was a space that was pleasant to be in, that felt 'homey' and 'cute' rather than cold and dirty. The space had to be comfortable rather than jarring or cold or unfriendly. Just as we saw earlier that Willow and Keira had felt

awkward and out of place in the dirty, 'boy's space' environment that
their makerspace had previously inhabited, Tiah argued that women –
and especially women with children – were more comfortable coming
into, and becoming part of, a space that was physically and aestheti-
cally familiar to them.

Beyond this, however, there was also the sense that the interper-
sonal culture of a hacker or makerspace had to be worked at, rather
than just left to emerge. Just as the location and fittings should be
consciously and thoughtfully selected, the kind of community that
this physical space housed needed to be designed and crafted. Many
diversity-oriented spaces are therefore even more careful about membership than other hackerspaces. Those that we spoke to were clear that
ensuring a diverse, women-centred community would mean selecting
for that community (for instance by inviting members rather than
opening up to anyone who might wander through the doors), at least
in the space's early stages. This is Kim talking about the challenges of
developing the right kind of 'dominant culture':

> And we're more careful about our community than maybe other spaces
> are because we have been cognizant of how other spaces – many other
> spaces have, like I said, very dominant cultures. We want to create our
> own dominant culture, but we want to be different. So we've been pretty
> deliberate in how we reach out. And that's probably not going to change
> soon. So eventually, we'll say, people, come to our space, once we already
> have a huge critical mass of people who can reflect what we want to do,
> because like attracts like.

Kim was extremely conscious of the way in which many hackerspaces
– and more broadly the tech industry generally – simply defaulted to
the 'dominant culture' of white middle-class men in both its demographics and behaviours. She wanted to ensure that the space she was
part of was different to this: gender-balanced, led by people of colour,
focused on social justice. The space should, she said, involve 'political
education as well as practical education'. Perhaps counter-intuitively,
at the stage they were currently at, this meant *not* advertising or publicizing themselves (saying 'people, come to our space'), but instead
deliberately reaching out to key figures and groups in the communities
they wanted to work with. They would craft a core group of users who
reflected the values they wanted the space to promote; this was, she
said, about 'establishing a community'. After that, 'like attracts like'.
She and others involved were confident that once they had created
their own dominant culture – one which was inclusive rather than
exclusive, non-threatening rather than intimidating, and oriented to

social justice rather than (or as well as) hobbyism – this would be self-perpetuating. Again, she was convinced that the interest, ability and economic drivers for participation in hacking and making were present in the communities the space was reaching out to; that, in other words, the fact that women and minorities and queer people and immigrants are under-represented in the hacker and maker movement isn't indicative of there being no interest in it. The problem is not with these groups, but with the 'dominant culture' that works to exclude them.

The dark side of social capital

It was too early, in the case of both of these spaces, to see how these plans were working out in practice. Both had only been open as physical spaces for a few months. However, the growth of feminist hackerspaces more generally suggests that there is a real hunger for such spaces. It suggests, in other words, that though the sense of community in hacker and makerspaces seems to be working fantastically well for some people, there are many others – most of whom we weren't able to meet and interview, simply because they are not hackerspace members – who feel excluded. However positive the majority of the stories we heard about hackerspace involvement, and however much hackers talk about being open to all, the power of community seems to have a dark side.

We can relate this to the notion of social capital discussed in the previous chapter. Social capital involves community, and the creation of connections between people. But Putnam, the popularizer of the term, also notes that social capital is not a singular thing. He distinguishes between *bridging* and *bonding* social capital, where the former is outward-looking and embraces diversity, and the latter is 'inward looking', tending 'to reinforce exclusive identities and homogeneous groups'.[20] The distinction is not always straightforward: some groups are bonding across some dimensions but bridging across others (churches might bring together people of the same religion but of different social classes). Examples of bonding social capital might be those found in an exclusive club or a small immigrant community; examples of bridging social capital might be volunteers working together to clean up a local park or campaigning in local politics. Putnam (and those who have developed his ideas) is also clear that social capital can be used to bad effect: he gives the example of a criminal who is able to use their networks and communities to allow them to commit or cover up crime. Social capital, in other words, doesn't have to be directed towards the good of a society. Community can do things that we might find deeply troubling.

So the question becomes not whether hacker and makerspaces enable the development of social capital – they certainly do – but of what kinds of social capital they enable, and to what effect. It seems likely that they, like many other kinds of association, involve both bonding and bridging (or inward- and outward-looking) social ties. 'Bonding' would seem to take place around an interest in hacking and making, or perhaps a commitment to the hacker lifestyle. If you're not 'one of us' in this regard, it's unclear why you would want to be involved in a hackerspace. We've seen this emphasis on the need for members to 'get' hacking and its practice as an active, self-reliant lifestyle in chapter 5, when Katie talked about people visiting her hackerspace and treating it as a service. Those visitors didn't get it; they weren't 'one of us'. The commonality around which the community gathers is being a hacker or maker – having those characteristics and interests of the hacker spirit that we saw back in chapter 5. In this respect, it is certainly inward-looking. But we might also expect hacker and makerspaces to mobilize plenty of bridging social capital, too. Other than having a focus on hacking stuff, we've seen that these spaces generally understand themselves as radically open to the wider world: 'anyone with a genuine interest is welcome', 'everything's very inclusive', we want to be 'accessible to all', we were told at various points as we visited hacker and makerspaces. Most spaces explicitly seek to be open to anyone, of any background, who is interested in participating, and in this respect hackers and makers imagine themselves as looking outward, beyond any particular age group, class or background.

The experiences we've looked at in this chapter, however, complicate this story. Clearly, not everyone feels welcome in (some) hackerspaces, and their demographics do not suggest a community where the commonalities are solely rooted in a particular lifestyle or interest (rather than in social class, economic resources or educational background). The success of hacker and makerspaces, in terms of the transformative experiences of community that people told us about, may therefore emerge not just from finding a community focused on hacking but one that feels cosy because it is full of people who are not that dissimilar to you. There are, it seems, also other forms of bonding social capital at work in (most) hackerspaces, that between people from the same intellectual, economic and social backgrounds. Perhaps the community spirit in hackerspaces is so exciting because in many ways it is relatively easy, focused not only on shared interests but on a shared set of experiences and assumptions. In this respect, some hacker and makerspaces are creating bonding social capital not around hacking but around hacking by certain kinds of people: those who are, or who are comfortable being around, young, educated, men. The irony is that these are the people who are least likely to require the empowerment that so many hackers and makers talk about their practices as bringing. By defaulting to the 'dominant culture' of the wider tech community, hackerspaces run the risk of neutering the power of hacking and making, and of turning it into just another hobby for the middle classes.

8

Cool Projects
Rather, It Was a Trojan Horse

Dave and I met Fee in Boston. She was a hacker in her twenties, with funkily striped hair and a passion for working with different media: her favourite projects, she told us, were those that combined technologies and materials that weren't usually thought of as going together. At the time she spoke to us she had a number of different interests. She was working with a friend to make a 'robotically monitored garden', where sensors for temperature and resistance (amongst other things) would alert you when you needed to water particular plants or change the light conditions. One of her passions was combining electronics with fabrics, and she was fixing up some shirts she had made herself on which, once ambient light dropped below a certain level, a set of LED lights came on to produce a pattern. In the past she had done simple electronics projects, like making a radio out of a cardboard tube and some wire. Her most useful project, she said, was a sweatshirt that she wore when she helped at a local astronomy club: in the dark, red LEDs picked out the shape of a constellation on the back of the sweater, so that others knew who she was and could ask her questions. (The LEDs had to be red, so that they wouldn't disrupt people's night vision.)

Fee was bursting with ideas and enthusiasm, interested in everything from aesthetics to how to make a washable fabric stuffed with wiring (the important thing, she said, was to take the batteries out before running your shirt through the laundry). But it was striking that she hadn't actually had any of these projects or ideas in mind when she got involved in the hackerspace she was part of. What had attracted her, she told us, was the environment and the people. She had stumbled across the space while looking for something else and was mesmerized by the machinery in use, and in particular the patterns that shards spiralling off aluminium made as it was cut, which she could watch for hours. Once she had made it inside the hackerspace, she found that she liked hanging out with the people who used it. But to participate, to become a member, she discovered she needed a project of some kind: it was expected that everyone was working on something. And there were no group projects that she could get involved with; 'other hackerspaces might do this differently', she said,

> but [here] people tend to work just on their own projects…so I decided to pick some really simple project of my own that I could make, like my own project at [the space]. So people are always happy to tell you about their projects or like show you what they're doing or explain what they're working on, but people tend to work on their own things in parallel. I started making this really simple stuffed doll; doll is a really generous way to describe this object. It was a fabric lump with two eyes and two switches, one in each hand, like – not really hand, it was like lumps coming off of the main lump and one of the – so there were LED eyes and LED ears, like sticking out of the top of the lump and one of the switches controlled the ears and they blinked and one of the switches controlled the eyes and that was my project. So sewing that – even though the project itself is not particularly exciting or complicated, working on something there allowed me to learn how [the space] worked and like learn where things were, and it was nice having something to work on…it was a good way to get to know everyone.

Fee's stuffed doll – which she resignedly described as a 'fabric lump' – was not a long-cherished dream realized through the technologies of making. Rather, it was a Trojan horse: it allowed her to become a part of the hackerspace – to 'get to know everyone', and to 'learn how [the space] worked and like learn where things were'. It also enabled her to grasp the rudiments of a technology she was not familiar with – LED circuits – and would later use to more interesting effect in her glow-in-the-dark shirts and sweaters. Even though the doll was not 'exciting or complicated' (and even though Fee talks about it with remarkedly little fondness), it served its purpose. It gave her access to the hackerspace, and to its community.

Fee's story is illustrative of the importance of the project in structuring hackerspace involvement. Though some people were open about being more interested in the hackerspace as a social opportunity than in actually using it as a space for making and hacking, this attitude was often frowned upon, at least implicitly. The hacker emphasis on doing and making meant that simply hanging out in the hackerspace could be seen as passive, uninteresting, not really in the spirit of things. It might mean, dangerously, that you were not 'one of our people'. The project, then, is a key organizing device for how hackers and makers use hackerspaces. Users of these spaces, like Fee, quickly learn that it's important to have a project (or many projects) and to be able to talk about them: as in the quote from Fee above, it's expected that those in the hackerspace will happily 'tell you about their projects or show you what they're doing or explain what they're working on'. At least one hackerspace we visited used this as an informal criterion for whether visitors might be potential members. Did they have a project, or ideas for one? Were they eager to get their hands dirty? Or were they only interested in, as one Arizonan hacker, Denver, put it, using the space for 'checking their email and listening to music, just kind of farting around'?

The role of the project

This chapter focuses on the role of the project in hacker and maker-spaces. Having spent most time so far looking at how hackerspace communities are organized and operate, I'll now turn to look more at the stuff that actually gets made, built and hacked by hackerspace users. Projects, as I've suggested, often seem to organize hackerspace involvement.[1] Some spaces told us that they had a high throughput of members, as individuals would join in order to access the knowledge and equipment necessary to complete a particular project, and drift away once they had realized this. One hacker told us that seeing whether someone had a project or not helped 'self-police' membership: he would, he told us, ask repeat visitors, 'Hey, where's your project? I want to see your project'. After that, any timewasters 'don't come back...because they don't have a project and they're not going to work on one'. Many of the hackers and makers we spoke to were, like Fee, managing a kind of personal portfolio of projects, of various types and at various stages of completion. But as well as describing some of the ways that projects are part of hacker and makerspaces, I want to discuss what the users of these spaces told us about why they chose to engage in these projects. What was it that drew them to these projects? What do hackers and makers get from the objects, code, systems and devices they create in hackerspaces?

Given the importance of community within hacker and maker-spaces, it's not surprising that, for many people, part of the appeal of particular projects came from their communal nature. In this respect Fee's hackerspace – where people tended to work on their own projects 'in parallel' – was unusual, though not unique. Many of the spaces that we visited would have one or two ongoing group projects that anyone could get involved in; in some cases, it was the chance to work on one of these projects that first got our interviewees involved in their space. Working together in this way was seen as exemplary of many of the aspects of the hacker spirit and the ethos behind hacker and makerspaces. Collaborative projects meant that hackers could learn from others with different skill sets, experience community being put into practice, and create projects that merged different approaches and techniques in interesting and creative ways. Ulrik was one hacker who was relatively upfront about the fact that, for him, the primary appeal of his hackerspace was that it was a social environment. At the same time, he was excited about a shared project he'd just been involved in, in which a group from his space had created a laser shooting gallery – a jukebox-sized frame in which targets popped up and down, to be shot at by two competing users armed with adapted laser pointers. Part of the appeal had been, he said, that the project 'had enough people interested that it looked like it had a chance of actually getting all the way through to what it is today'. In practice, what he'd enjoyed was not so much the actual making and hacking as the interplay between people with different skills and interests, all working together towards a shared goal; a kind of collaboration, he was at pains to point out, that he had rarely experienced in his professional life. This is how he described the process:

> Phil, who is one of the founding members here, did all the Arduino and electronics components to it. Someone else did all the soldering. We had an artist come in and do the art who isn't a member here but we persuaded her to come in and help out and it was like – it was really interesting to watch. Because it was like this – I don't know. If you paid these people to work together, they wouldn't work together as smoothly as they did for free. And everybody contributed. [...] So it was great. It was this awesome idea that like everybody came together with this deadline and this kind of idea that they were going to get it done and they did it.

Ulrik had, he said, offered to help with 'everything', and in the end hadn't worked on any one specific component of the shooting gallery set-up: there had been plenty of people focused on the different aspects that it required (a wooden laser-cut frame, electronics, soldering, the artwork). What he had found powerful, though, and what he had got out of the project, was exactly the social dynamics that it had entailed – the amazing way in which people worked together 'smoothly', all contributing, with 'everybody coming together' rather than complaining or withdrawing. When he talked about it, it was these that he highlighted, rather than the technical set-up or its aesthetics, impressive though these were.

Many others that we spoke to similarly told us that it was the merging of people and disciplines that could take place around shared projects that they found particularly pleasurable. 'What I love', said one hacker, 'is the cross-pollination'. Others talked about the 'multidisciplinary' or 'interdisciplinary' projects that emerged from their spaces and how, even if specific projects didn't always develop, it was exciting to hear conversations which ranged from 'chromatics to sculpture to new materials to [...] DNA [...] to philosophy'. In this respect shared or hackerspace-sponsored projects were a vehicle for the creativity and passion understood as part of the hacker spirit. By bringing together a mix of members – and sometimes, as in the project Ulrik described, non-members – with different skills these projects could spark new kinds of creativity, resulting in something far better than if individuals had worked alone.

Not everyone chose to work on shared projects. Experiencing community and sharing knowledge are, after all, integral to hackerspace membership, not something that you have to be involved in communal projects to access. Individual projects took a number of different forms. A few people that we spoke to had commercial projects that they had or were planning to develop using their hacker or makerspace facilities. These included the founders of the space focused on diversity discussed in the previous chapter, who were explicit in their aim to encourage entrepreneurship amongst their members: this was, they said, about enabling people to take 'control. You can create the situation that you need in order to thrive'. One of their hopes was thus that skill sharing between members could lead to new cooperations and business opportunities on members' terms, rather than those of employers and big business. Someone who could sew but had no computer skills might discover how to set up their own Etsy business. A part-time programmer might collaborate with a designer or artist to create a new app.

The use of hacker and makerspaces for entrepreneurial activities is in line with the excitement that has emerged around hacker and makerspaces in recent years, much of which has focused on their potential as sites of new kinds of innovation. Enthusiasts such as Chris Anderson and Mark Hatch see makerspaces as the starting point for a 'new industrial revolution'. Academic commentators have also discussed 'community-based digital fabrication workshops' (used as a catch-all term for hacker and makerspaces, Fab Labs, and other public spaces with digital fabrication equipment) first and foremost in the context of 'the possibilities for civil society contributions to innovations'.[2] The emphasis is squarely on entrepreneurship, commercial development and economic growth.

This rhetoric was also present in our interviews. A number of people mentioned well-known businesses that had emerged from hacker or makerspaces (like MakerBot or Pinterest), or told us about people who used their spaces as sites to incubate start-ups or commercial ideas. One or two that we spoke to were nurturing their own business ideas, or, as in the diversity-oriented space, saw their hackerspace as a potential venue for collaborative entrepreneurship. People were, for the most part, not averse to hacker and makerspaces being used as the starting point for innovation and commercial development. At the same time, commercial projects were rarely the central interest of those we spoke to. A few talked about start-ups as side projects, or about how their involvement in their hackerspace supported their day job (for instance by providing contacts or know-how). But some spaces had also experienced tensions between those using the space for their own commercial projects and those who saw this as unacceptable in a shared space. Some people, we were told, 'don't think that money should be involved' in hacker and makerspaces.[3]

Innovation and commercial activities were therefore not as central as we might have expected from public discussion of hacker or makerspaces, and were certainly not a key motivation behind the kinds of projects those we spoke to worked on. According to our interviewees, it was the sense of community that drew people to these spaces, rather than the pull of particular technologies or commercial opportunities. No one told us they were part of their hackerspace because they had a brilliant commercial idea and wanted to develop it; no one was working on a project solely because they thought it could make them a lot of money. Hackers' and makers' projects tended not to be selected because of their potential for innovation or commercial development. Instead, there was a sense that choosing your project was something that was personal, even emotional. It was about you, and your passions and interests. Indeed, this was true even of commercial projects. 'I want to be in that field', one hacker told us in discussing their business ideas. Commercialization often meant the commercialization of private enthusiasms, as and when opportunities to do so appeared. Your projects were also community-focused in that they might be a way in which others would judge you, and through which you could become respected within the hackerspace community. 'You gain respect and you gain credit', we were told, 'by doing cool things and teaching cool things and proving that you know a lot about something that you care about'. Your projects, ultimately, should be things you 'care about'. Efficient but passionless disinterest, or purely monetary calculations, had no place in hacker and makerspaces.

If choosing a project wasn't about having ideas for innovations, how did hackers and makers select their projects? We spoke to people working on everything from cutting-edge genomic sequencing to pinball machines, musical stairs, tabletop touchscreens and Fee's light-sensitive clothing. But perhaps exactly because project choice was personal, tied to who you were as a hacker or maker, people often found it hard to articulate why they worked on what they did, and what it was that drew them to particular projects, technologies or concepts. These pulls were something inchoate, about who you were as a person; they were 'definable to each individual', as one hacker, Dave, tried to explain to us. One concept did emerge: people liked to work on cool projects. 'You don't really need a reason to do things', Reg told us. 'Just because it's cool or to see if you can is good enough reason here.'

Of course, we then wanted to know what it was that made something cool. Perhaps unsurprisingly, this was not any easier to articulate: 'I know it when I see it', Reg said to us, trying to explain, 'that's how cool is. So I'll work on it if it's cool.' Cool is a notoriously slippery concept: a hallmark of subversive youth culture that has itself gradually been subverted, shifting shape into a brand to be commodified and marketed.[4] Its meaning cannot be taken for granted as it is highly context-dependent: as many of us have discovered, what is cool in one place – a school, a country, a generation – can be viewed as uncool in another. Its original sense seems to reflect the importance of being nonchalant, calm or unimpressed,[5] but this kind of coolness, with its ironic distance to life, is out of place in a hackerspace. If anything the reverse is true: it is cool to care about things, to enthusiastically engage and share and teach and build.

What makes a cool project? Coolness in a hackerspace context seems much warmer than in other counter-cultural spaces. It is about individual enthusiasms, the pleasures of hands-on engagement, newness and cleverness. Cool is playful, rather than distanced or severe. Despite the difficulties of expressing what makes a project cool, or appealing, those we spoke to did have some answers as to why they worked on the projects they did. Ultimately this was about different kinds of pleasure. Hackers' and makers' projects satisfied different personal needs. A project was certainly cool if it earned you 'bragging rights' – but it was also uncool to do a project just to gain those. A project was cool if you cared about it.

What makes a cool project?

Sometimes this coolness related to the hacker emphasis on understanding and learning. If hackers and makers see themselves as people who love to learn new things and to understand the black boxes of the world around them, then it's not surprising that projects that offered the opportunity to learn or be challenged were highly valued. One New York hacker, Ed, was working on fixing up an old oscilloscope when we met him (he had, he said, 'an affinity for things that make me look like a mad scientist'). What attracted him to projects like that, he told us, was the challenge they represented – that it wasn't just another technology that he'd seen before, thoroughly understood, and could get working pretty easily. There was a 'voodoo' to getting to know something so thoroughly alien, even though that process might be frustrating or difficult or slow.

> I feel like it will be a learning experience to try to get something [like this] working again. Like even though I've had projects that have been close to failures, I look back on the fact like, yeah, that project may have come out ugly and I may be embarrassed by the finished project. But during that project I learned how to make a motor control circuit. Or during that project I've done a lot of things that I haven't done before. I learned how to program in a different language. I learned how to make things move or count the number of steps in a stepper motor and things like that. And that's sort of what I take away from the projects that I do. So perhaps the next project won't be as ugly looking or won't be such a failure.

Each project, then, is exactly not about the final outcome, which may well be ugly or embarrassing or simply not function very well. Rather, it represents an experience in which challenges were overcome, new techniques mastered and skills learnt. Importantly, this was not seen as a drily educational process. Projects were not worked through methodically so that you built up a comprehensive skill set; rather, learning itself was seen as exciting and pleasurable. Ed was salivating at the thought of the challenge the oscilloscope was going to present: this kind of hacking was 'the juicy stuff', because the 'things that are interesting are hidden'. The oscilloscope project offered an opportunity to go behind the scenes of a new technology and to test and stretch himself (and, of course, to look like a mad scientist). As such, it was cool. We can see a similarity here with the stuffed doll Fee described right at the start of the chapter. This, too, was ugly and misshapen, not 'exciting or complicated' as a project in and of itself. But it embodied the experiences and knowledge that were gained through

its production. Cool projects in hackerspaces were therefore not necessarily about the thing itself being produced; rather, they held value as
the set of processes, potentially frustrating but ultimately pleasurable,
that they had involved.

In popular culture coolness is often related to novelty. (According
to research done in schools in Norway, iPads are cool, and confer coolness on their users, in part because they are new; an iPad2 is cooler
than an iPad1[6] – or was when the research was carried out.) Novelty,
innovation and originality were also valued in hackers' and makers'
projects as something that helped to make a project cool. In contrast
to much of mainstream culture, though, novelty couldn't just involve
something that you found or bought or copied (the buying-a-brand-
new-iPad effect). A project was cool when its originality or quirkiness
was something that you brought to it yourself – when it was something
that you thought of, or designed, or tweaked in a new way. As such, it
might become a 'trophy object' or win you 'bragging rights'. It earned
you respect because your innovation or skill was invested in it.

Fee summed up the hackerspace she was a part of as 'a place for
people to make cool projects'. But what, we asked her, makes a project
cool? She was hesitant to give a definitive answer because 'if you want
to do it, it's a cool project' – because, in other words, coolness is in part
attached to your personal passions and to living out your enthusiasms,
whatever they are. Wanting to make a project, and caring about it,
automatically made it cool to you. But at the same time she wanted to
highlight the role of creativity and originality:

> I think any project that people want to make that's something that you
> – that's not completely trivial to make that requires you to sort of think
> about it and be creative about it, and like if you were to build something
> from a kit, that might be fun and interesting but the result wouldn't be
> as cool a project as something that you made up yourself and had to
> tinker with. So I guess it probably involves creativity and maybe doing
> something that hasn't exactly been done before, trying to make some-
> thing yourself that you have not made before. I would call those cool
> projects, I guess.

Fee was unwilling to say that any kind of project was uncool. But it was
definitely more cool to make from scratch, 'tinkering' with a project
and doing something new, than to 'build something from a kit'. Creativity was key. It was cool to do something 'that hasn't exactly been
done before'; to be novel, ingenious, quirky. In this respect there is a
connection to the norms which govern computer hacking. As Gabriella
Coleman has shown, coding culture values cleverness, ingenuity and

skill: hackers, she writes, 'define the meaning of the free individual through this very persistent inclination to find solutions; they revel in directing their faculty for critical thought toward creating better technology'.[7] There's also a connection with the notion, described as part of the hacker spirit, that hacking means making technology work better for you. Fee says that coolness is connected to projects that you had 'made up yourself'. If projects are chosen according to one's personal passions and interests, then novelty is best applied in finding solutions to one's particular needs or in tweaking a technology so it is the best possible fit for your life.

Creativity and originality didn't have to result in serious, useful technologies. Quirkiness was also valued, and many hackers were explicit that they saw their activities and their projects as fundamentally playful.[8] You might do a project 'just for the grins', or view your hacker or makerspace as a 'playground'. As we heard Reg comment earlier, you didn't need a reason to work on a project: you didn't need a solid outcome, or business plan, or understanding of what it would be good for. It was enough that you were interested in it and wanted to see if you could build a working motor, or identify the DNA in your sushi, or fix up an old piano, or whatever else took your fancy. Again, it was hard for people to articulate what drew them to these fancies. Often, they told us, they emerged from long-term personal fascinations with computers, or technology generally, or tinkering. They might have been interested in these kinds of activities and tools since childhood, or work in a technological area. Some people 'just have an itch that they want to scratch'. The sense was that the appeal of particular projects, and indeed hacking and making more generally, was something deeply personal, connected to who you were as an individual. It could not be readily explained by the need to create something instrumentally useful to yourself or others, or by commercial drivers.

Cool projects, then, were those that were personally meaningful, novel and creative, and challenging. Those we spoke to had an intuitive understanding of this. Even where they couldn't articulate what drew themselves or others to particular projects, there was a sense that 'you knew it when you saw it'. There was, however, one other important factor that some hackers and makers discussed as drawing them to their activities or projects, one which wasn't necessarily explained in terms of coolness but which nonetheless seemed to be an important driver in structuring what people got from participating in hacker and makerspaces. This was a desire to be hands-on: to actually engage with the messy, resistant physical stuff of the world around you. Some people, at least, were drawn to hacker and makerspaces exactly because they offered a focus on physical materials, creation and community that stood in contrast to their increasingly digitized and mediated experience of everyday life.

While hackers and makers didn't tend to draw a sharp distinction between computer-based hacking and more hands-on making or hacking (those in hacker and makerspaces were often involved in both), they did at times talk about an over-engagement with the digital that led them to the pleasures of making. There were a number of IT professionals amongst our interviewees; one explained that his 'after-work interest is in physical stuff' like soldering electronic systems or making a robot rather than in the computer work he spent his days doing. Exactly because these individuals already spent their time coding – something which made them an important resource for the hackerspace – they liked to immerse themselves in making and creating physical things. More generally, people spoke of the value of a space where they could get their hands dirty and thereby learn, know, in a different way. You need, one hacker told us, to 'tickle the parts of the brain that are not satisfied with a completely virtual pursuit'. Someone else, whose previous creative activities had involved writing, had 'felt that need to get the rest of my body involved in making'. Many others spoke about the difference that getting to do and make with your own body, as opposed to watching or reading or hearing, could make to your understanding of a material or technology – a difference that at times would lead to a kind of flow experience, as you started to realize 'oh, these things actually connect together'. Many hacker and maker projects involved a mix of different techniques and technologies: sewing and electronics, say, to build Fee's stuffed doll; or mechanics and software to make a set of musical stairs. Part of the value of such projects was not only that it forced you to learn a new set of techniques or skills – given that you might be great at electronics but know nothing about sewing, or vice versa – but that it gave you new physical experiences. Hacker and makerspaces were places where you could 'learn by doing'; places that were dirty and messy in an aestheticized world. Even if you personally wanted to hack software and programs, this 'artistry' of the physical world was something that was valued.

The Pleasure of the Hack

Cool projects therefore provide a number of attractions to their creators. They may present an interesting challenge and thus provide opportunities for learning: someone told us that one thing that made a project cool for them was when 'it's not expected that...someone at my level could do it'. They could be fun, quirky or playful, like the swarm of flying robots one of our interviewees had dreamt up (downgraded to a single robot, in the cold light of day, but still an inarguably cool project). They might provide an opportunity to engage with the material world, to 'get your hands dirty' after a 9-to-5 in an office. Their pleasures might ultimately escape language: plenty of people were lost for words when asked about what drew them to the projects they worked on. 'It's more, you know, just being who you are', said Winni, when we asked her what made a project cool or appealing.

What is clear is that – just as the emphasis in the hacker spirit on creativity and passion would suggest – hackers' and makers' projects were often invested with passion and emotion. Those we spoke to were excited about the projects that they worked on. Projects are deeply meaningful to hackers and makers as an expression of their personalities, interests and desires. This was often articulated through language in an emotional register. 'I'm completely in love' with a 'really nice bacteria', Orla told us. 'I fell in love' with programming, said Nina. A barbot project – a robot that serves drinks – was described as 'just funny...It was fun'. What attracts particular individuals to particular projects, from barbots to home-turned motors, is exactly intangible because it is an expression of who those individuals are and of their deepest passions and affects.[9] Coolness in this context has to be unique, rather than mass-produced, to the extent of being defined by the nature of a single individual.

The difficulty of pinning down the nature of pleasure in hacker and makerspace projects comes through in a short film, *The Pleasure of the Hack*, produced by researcher Kevin Gotkin.[10] The film, made as a graduate student project and shot in the Philadelphia hackerspace Hactory, attempts to represent the unrepresentable: the emotions and experiences that constitute hacking. It traces some of the pleasures of hacking – things like the joy and frustration of working at, and eventually overcoming, problems; the thrill of learning; the satisfactions of community. Just as the hackers we spoke to talked of the pull of hands-on engagement with the physical world, and struggled to articulate what drew them to their projects, the film acknowledges that the pleasures of hacking can never be conveyed through text or even images on film. To a non-participant, there is something intangible about them; like playfulness generally, they can never be fully explained, or analysed, or conveyed to another. 'Hacking', Gotkin's voiceover says, 'escapes how we describe or explain it in language or images. It's almost there, in words, and then not.'

Throughout the film hackers talk – or do their best to talk – about what they get from hacking. A key aspect of this relates to the sense of community that we've seen repeatedly is so important to hackers' and makers' imagination of hackerspaces. Gotkin's interviewees talk about the satisfaction of working with others, and of having the community as a resource when the frustrations of hacking get too much. There's always, they say, the possibility of reaching out for assistance when the problem you are working on seems simply to be intractable. But there is also mention of a slightly different kind of satisfaction of community, one that relates to feeling part of the 'in-crowd'. 'It's kind of cool', one interviewee says, 'to be part of a subculture'. Though the film emphasizes the openness of Hactory – which, like the hacker and makerspaces we visited, seeks to be accessible and welcoming to all – it also gives the sense that there is a definite pleasure in being part of a group which, as one of the interviewees says, is 'special', in that it has its own jargon, events and knowledge. This specialness and coolness relates to the distinction that Fee made in trying to define what made a cool project. Hacking, says one of Gotkin's interviewees, is *not* DIY or making things from kits. Things have to be done the hard way: the frustration of getting stuck, sometimes permanently, is worn as a 'badge of honour'. People who use kits, who 'make' by following instructions, are not hackers.

Gotkin's film points us to the fact there are multiple layers of pleasure involved in the production of cool projects. I've discussed the immediate enjoyments and impacts that hackers and makers experience: the satisfaction of physical engagement with tools and materials, the joys of learning, the excitement of developing creative, novel solutions. But cool projects can also have more instrumental purposes. In Fee's case, for instance, her stuffed doll project was a means to an end: legitimate involvement in the hackerspace community. Simply hanging out in the space wasn't an option. She needed a project – any project – so that she could get to know other users of the space and the tools and technologies it provided. Gotkin's interviewees relate their projects, and their involvement in their hackerspace, to another pleasure, that of feeling part of a subculture or in-crowd. Their projects – and specifically the challenging nature of those projects – are used to separate themselves from other groups and individuals. Engaging in these innovative, frustrating projects marks them out as members of a special kind of community, involvement in which entails satisfactions above and beyond those of carrying out the projects themselves.

The hackers and makers we spoke to similarly suggested that cool projects could have other, more diffuse, benefits beyond their immediate satisfactions. There was a sense, for instance, that cool projects would render their creators cool. Alongside a consistent understanding of hacker and makerspaces, and the culture of hacking generally, as open and welcoming to all, it was also clear that there were differences in skilfulness and technical ability between hackers. Some people that we spoke to talked about 'noobs', or 'newbies', who didn't deserve the respect of others – not because they were new but because they should have known better.[11] This is Yan talking about some of the people that they had found weren't a good fit for their space:

> I don't know anybody personally who would encourage and maybe participate in the Sony and PlayStation hacks of last year because those were just blatant: We think you're stupid, you're arrogant, you're going down. It's a very childish – what we call script kiddie mentality. So people who come in and want to hack Chase or Google or whatever, we show them the door. They're really not welcome. They're noobs and misunderstand what we're about.

For Yan, black-hat hackers are noobs not because they aren't skilful (though, in computer hacking lore, 'script kiddies' do tend to lack genuine expertise),[12] but because they 'misunderstand' what hackerspaces are about. What gains you respect in the 'meritocracy' of hacking and making, he told us at another point, is having 'a head on your shoulders and…trying and learning'.

Having the right attitude is therefore key to gaining respect in hacker and makerspaces. Are you making an effort? Are you doing things, rather than sitting back and waiting for someone to help? But there was also an expectation that having this attitude would be expressed through the production of cool projects. If you had a cool project, you would be keen to show it off, in your hackerspace or beyond. This was, people told us, one rationale behind publishing project details online. It would gain you credit. Openly publishing your project on the net was, Kip said, 'sort of showing off to the hacker community', involving explaining 'here's what we did. We're cool because we were able to do it'. Cool projects reflected well on a hackerspace as a whole, and on particular individuals. Hacker culture functions, one hacker told us, through the 'transfer of prestige'.

The pleasures of cool projects therefore operate at a number of different levels. There are the immediate satisfactions – gaining victory over recalcitrant materials, learning new skills, or making something (like a barbot) that makes you laugh. But there are other things that hackers and makers can get from their projects. They can use them to experience community in action, as they collaborate on shared projects and solve problems together. Hackers and makers might work towards completing clever, innovative projects that will bring them prestige and give them 'bragging rights'. Their projects might show that they are part of an elite community, one which is counter-cultural and self-reliant and which depends on skill rather than on consumer products.

Looking at the projects that hackers and makers get involved in, and why they do so, points us to the way in which the material practice of hacking and making is always located within wider social worlds. The pleasures of hacking are in some respects inexpressible, and can be experienced only through actually getting your hands dirty (whether with wood, metal, solder or code). But more social pleasures leave the material domain and are experienced in the form of congratulations from your peers, number of downloads on Thingiverse, or photos on a wiki. Hacking and making, in other words, are not just about the project itself, but about the social, economic and political worlds that that project is part of. It's these wider resonances and ramifications that I look at further in the next chapter.

9

Emancipation and Commodification
This Was a Movement That Could Do Something Good

'I want to change the world', said Nick, and Kerry, and Lynn, and Willow. Different people in different hackerspaces and different locations around the US, and they expressed themselves in slightly different ways – but they, and many others that we spoke to, had a desire to be a part of changing society for the better. They loved the individual projects that they worked on, certainly, and enjoyed the practice of hacking and making. But they were excited about hacker and makerspaces for other reasons alongside such personal, private pleasures. They had high expectations for hacking and making as it spread around their local communities and the globe. 'I feel like history is being made', Keira told us, 'and I'm a bloody part of it'. In part this was about the rolling out of forms of personal empowerment that they had experienced. Hacking was about 'reclaiming ownership' of one's devices and neighbourhoods, Ulrik told us. Hackerspaces provided the resources for people to go out and learn and do what they wanted, said someone else. But change was also envisaged as stemming from a more general cultural shift towards new kinds of creativity and innovation. Hacking has the potential, said Kerry, to solve 'really interesting problems in really interesting ways'.

Many others are excited about the potential of the maker movement. Earlier in the book I quoted Professor Danielle George, who delivered the Royal Institution's 2014 Christmas lectures: if we 'take control of the technology around us and think creatively', she said, 'then solving some of the world's greatest challenges is only a small step away'.[1] Her lectures suggested that this control of technology can be accomplished by becoming a tinkerer and learning to hack everyday devices like light bulbs or electric motors. Dale Dougherty, the founder of *MAKE* magazine, has argued that making has the potential to revitalize education, spark economic growth and development, and help those in the poorest parts of the world. US government, business and education should, he writes, 'look to the maker movement for tips on how to create an ecosystem of talent, connections, and learning that will lead to a truly innovative economy and society'.[2] The Fab Foundation, which coordinates Fab Labs around the world, aims to provide access to the tools of digital fabrication and thereby create 'opportunities to improve lives and livelihoods around the world'.[3]

We saw in the previous chapter that makers and hackers presented their projects as personal and individual, and as something that involved a high degree of emotional investment. At the same time, making and hacking were not seen as a solely private project, but as something that could, to greater and lesser extents and in different ways, impact the wider world. Making might lead to innovation or new scientific knowledge; change the lives and opportunities of young people; empower those in majority world countries; or simply point the way to the technologies that will become mundane in ten or twenty or thirty years' time. As we visited different hacker and makerspaces and spoke to different people using them there was often a palpable sense of excitement. This was something bigger than any particular space or set of individuals. This was a movement that could do something good.

Hacking and making were seen as something intrinsically positive, which could impact the world for the better. Hacker and makerspaces, we were told, could be a 'force for change'. Sometimes this desire to make a difference was overt and immediate, taking concrete form within the physical and social environment of the local hackerspace. Kim, who was involved in the diversity-oriented space we visited, was quite clear that this space had a political agenda which involved empowering particular local communities. She was interested in supporting entrepreneurship in these communities and in helping to improve the monetization of traditional skills, such as sewing or carpentry, that might benefit from having the 'maker' label applied to them. The space also wanted, she said, to 'address the deficit of people of colour and women in some fields', and in particular in programming and STEM (science, technology, engineering and mathematics) subjects. This makerspace, and others like it, were explicitly seeking to change the lives of its members for the better and, through them, to impact society at large.

More generally many of the hackers and makers we spoke to saw their space as having what one biohacker called a 'community education mission'. This might involve reaching out to adults, or children, or both. Even if such education programmes weren't formalized, or weren't immediately practicable because of constraints in the physical space, 'all of us', New York-based hacker Nick told us, 'have an interest in teaching children to be more like us'. Many hackers were evangelistic about the benefits of the hacker lifestyle, and it was taken for granted that hackers and makers would be interested in allowing more people access to this lifestyle. This came through, for instance, in a sense of the importance of supporting children and young people's STEM education, which many people felt was lacking in the US. This is one biohacker, Kerry, talking excitedly about some of the workshops they'd run for children at their space:

> We've got a whole series for kids in the summer [...] In fact, there's a great photo, one of the founders took it actually, there's a girl that's come into class, who's what? 8? She can do a hack with the GFP.[4] And she could teach the class she understands it so thoroughly. It's amazing. You give kids the tools and basically explain it, and they're off and running. [At another class] we had fourteen kids and seventy per cent of them were girls. Which I thought was really awesome. Get as many women in science as possible.

Kerry had told us there had been a good overall response to the classes they were running, but that she was particularly pleased that they were reaching, and enabling to become skilful, girls and young women. Others talked about giving people who'd been put off science at school a chance to access it again through hacking and making, or about wanting to patch the gaps in a failing or inadequate education system. In all of these conversations, hacking and making were seen as relating to wider educational goals. Participation in a hackerspace might help boost interest in science and technology, give you skills that related to your formal education, or recruit young people into STEM professions.

There were other, more diffuse, expectations attached to hacking and making. The hackers and makers we spoke to were excited about the development of a movement around hacking and making, and felt that it could change things in a powerful way. But it wasn't always clear what that change would look like. Katherine, for instance, was a Boston-based hacker who saw the rise of hacking and making as part of a much-needed creative wave in US culture. 'We've lost all manufacturing in this country', she said. 'And I think this is part of the move to bring it back.' The creativity and meeting of minds that took place within her makerspace felt to her like 'the kind of thing that spawned the space programme'. Yan, the Arizonan hacker, similarly had hopes for national development through his hackerspace and others like it. They didn't just want more members for the sake of it, he said:

> We're not about getting more money. We're about getting more people interested in doing awesome stuff, advancing technology and learning forward, and advancing America in world STEM and science and innovation and that kind of stuff. And not even nationally. There's hackerspaces internationally. [...] Let's transcend that stuff and bring awesomeness to the world.

Yan had been talking about rivalry between local hacker and makerspaces. Such rivalry, and petty concerns about getting more money, is the 'stuff' he says needs to be 'transcended'. Many hackers would agree with Yan's mission to 'bring awesomeness to the world' regardless of national or international politics. Awesomeness might involve 'advancing technology and learning' and 'advancing America', as in Yan's account, but also providing services to a local community, changing society from the bottom up to become more active and less consumption-oriented, or connecting people in ways that would bring about new kinds of innovations and technologies. At the very least, hackerspaces involve 'a lot of people who are willing to be invested and help out'.

Self-actualization and serious leisure

There was therefore a clear value placed on hacking and making – and through them, hacker and makerspaces – above and beyond the personal benefits that hackers and makers gained from participating in the movement. At the same time, those we spoke to had much more to say about those personal benefits than about the wider changes they told us hacking was producing. They had high expectations of the maker movement: it would create innovation, help the disempowered, boost national economies. In this respect there were echoes of public discussion of hacking and making, and of promises of paradigm shifts, disruptive innovation and a new industrial revolution. But when it came to it, the hackers and makers we interviewed said rather little about what this disruption looked like, or how it was happening in and through their hacker and makerspaces. Aside from those involved in women- or diversity-oriented spaces, few people had specific examples of how local, societal or international change was being triggered by hacking and making activities, whether their own or other people's.

It was much easier to locate the power of hacking and making at the level of personal change and empowerment. For many that we spoke to, the experience of hacking was connected to self-actualization and fulfilment: it was this that made it so emotionally and personally resonant. While hackers and makers might also talk about hacking's potential for wider change and social good, their immediate concern was its effects on their own lives.

In our interviews, this came across in the ways in which people talked about hacking as a lifestyle or hobby, or as they explicitly described their hacking and making activities as personal projects for self-actualization. For many users of hacker and makerspaces, hacking did not necessarily mean adopting a particular political or social mission, opting out of mainstream society, or indeed doing anything radically different from those with other kinds of hobbies. The pleasures of hacking were personal pleasures, realized on the level of individual satisfaction rather than that of social change or economic innovation. Hackers and makers were seen as tinkerers or 'hobbyists'. Many happily acknowledged that hackerspaces had much in common with other kinds of hobbyist associations, from motorbike clubs to quilting circles.

What did it mean to have hacking as your hobby? For Denver it was a way of making sure he kept learning while in a 'brain-dead job'. He had been working, he told us, for a great company but in a role that simply didn't challenge him enough. One day, he said:

> I was sitting in my office and I was thinking to myself I'm actually getting dumber every day, like I feel less intelligent than I did last week, and it's only going to get worse. And I thought to myself I need a hobby or something to get my brain working again [...] And it's kind of branched out since then and it kind of dovetails with my hobbies, and I've gotten much better over the years. So now, like now I honestly feel smarter every day than I did before.

The project Denver started working on after his moment of crisis was building a toy steam engine from scratch; this was, he said, something he'd always wanted as a kid. This was before hackerspaces took off in the US, so he was, more or less, on his own. He bought himself a CNC router, did a lot of Googling, and got to work, teaching himself how to machine the different components he would need. Since then, he says, his projects have 'kind of branched out' and he's 'gotten much better over the years'. He mentions two benefits of this self-taught ability in machining: it 'dovetails with my hobbies' (and therefore relates to other interests he has) and, thanks to the constant learning it involves, 'now I honestly feel smarter every day than I did before'.

Lou worked on very different kinds of projects to Denver: she was part of a large makerspace and her particular interest was in welding large metal sculptures. But her approach to her making was similar in that she emphasized its personal benefits and its status as a means of self-actualization. At the time that we talked with her she had recently left a high-powered job as a consultant and was 'gifting myself at least twelve months of whatever I want'. What she wanted, she had found, was to invest time and energy in making and in developing the creative visions she had nurtured throughout her career. She had had a ritual, she told us, throughout her career, in which each morning she would meditate and make a drawing. By this point in her life she 'had hundreds of sculpture ideas that were all unborn in the physical world'. This period was her opportunity to realize some of them:

> I'm creating out of pure joy, right? Because the other thing about this year, for this twelve-month period, I'm not trying to sell anything. It has nothing to do with money. So I have allotted this time where everything I create is because I'm curious about it, because I want to learn about some technique, because I have some image that I want expressed. So it means that I get to kind of dabble and do all sorts of things.

Lou's making was explicitly tied to self-expression and to the development of creative skills that had – she implied – been on the back burner during her four years as a management consultant. Her making had 'nothing to do with money': she wasn't thinking about how her work could be sold, or commercialized, or made more attractive to potential customers. It was self-indulgent in the sense that it was driven solely by her own interests. Ultimately, she said, it was creation 'out of pure joy'. The impression she gives is that her creative activities are not only more joyful than the work she had been doing previously, but more authentic. Her twelve months of making was designed to be a period where she could explore the possibilities available to her. If she followed her desires, her passions, for a year, where would she end up? Who would she be?

For both Denver and Lou the spaces they belonged to were in some senses a means to an end. Though they both enjoyed the community within them (Denver, for instance, talked about enjoying being 'inspired. I want to see what people are doing because it's going to increase my capability'), this, again, related to their personal projects and their effects on themselves, as individuals. Their priority was not the gathering movement around hacking and making, wider social change, or the revitalization of US innovation. Rather, they used hackerspaces because these spaces, and the community in them, allowed them to develop new aspects of themselves.

This way of using hacker and makerspaces brings us back to the notion of serious leisure. Serious leisure, as I discussed in chapter 2, is the sustained pursuit of some hobby or activity. It has the seriousness of work – it requires effort and training, involves a 'career' through which one's skills and involvement develop, and results in long-term satisfactions rather than short-term pay-offs – but without the remuneration. Theorists of serious leisure view it as a means of gaining the kinds of psychic benefits and social interactions that paid employment has traditionally been assumed to provide. Robert Stebbins, who popularized the concept, is clear that serious leisure is a project of the self as much as being about the chosen activity in and of itself. He argues, for instance, that there are

> eight durable benefits, or broad outcomes, of serious leisure [...] They are self-actualization, self-enrichment, self-expression, regeneration or renewal of self, feelings of accomplishment, enhancement of self-image, social interaction and belongingness, and lasting physical products of the activity (e.g., a painting, scientific paper, piece of furniture).[5]

Serious leisure is therefore about developing an enhanced sense of self. The benefits are only in part the products of your activity (Stebbins' examples are 'a painting, scientific paper, piece of furniture', but we might just as easily substitute open-source code, a working steam train, a sculpture or a robot). In addition to the things that you make, satisfaction comes from 'self-actualization...self-expression...enrichment of self-image', as well as 'social interaction and belongingness'. Stebbins is clear that these satisfactions are in part derived from the challenges that serious leisure involves. The creation of a painting, or a steam engine, cannot be too easy; such creation is psychically pleasing exactly because it requires deep thought and concentration, the slow resolution of problems and challenges, and learning that stretches you to the limit of your abilities. Denver and Lou describe their making as a means of learning or the expression of creativity, and thereby a development of their authentic selves, the people they are or want to be. Their making activities are exactly about 'self-expression' and 'renewal of self', as well as the construction of particular kinds of identities. At least implicitly, these are projects that are focused on personal development.

Serious leisure is about becoming the person that you want to be, but it is also about being part of something. One of the benefits of a serious leisure career is 'social interaction and belongingness'. To use

Putnam's language, serious leisure gives you social capital. Through engaging in a community around your chosen activity, you gain not just networks of friends and acquaintances but the sense of being part of something bigger than yourself. In this respect, too, there are clear parallels with how people experience involvement in hacker and makerspaces. Community is key to hacking and making: by signing yourself up for involvement you commit to mutuality, the sharing of knowledge, and grassroots governance and administration. By aligning yourself with the characteristics of the hacker spirit, and thereby choosing to value things like creativity, being proactive, and learning by doing, you become part of a wider fraternity of hackers, a movement that reaches beyond yourself or your local hacker or makerspace to encompass a way of life followed by people all over the globe. Again, the psychic benefits are clear. Through your leisure activities you are able to experience a sense of meaning and purpose, alongside the more immediate benefits of social capital (friendships, contacts, professional and personal networks).

On not being political

Thinking of hacking and making as a form of serious leisure both emphasizes its status as a hobby, for many involved in it, and raises questions about the relation of such hobbies to wider landscapes of innovation, entrepreneurship and technological development. For most of those we spoke to, hacking and making are, indeed, a leisure activity, and is pursued for reasons of self-actualization. Despite public rhetoric around it that suggests that it is something more – a technological revolution, or an opportunity for economic regeneration – hacking and making were primarily viewed as personal projects of enjoyment and self-improvement. They can enable you to explore who you are, make the stuff that you want, build an identity as part of a select community, or develop your skills. Certainly, we were told, these activities might also empower others, stimulate innovation and change the world. But these aspects were less visible in the experiences of the hackers and makers we talked to. They were gestured towards, rather than described as a part of the everyday experience of hacking and making.

There was a similar emphasis on the personal when we spoke to hackers and makers about politics, and the role, if any, that this played within their spaces. Few of the spaces we visited saw themselves as politically active. At the very least, there was a shared sense of the importance of openness and the need to be welcoming to anyone, regardless of their political affiliation; some spaces, for instance, had members who had been involved in the Occupy movement, but this was generally kept strictly separate from their activities in the hackerspace. It needed to be clear, Nick said, that their space didn't 'have a unified point of view and that individuals are free to do what they want'. The hackerspace was thereby viewed as politically neutral, somewhere that Democrats and Republicans and anarchists might rub shoulders without their different views becoming an issue. A few people told us explicitly that what they did was different from more 'political' versions of hacking. This tended to be based on a distinction made with hackers and hackerspaces, in Europe or elsewhere, which were overtly part of an actively resistant counter-culture. This was fine, people said – but it was not for them. 'We're very much a hackerspace', one hacker, Dan, told us. 'But we're also not because we don't have a lot of the cultural political baggage that a lot of the hackerspaces have.' Dan's space, he told us, didn't want to be a 'cause'. They didn't want to get distracted by wider social or political projects as some other hackerspaces had been; for them, the emphasis had to be on making stuff (and on building a community based around these activities: they saw themselves as a 'clubhouse'). Because of this they occasionally got some pushback:

> Well, we'll get some people from some European countries coming in, like, This isn't a hackerspace. I know what a hackerspace is. Our hackerspaces are political. One of our earlier members, he's Austrian and his wife is involved at Metalab, the hackerspace. You know, where this current trend has started from. And they're very much – they are active. They are political. This is like, We're doing cool things with electronics so that we can subvert the paradigm. Or it's like, This is a GPS tracking, slash, quadcopter spying on the activist, whatever. We've got a laser shooting gallery over here [laughs].

Dan is, perhaps, a little sensitive about an implied criticism of his space: he spent some time in his interview reflecting on what members wanted the space to be and how that differed from other kinds of hackerspaces (such as those in 'European countries'). He laughs about the contrast – 'subverting the paradigm' versus 'we've got a laser shooting gallery over here' – but at the same time his point is clear. This space is about fun, about leisure and pleasure. It is, perhaps, slightly less worthy and earnest-seeming than the political hackerspaces he is caricaturing. The activities at Dan's space are focused on change at the level of the individual, or at least that of the small group (as we saw in the previous chapter, the laser shooting gallery was a collaborative project). Just as with Denver and Lou, and other hobbyist hackers, hacking's effects are first and foremost on hackers themselves. Politics – and the wider world generally – is something that exists outside the world of the hackerspace.

Many hackers and makers, then, are happy to see their activities as hobbies: leisure projects which enable them to develop into more authentic or satisfied versions of themselves. Hacking and making are personal rather than political. Affiliating yourself to hacking and making is a lifestyle: a personal choice that is used as a means of identity and community building. In this imagination of hacking and making, becoming a user of hackerspaces is one possibility among many. Some people are into dog breeding, or learning to bake the perfect sourdough loaf, or becoming expert in pre-war cinema. Others like making. Hackers and makers tended to argue that their lifestyle was better, more independent and self-reliant, than those that other people chose, but there was still no question that any of these choices were valid. The developing movement around hacking and making was described as both a world-changing revolution and, at the same time, a personal choice enacted at the level of the individual.

This points to a central tension within the growing movement around hacking and making, one that is expressed not just at the local level on which our interviews focused, but within the movement as a whole. The expectations being placed on the power of hacking and making are incredibly high. Its advocates are evangelistic about its potential to change individual lives and whole societies, whether that is through personal empowerment or through innovation and new business opportunities. But in many ways the practice of hacking and making is business as usual. On the one hand, we were told stories of empowerment, of 'changing the world', and of hacking's potential to revitalize US manufacturing. Hacking and making were described as counter-cultural and revolutionary: as we saw in chapter 5, the hacker spirit was portrayed as a reaction against passivity, and specifically against passive consumption. It's a choice that involves a commitment to self-agency – 'doing things' – as much as to the actual practice of hacking and making. On the other hand, hackers were often happy to see themselves as hobbyists, occupying their leisure time with tinkering activities with no pretensions to wider social change or to the production of grassroots innovations. In many cases, hacking and making were reliant on traditional commerce and indeed on mundane, but perhaps troubling, patterns of global manufacturing and consumption. Many of our interviewees got their supplies from Radio Shack, or other mainstream businesses. Ultimately, much of the material they used, from electronics components to equipment such as laser cutters, had been produced in factories in China. The hacker lifestyle might look rather different to mainstream North American consumption, but it was still primarily meaningful on the level of the private and individual, rather than the societal or political. It was not disrupting manufacturing as a globalized enterprise, or changing the conditions of production aside from in a very few, specific projects.[6]

We have seen something of this tension before. In chapter 3 I quoted the European hackers Johannes Grenzfurthner and Frank Apunkt Schneider on the loss of hackerspaces' counter-cultural emphasis. While early hackerspaces, they wrote, 'fit best into a counter-cultural topography', later spaces had turned into 'tiny geeky workshop paradises' devoid of political awareness.[7] For Grenzfurthner and Apunkt Schneider, this change was normative. Hackerspaces, they believed, *should* be political. They should provide a space for 'an alternative lifestyle within the heart of bourgeois darkness'. But for many of the spaces that we visited, and the hackers and makers we spoke to, this was a false understanding of what hackerspaces are and should be. 'It wouldn't help our cause', Nick told us, if their space was 'to be political in any particular way'. Hacker and makerspaces were 'neutral'. Politics, like the projects one chose, was a matter of individual choice. Hackerspaces were exactly not about collective action, but were instead concerned with resourcing individuals. 'Neutrality' meant that hacker and makerspaces were not really concerned with what this resourcing was for: it might be to help people develop stable and satisfactory identities, or (more rarely) to equip them for wider political engagement or business development. The spaces that we visited tended to cultivate a studied neutrality on wider political dynamics, whether relating to social justice, the role of corporations and business in hacking and making, or one's political affiliations.

Commodifying the counter-culture

I've already discussed (in chapter 3) MAKE as a key commercial presence in hacking and making – one which has rather more street-cred than TechShop, which most of those we spoke to saw as a resource rather than a community. MAKE, with its suite of related offerings (the magazine, the Maker Faires, the online store) has pretensions to represent and to connect makers everywhere. Many of the hackers and makers we spoke to had visited, displayed at, or organized Maker

Faires. 'Maker Media', its website says, 'is a global platform for connecting Makers with each other, with products and services, and with our partners.'[8] (It also suggests, somewhat opportunistically, that its activities 'jumpstarted' the maker movement around the world.) MAKE promotes an image of makers which draws on the characteristics of the hacker spirit: they are 'creative, resourceful and curious', for instance, and bring a 'DIY mindset to technology'.[9] At the same time, the organization is also about equipping makers in a way that doesn't necessarily require creativity, resourcefulness or curiosity. Why build your own toy steam engine from scratch when you could buy a kit with the parts ready milled?[10] Why wrestle with fabric and waterproof wiring when you could buy the 'Smart Sewing Basic Kit' for only $15?[11] Why figure out how to hack your own code when you could follow a step-by-step guide?

MAKE can be understood as one example of the phenomemon that Kevin Wehr has discussed in the context of DIY: the commodification of self-reliant, from-scratch approaches, such that an edgy and countercultural vibe is sold to willing consumers.[12] MAKE's products bring with them the ethos of DIY without necessarily requiring the work involved in actually doing it yourself. At least part of what is being sold is a vision of yourself, the consumer, as a creative, hands-on kind of person. Perhaps it's not surprising that MAKE is wildly successful. It hasn't yet been going a decade but continues to expand rapidly: every year, there are Maker Faires in more places, its professional activities grow (most recently with Maker Con and Maker Camp), and the magazine circulation increases.[13]

I'm not the only person to notice that MAKE is doing pretty well out of commercializing the ostensibly counter-cultural spirit of hacking and making. The technology writer and critic Evgeny Morozov has written about the long history of technological optimism – access to tools will change the world! – of which MAKE, and the boosterism of people like Chris Anderson, Dale Dougherty and Mark Hatch, is the latest manifestation. Such boosterism, Morozov argues, not only ignores the ways in which access and opportunity continue to be structured by enduring inequalities (as he writes, 'if you need to raise money on Kickstarter, it helps to have fifty thousand Twitter followers, not fifty'),[14] but fails to reflect on how proximity to power, in the form of big businesses like MAKE, might limit or re-direct any revolutionary or emancipatory potential of maker-oriented technologies. The blogger David Bollier, commenting on Morozov's arguments, relates this process of commercialization back to the early computing pioneers and the appropriation of the DIY ethic by the business behemoths who would come to define our experience of personal computing. Apple, he writes, 'adopted the patois of personal empowerment, but shrewdly ignored the substance. There would be no freedom to examine the source code of software and modify it to suit individual needs'.[15] Just as most of us are handcuffed by the blackboxed settings of our operating systems or iPhones, a commercialized maker movement runs the risk of allowing us to tinker only within certain pre-defined limits.

These concerns also emerged, though to a very limited degree, as we spoke to hackers and makers. For a few people, at least, there was some unease about the ways in which hacking and making was becoming something to be bought and sold. This was often hard to articulate, and emerged around the edges of our conversations: a comment about 'selling out' here, a concern about overly commercialized spaces there. Nick, the New York-based hacker, was perhaps most aware of the way in which the language of hacking and making was starting – at least in his view – to reflect different relations to the market. 'Maker is a very new term', he told us. 'Who has a vested interest in bringing that up, and why would they overwrite or attempt to overwrite hacker, and what purpose does it serve?'

> There are a number of organizations such as O'Reilly [the group behind Maker Media] that publish things built around the maker model or the maker term in that community that they're building, the Maker Faire, that sort of thing. So it's almost a branding approach if you think about it in those terms....there's a large industry that's growing up around building – there's a lot of companies like Radio Shack that have a vested interest in fostering more making, DIY-type stuff because that's their target market....So if you look at maker and making as a potentially commercialized version of this movement and you see hacking and hackerspaces as a grassroots side of it, you see the contrast there.

In contrast to others we spoke to (such as Clare, who was adamant that hacker and makerspaces were the same thing), Nick explicitly wanted to distinguish between hacking and making: the terminology, he felt, reflected how commercialized the activity was. For him, hacking and hackerspaces were more 'grassroots', while the language of 'making' was more of a brand. There were plenty of businesses, he pointed out, who had an interest in selling stuff to DIY-ers and makers. If there is a coherent 'maker movement', Radio Shack or Best Buy or MAKE can target it as a market, selling makers not just the components and tools and technologies they need, but kits, introductory projects and advice. 'Maker' becomes a category of consumer, rather than being synonymous with the more transgressive figure of the hacker – a figure which, someone told us, was still 'not socially acceptable'.

Rather few people, however, picked up on this distinction, or showed much concern about how commercialization might encroach on the spirit and practice of making and hacking. There was therefore a tension, in our interviews, between discussion of hacking and making as something that pushed you out of your comfort zone and was 'subversive', rule-breaking and maybe even 'anarchistic', and the ready acceptance of the market as an unproblematic mechanism for developing hacking. Hackerspaces were both free-wheeling spaces of creativity and counter-cultural thinking and potential spaces for new kinds of markets. As we've seen, few of those we spoke to were interested in innovation and commercial development. It was, however, generally taken for granted that traditional markets were what hackers and makers would turn to if a business opportunity did emerge. Tiah, for instance, was in the throes of setting up a hackerspace, and had been inspired by this process to think about starting 'a business, like a little business, a hackerspace business [...] I have found in starting this, that I am interested in people, organizing people'. Her vision was of commercializing her space, spinning it out so that it could reach more people, in the manner of TechShop or other makerspace franchises. Most of the hackers and makers we talked with similarly operated in a universe in which entrepreneurial activities were the natural way to develop new ideas and to effect social change.

Hacking, governments and educators

The dynamics around MAKE, TechShop and other forms of commercialization show how big business is becoming intertwined with hacking. But increasing commercialization is just one way in which hacking and making are entering the mainstream, being taken up by traditional authorities, and, perhaps, losing something of its countercultural edge. The promotion of hacking and making by governments offers further insight into the tensions that underpin the growth of the maker movement.

Take China. A couple of people we interviewed had recently visited, or were planning on visiting, Chinese cities in order to check out the hacking scene there. China was seen as a Mecca for making: just as Chris Anderson celebrates the opportunities China presents as a low-cost labour centre for makers wanting to scale up their production, those we spoke to talked dreamily about being able to go down to a factory or to a 'skyscraper' full of electrical components in order to test out your ideas on the spot. More than this, though, they told us that

China was an exciting place for hacking right now because the government was actively supporting the development of hackerspaces, in universities and elsewhere. ('The Chinese government doesn't care as much about liability as US universities', one hacker told us, 'and they're starting to give universities money to make hackerspaces inside their schools.') In 2011, for instance, there was a government call to develop 100 new community hackerspaces, or innovation houses, which was, as academic Silvia Lindter writes, widely interpreted 'as an endorsement of China's fledgling hackerspace community'.[16] The government-sponsored Maker Carnival has now run for three years, drawing some 100,000 people.[17] North American hackers, including our interviewees, talk enviously about this level of support. This, the hacking website Hackaday wrote triumphantly, is what happens 'when a government is run by engineers'.[18]

As Lindter has argued, at least some of this high-level support seems to stem from China's perceived 'creativity problem', and the concern that its educational system penalizes originality in favour of rote learning and a reliance on established authority.[19] Hackerspaces are seen as a way of nurturing independent thought and enabling a shift from manufacturing (the 'Designed in California, Made in China' effect) to home-grown innovation, design and invention. But this is not just about creating a more robust educational experience. 'One of these tinkers might develop the next groundbreaking technology,' Emily Parker writes, in the *Wall Street Journal*, as she reports on a Bejing hackerspace, 'or at least that is the hope of Chinese policy makers'.[20] Government support is tied to the notion that the creativity, independent thinking and tinkering spirit that are ostensibly incubated in hackerspaces will lead to the new Apple, or Google, or Pinterest, and the economic benefits thereof. Some of those we spoke to thought the same thing. 'What's your feeling about state-sponsored hackerspaces?' I asked one hacker who'd visited China, curious about how the hacker spirit meshed with intervention from a state with a poor humans rights record. Fantastic, they replied. 'You just have all this like amazing do-it-yourself low-cost open-source information flow being generated. I just think that's what we need [in America].'

The US government has the same idea. And though no one we spoke to had anything bad to say about Chinese government support for hackerspaces,[21] DARPA (the US Defense Advanced Research Projects Agency) interest in hacking has been received more critically. In 2012, DARPA announced it was working with MAKE in order to expand educational activities based around making;[22] it is also involved in Maker Faires[23] and gives grants to individual hackerspaces and hackerspace projects.[24] For Dale Dougherty, the founder of MAKE, 'DARPA funding [of MAKE's activities] signifies that a revitalized manufacturing capacity is a national priority':[25] supporting hacking and making in schools, in other words, will create a generation of 'bits to atoms' technological entrepreneurs (military and otherwise) who will boost the US economy. For many other hackers, the combination of young makers and the military is a queasy one.[26] DARPA's goal 'is to advance our military', one hacker told us. 'There's nothing fluffy about it. There's a little bit of euphemism, but they are there to make sure that our people who kill people get better at it'. The controversy led a number of high-profile hackers (including the founder of San Francisco's Noisebridge, Mitch Altman) to publicly disassociate themselves from MAKE activities, including the increasingly ubiquitous Maker Faires, and to a thousand angry internet comments arguing one way or the other (DARPA are evil...but their activities spawned the internet...but they kill people...but we need to revitalize US education).

Arguably, however, DARPA's involvement in the hacker and maker movement is a distraction.[27] It is too easy to criticize the way in which they seem to be co-opting making. What might be seen as more insidious is the gradual mainstreaming of hacking through its integration with education via the creation of makerspaces and making workshops in schools, libraries and museums.[28] Makerspaces are popping up in schools all over the US, often funded or part-funded by grants from businesses.[29] MAKE offers a 'Makerspace Playbook: School Edition', which provides a guide to setting up a makerspace in educational environments.[30] In *Make It Here*, a 2015 volume, librarians Matthew Hamilton and Dara Hanke Schmidt discuss 'inciting creativity and innovation in your library'.[31] 'The job market now requires new skills and technological fluencies', they write, and argue for the importance of creativity and playfulness in equipping students for the working world. Libraries can play a crucial role in this, offering trusted environments that, through the incorporation of making activities, go beyond their traditional role of information provision to support active, creative and self-directed learning. Similarly, museums and science centres have seen making as an opportunity to encourage learning about STEM in new and engaging ways. San Francisco's Exploratorium now hosts a 'tinkering studio' where visitors can 'slow down, become deeply engaged in an investigation of scientific phenomena, and make something'.[32]

What values are being inculcated through the promotion of hacking and making in educational environments? Unsurprisingly, it's not the anti-establishment, anti-corporate imaginations of hacking – those pushed by the likes of Johannes Grenzfurthner and Frank Apunkt

Schneider – that are being promoted here. One study of the Exploratorium's tinkering studio sets the focus firmly on tinkerers' learning: using the studio, the researchers suggest, may promote 'four different Dimensions of Learning: Engagement, Initiative and Intentionality, Social Scaffolding, and Development of Understanding'.[33] Making in this context is highly instrumentalized, seen as an activity that is simply a better, more effective means of getting museum visitors to learn about science and technology than traditional exhibits. The priorities of Hamilton and Hanke, the librarians encouraging the development of makerspaces in public libraries, are similarly clear:

> The skills needed by today's employers are communication, collaboration, and innovation. As STEM (Science, Technology, Engineering, Mathematics) education rises to prominence, it's become clear that hands-on modalities, such as Problem-Based Learning, are more effective pathways to education.[34]

Making, in other words, makes not just for good learning, but for good employees.

Few of these developments had impinged on the experiences of the hackers and makers that we spoke to (though some mentioned, with approval, concomitant educational enterprises like Khan Academy and, as we've seen, most were happy to view community education as part of the general mission of a hackerspace). The appropriation of hacking and making by educators can, however, be seen as part of a wider trend in what scholar Christo Sims has called progressive technological education, one that seeks to reinvent education for the twenty-first century through the use of new media technologies, gamification and real-world problems and cases.[35] This appropriation seems to be largely managed by MAKE and other arms of the commercial wing of hacking and making. Contrary to the priorities of those we spoke to, and their focus on hacking as self-actualization, it once again connects the practice of hacking with innovation and commercial development: the assumption is that by nurturing student makers, US education will produce a generation of employees and entrepreneurs equipped for twenty-first-century economies. As Sims suggests, such models of education assume that children are naturally creative, curious and innovative, and that these characteristics are exactly the ones that are required in future businesses. While they may not have been aware of these developments, this is a vision that our interviewees would probably agree with. As noted earlier, many hackers and makers *did* think that educational outreach was important, and that their activities do offer a good model for young people. Hacking and making were framed as being about learning in new, hands-on, mutualistic ways. There were rather few concerns about commercialization or appropriation of hacking generally. It seems likely, then, that this is one aspect of mainstreaming that would raise particularly few anxieties from hackers and makers.

There are deep tensions and contradictions both in what the hackers and makers we talked to told us and in public discussion of hacking and making generally. Hacking is something that will both change the world and that is primarily meaningful at the level of individual satisfaction and self-actualization. It is edgy and counter-cultural but also readily commodified. It is a radically alternative way of looking at the world and something that is excitedly adopted by mainstream educators. It celebrates a self-reliant, DIY ethos but is being framed as the solution that businesses and national economies need to spark their growth. It is a relaxed leisure activity but also a means of empowerment and transformative social change.

Some hackers would say that there is a battle for the soul of hacking and making going on. Johannes Grenzfurthner and Frank Apunkt Schneider, who wrote about the need to 'hack the spaces', or Mitch Altman, who withdrew from MAKE activities after they accepted money from DARPA, believe that hacking is something that is intrinsically political and counter-cultural. But there were few traces of such a battle in the interviews and visits we carried out: only a few people were concerned about commercialization or saw anything to criticize in the way in which hacking and making was spreading and taking shape. The question arises, then, as to whether hacking as an anarchistic, counter-cultural, transgressive form of resistance to consumption has ever been a stable phenomenon in North American hackerspaces. Perhaps the original, 'European', 'political' notion of hacking only ever existed in a few isolated enclaves. Perhaps the need to 'hack the spaces', to use the language of Grenzfurthner and Apunkt Schneider, has been incipient from the very start.

10

Who Is a Hacker?

No One Is Claiming that Involvement in a Quilting Circle Is Going to Prompt a New Industrial Revolution

The sourdough that lives in my fridge is getting on for two years old. I grew it myself, from flour and water and some mushed-up apple, and it's become a resilient and active starter, able to cope with being forgotten for a few weeks (ideally, it should be fed every week with more flour and water) and to act as an enthusiastic raising agent for all kinds of wheat, spelt and rye breads. Now that I've got the hang of keeping it alive I'm experimenting more with what I can do with it. Sourdough pancakes are a hit, and have the happy effect of using up a lot of starter: if you are feeding your sourdough every week, you inevitably have more than you can get through. Lately I've been trying to bake with heritage flours, and making dough with mixes of different flours and seeds. Sourdough breads tend to involve long proofing stages at low temperatures. Here in Copenhagen I've found that I can just stick a bowl of dough out on the balcony throughout the winter, to prove for a day or so before bringing it back inside to bake.

My experiments with sourdough culturing and baking have parallels with other kinds of DIY, serious leisure, and 'New Domesticity' projects. I like saving money on bread, and cooking for myself rather than relying on store-bought food. There's a satisfaction, an element of self-empowerment, to having mastered my at times unruly sourdough starter. Baking is a hobby, and something that has become part of my identity: to use the language of the serious leisure literature, there are aspects of self-actualization to it. There are social pleasures – being the person who brings gifts of home-baked bread – alongside the physical pleasures of the taste of the bread and the satisfaction of (a rather small-scale) self-reliance. At the risk of becoming a baking bore, I'm always keen to pass my starter on, and to talk about how I culture and use it.

Could we understand my activities as hacking? In chapter 5 I described the ways in which hackers and makers characterize their lifestyles. This 'hacker spirit' involved making things, doing things, understanding the world around you, tweaking aspects of that world to fit you, creativity, learning by doing, and a commitment to sharing knowledge and to community. Hacking was a mindset, one that involved self-reliance, a curious spirit and being active rather than passive. It was about claiming agency over the material world and the circumstances around you and, having done so, supporting other people in doing the same. A hacker has a particular attitude, a resistance to the mainstream, rather than any particular relationship to specific technologies. As we've seen, one can be a hacker or maker by fixing up an old piano, tinkering with DNA, writing open-source code, unlocking region-specific DVDs or making glow-in-the-dark clothing. How could this relate to sourdough baking?

Homebaking is certainly an active way of engaging with food: I'm not satisfied by buying bread from the supermarket or local bakery, however delicious it is, but want to make it for myself and understand everything that goes into it. Although I don't have detailed knowledge about the microbiology of my sourdough culture, I do now have a better understanding of how yeast can be cultured, what exactly is going on in the thick mix that is my sourdough starter, and the role of microbiological cultures in how bread behaves. I've learned by doing: as anyone who's tried my bread will attest, there were a few disasters in the early stages before I worked out the almost unconsciously recognized signs that tell you how to manage your sourdough culture. Simple experience, and repeated experimentation, have taught me things like what healthy sourdough should smell and feel like (rich and hoppy, like beer, and somewhere between spoon-sticking-up-in-it thick and watery thinness). And I certainly tweak and adapt my baking to suit my own needs, adding seeds and using different flours depending on my mood (and what's in the cupboard). I don't really feel part of a community, but I am an avid Googler, and use blogs and wikis to help me when I'm stuck on something, so I'm definitely learning from the knowledge and expertise of others in that respect.

Am I a hacker? My rather limited experiments with sourdough baking do seem to fit at least some of the characteristics of the hacker spirit.[1] And if my baking does, then so will many other activities: crafting in its various guises; DIY; the New Domesticity activities that Emily Matchar describes; creativity and connectivity through Web 2.0. Even the 'Do Something' *Guardian* newspaper campaign, with its emphasis on easily accessible, thrifty, creative, sociable and (above all) active leisure could be understood as incorporating some elements of the hacker spirit. If the hacker spirit, or lifestyle, is what it means to be a hacker, then the term seems to be open to many people outside of hacker and makerspaces. If it's about creative and active engagement with the world around us, about not being content with the systems that surround us but tweaking them to fit us, then maybe many of us, if not all, are hackers now.

The difference, of course, is that no one would claim that sourdough baking is new, innovative or heralding a new technological and economic era. For some enthusiasts, the older the sourdough starter the better the taste (there are starters around that have been grown since the 1800s);[2] for others, the whole point of homebaking is to go back to an age when food production was not carried out on a massive industrial scale.[3] The same is true of DIY, or dressmaking, or – to use an example given by one of our interviewees – being a member of a motorcycle club. These activities, and the kinds of clubs and associations through which people may get involved in them, have been around for decades, if not centuries. The spirit behind them might be the same as that found in hacker and makerspaces: interest in making and doing, a community orientation that encourages learning from others, hands-on engagement with the material world. But no one is claiming that involvement in a quilting circle is going to prompt a new industrial revolution.

This raises the question of the newness, or otherwise, of hacker and makerspaces themselves. Certainly, the spaces themselves are new. I've talked about the meteoric growth of hacker and makerspaces in North America and beyond: around 30 worldwide in 2007; almost 500 in 2011; 1,233 active spaces when I checked on hackerspaces.org in 2016.[4] Businesses like TechShop, MAKE and other makerspace franchises have emerged over the last decade. The terminology of hacker and makerspaces and that of the 'maker movement' is certainly an innovation. But are the practices that these spaces host anything different from those found in other kinds of craft or making-oriented associations? Is the sociology, the way in which hackers and makers interact with each other and with their tools and projects, different – or are hacker and makerspaces old wine in new bottles?

The novelty of hacking and making

Plenty of people have argued that the rise of hacker and makerspaces does represent something dramatically new. For many proponents,

the maker movement is both a discrete, clearly identifiable development and a step-change in how entrepreneurship and innovation are
imagined and carried out, something that is radically different from
what has gone before. One academic analysis of current discussion of
the maker movement notes the frenzied nature of much discussion of
hacking and making:

> Excited claims are made about workshops transforming practices of
> design, innovation, production and consumption; 'how you live, work
> and play in a world where anyone can make anything anywhere'.
> Excitement includes claims for a 'third industrial revolution' and post-
> consumer sustainable societies.[5]

Chris Anderson, Dale Dougherty and think tanks like the Institute for
the Future do acknowledge that making draws on well-established
modes of creating community or on humanity's natural ingenuity and
curiosity. In that respect, making is something that is very old. But the
distinctiveness – the newness – of this particular moment is, they say,
to do with emerging technology, and what that is enabling hackers,
makers and tinkerers to do. The internet has brought about 'a level of
interconnectedness that has helped to build a movement', writes Dale
Dougherty, the founder of MAKE.[6] That same interconnectedness can
allow an enthusiast in Michigan to contact, and get their ideas proto-
typed by, a workshop in India, or a budding entrepreneur in Switzer-
land to put in a bulk order from a Chinese factory. Technology is also
ushering in an age of rapid, cheap digital fabrication, in the shape of the
ever-increasing availability of 3D scanners and printers, among other
tools. 'Advanced fabrication tools', write the authors of a 2008 Institute
for the Future report, 'are falling in price, driving a shift in manufacturing from massive, centralized factories to flexible, lightweight, and
ad hoc production.'[7] What is new, according to these accounts, is the
way in which technologies like laser cutters and 3D printers are allowing garage tinkerers to become manufacturers on their own account.
Making things is simply becoming easier.
    This is true. But it is also something of an oversimplification of what
we found when we visited hacker and makerspaces. The stories we
were told weren't just about new technology as the driver for the rise
of making and hacking, or about new kinds of connectivity leading to
easy prototyping and manufacture. Instead, we heard about anything
from the passionate attachment some spaces had to their hard-earned
laser cutters to the protracted technical struggles 3D printers tended
to involve or the deliberate rejection, on the part of some hackers and
makers, of the new digital technologies that are meant to be so integral

to their activities. (Think about Ed, whom we met in chapter 8, and the antique oscilloscope he was fixing up. Its outdatedness was exactly its appeal.) What our interviewees told us was that, often, new technologies and the opportunities they offered were only tangentially important to their experiences of being a hacker or maker.[8] Other things were more vivid, more central to their understanding of the hacker spirit: finding a strong community, getting your hands dirty, doing rather than talking. Access to new technology was nice, sure, but it didn't define a hacker or makerspace.

This isn't to say that makers and hackers didn't describe what they were doing as distinctive or innovative. Those we spoke to did sometimes emphasize that the movement they were involved in was something different from other forms of leisure or making: as with many public commentators, they saw the activities hosted by hackerspaces as qualitatively different from those found in wider society. This distinctiveness, however, wasn't to do with particular technologies or the new opportunities enabled by the interconnectedness of the internet age. Rather, hacking was portrayed as something that is exclusive and special because of the ethos it involves. It's different from what has gone before, and from mainstream culture, because of its emphasis on being active. It's this emphasis, we were told, that makes it distinctively counter-cultural, and which marks out the maker movement as the vanguard of a new way of life.

We have seen something of this already, when I've discussed the hacker spirit. The hacker spirit was portrayed as something that was open and accessible to anyone. Anybody can become a hacker: you don't need to be a tech genius or have a degree or own lots of tools or equipment. But taking up this opportunity and becoming a hacker was also a choice. Some people, we were told, simply preferred to be passive. We saw this in Katie's comments about her flatmate, a woman who, Katie said, was 'just like, I just want to watch TV and that's all I want to do'. In emphasizing her flatmate's passivity, her contentment with Netflix as her sole leisure activity, Katie makes the point that this is someone who is fundamentally different from her and from her active, engaged, hacker lifestyle. Hacking is different from mainstream society, as exemplified by TV-watching flatmates, because the hacker spirit involves the decision to be active and do things. Such activity is the fundamental requirement for entry to hacker and makerspaces and to becoming a hacker. If you want to learn from others, you need to show that you are prepared to make an effort. If you want to hack and make, you have to *do* those things, not just talk about your projects. Passivity is never an option. Hackers need to be hands-on and to push themselves beyond their limits; they are expected to have opinions and to express them. As one hacker told us, 'we don't want wallflowers'.

It's this emphasis on active engagement that we were told made hacking and making distinctive. Hackers and makers did see themselves as counter-cultural and unusual, part of a new tide in how to live in majority world societies, but this difference was derived from their agency rather than their access to technology. In a country where most people are 'wage slaves and slaves to Starbucks and McDonalds and Walmart', one hacker told us, hackers and makers are the people who get fed up with the system and decide to escape its endless cycles of passive consumption. This escape, as of yet, remains niche. Hacker and makerspaces were sometimes portrayed to us as embattled enclaves, groups who were viewed by the wider world as quirky or hippies or drop-outs. Hacking is 'subversive', Nick told us. It involves 'breaking these general walls that we might have in our minds', said Kip.

This conception of the differentness of hacking and making, its newness when contrasted with mainstream North American culture, brings a rather different sense of the dynamics of hacking and making from that found in those public accounts which emphasize its entrepreneurial dimensions. In chapter 8 I mentioned some of the social pleasures of hacking. Community is central, I argued, but there are also satisfactions relating to being part of an elite group, a specialized subculture that sees itself as more wide-awake than society as a whole. Just as there are emergent faultlines around the degree to which hacking and making can and should be commodified (as we saw in chapter 9), this sense of being an elite subculture also leads to tensions as it comes into contact with the notion of hacking and making's accessibility. Hacking is open to anyone – but it's also closed to certain kinds of people (like Katie's TV-watching flatmate). The hacker spirit is widespread, found in anyone from DIY-ers to sourdough bakers – but it's also an attitude that is niche and counter-cultural. There are no requirements for becoming a hacker or maker – apart from the fact that you need to be able to demonstrate your interest and agency to those already in the hackerspace.

In the context of our interviews, these tensions were sometimes managed through ideas about 'our people'. Did hackers recognize newcomers or visitors as having the hacker spirit, and thus being 'one of us'? As our interviewees discussed hackerspaces and the community that forms through them, there was often a sense that there were 'right' and 'wrong' people for hackerspace involvement. Some people who visited hackerspaces were hackers, 'our' people, who were ripe for further participation. Others were not. 'You can tell the difference', one hacker told us, 'between somebody who gets it and somebody who doesn't'. As we've seen, this worked extremely well in terms of forming close, supportive communities. Many people spoke about their relief about finding 'their' community, their 'tribe', their 'safe haven'. If you are someone who is quirky and counter-cultural and likes things that the people around you are not so interested in, like electronics or programming or metalwork – which is how some, at least, of our interviewees described themselves – then it is incredibly exciting and empowering to find a group of other people who care about the same things and who make you feel at home. The relief that many hackers expressed, and the difference that joining a hackerspace had made to their lives, was something that was powerful and real. On the other hand, as we saw in chapter 7, the flip side of such communities is that they can function in equally powerful ways to exclude those who are 'not my kind of people' (to quote one San Francisco hacker). As several people pointed out, any kind of social group or community can only function by drawing boundaries between itself and the wider world. To ensure a sense of inclusion, certain people or groups have to be excluded. Distinguishing between 'our people', who have the hacker spirit, and others, who appear to be passive or lazy, is one way of doing this.

Overlapping communities

What I've discussed so far suggests that both public cheerleaders for the movement and hackers themselves would argue for the novelty of hacking and making; the former because they see new digital fabrication tools as defining the movement, and the latter because they view the hacker spirit as distinctively counter-cultural. Hacking and making, we were told, run counter to the mainstream in their emphasis on active understanding of and engagement with technology specifically, and the world at large generally. But the story is a little more complicated than this. While at times our interviewees emphasized hacking's novelty and difference, at others they talked about it as both very old and very similar to many other, non-hacking activities and groups. It was clear, for instance, that the hackers and makers we spoke to often saw their connections to groups outside of the hacking and making movement as just as, if not more, important than those within it. Even when people emphasized the innovative nature of hacking and making, they also noted that there was a high degree of continuity with other kinds of practices. Hacking and making were pretty much the same as quilting, they said, or online learning, or the back-to-the-land movement, or tech incubators. In this sense the makerspace movement is nothing new, but a slightly different iteration of a kind of community that is as old as human curiosity or collaboration itself.

One way these similarities became visible was when hackers and makers talked about other organizations their spaces were connected to or had parallels with. We had been surprised – as I noted in chapter 4 – by the relative lack of interest in the wider movement around hacking and making from those we spoke to. Few people were aware of wider networks like Space Federation or the hackerspace passport; instead, their attention and interest was focused on their local hacker or makerspace, and the community they found there. At the same time we were often told about parallels or connections between a hacker or makerspace and other local communities or activities. While they might not know about or show much interest in the maker movement as a large-scale community, hackers and makers did see plenty of connections between their activities and those of other individuals, groups or organizations. Rather than (or as well as) emphasizing how different hacking and making are to the rest of society, these conversations focused on how hackerspaces are the same as other ways of approaching life or finding community.

The diversity of the different groups and kinds of activities that hackers and makers drew parallels with was pretty astonishing. Those we spoke to mentioned everything from communes to guerrilla gardening, DIY, an acrobatics centre, automotive shops, co-working spaces and the Kahn Academy (an online learning environment) as in some way similar, or related to, the hacker or makerspace they were a member of. As points of comparison, of course, these were used at particular moments for particular purposes: no one was saying that their hackerspace was exactly the same as guerrilla gardening. But many people thought that their hackerspace had some important, perhaps even defining, features in common with these different groups, organizations or activities. Hackerspaces were counter-cultural like artists' collectives or homesteading; they were innovative learning environments like the Khan Academy; they were close-knit communities like co-operatives; they had the same equipment as university or automotive workshops. Hacking and making were, people told us, largely continuous with these instances of the outside world.

Lynn was one person who explicitly told us that her hackerspace had more in common with local community-oriented organizations than with other hackerspaces around the country. What defined her space was, she said, the sense of community she had found there.

According to her, the hackerspace she was part of didn't fit into the model of the European hackerspace brought back from the Chaos Communication Camp: her space was more friendly to entrepreneurship and start-ups, and less part of the open-source community than these other hackerspaces. To her there was simply nothing in common between her hackerspace and some of the other groups that used the term: they were different in size, style, interests and venue. But if we were interested in hackerspaces we should, she added, visit a local acrobatics and athletics centre:

> Lynn: I think they're wonderful. They're a – they teach – it's just a warehouse filled with kind of a foam. And they teach aerial trapeze and aerial silks and Parkour. And it's just a very – but they also have movie nights and a community to them. But it's a very peer-teaching, wonderful kind of community. Athletically oriented, which, of course, is heresy. But I think they're phenomenal.
>
> Sarah: And so the things that you guys would have in common with them would be the community?
>
> Lynn: We're a community center. I think that the hackerspace model in our mind is a community center, that we are proud of the community's accomplishments.

Lynn felt that the hackerspace she was part of was closer to this acrobatics centre, with its peer learning and community feel, than it was to some well-known hackerspaces (specifically, those set up after the 'Hackers on a Plane' trip described in chapter 3). Being a 'community centre' and enabling 'peer-teaching' were, to her, the key features of her space, and these were things that might or might not be found in other hackerspaces, but which were definitely present in other groups or organizations. Her hackerspace was essentially the same as other 'community centres', whether they focused on acrobatics, making or anything else.

Lynn and many others that we spoke to didn't view hacker and makerspaces as particularly new or as fundamentally different from other types of organization. Several people pointed out, for example, that many of the skills that are being (re)developed in hacker and makerspaces are actually fairly ancient: fixing up motor engines or electrical equipment, making your own thread or cloth, hacking together useful technologies, or preserving food have all been around for anything between decades and millennia. These hackers saw the community aspects of the hackerspace as central to their experience of it, and therefore readily identified commonalities with other kinds of clubs or social groups. 'I don't think hackerspaces are any different to any other group of people', one hacker told us. 'You know, like some motorcycle club or quilting club or whatever.' This view of what a hacker or makerspace is draws on the centrality of social interaction and togetherness in people's experiences of them. If community is integral to one's experience of hacking and making, and is the thing that really makes being part of a hackerspace distinctive and valuable, then it is easy to recognize groups that also develop a strong sense of community as similar in all the most important ways. Technology, even the idea of hacking and making itself, fades into the background. Hacking is one hobby among many, and hackerspaces just a particular kind of club.

This sense of continuity with wider society also emerged as hackers and makers reflected on other groups and people who shared aspects of the hacker spirit. We've already seen that this spirit is rather nonspecific. It's not about technology so much as an attitude to life, and one that can be applied to anything that you encounter. Those we spoke to frequently recognized this, identifying the same approach in anyone from DIY-ers to motorcycle enthusiasts. Some drew parallels, for instance, with other kinds of counter-cultural activities or movements, which they saw as having the same egalitarian, hands-on spirit as hackerspaces. Others pointed out that, around the world, many people hack and make simply to make ends meet: as Kim told us, making your own furniture and food and technology is essential for survival for many people, rather than a leisure activity. Even communities with a specific focus on making and hacking technology had plenty of precursors. One hacker told us about a group that had existed in their state in the 1960s and 1970s which had brought together 'tinkerers and hackers', just like his hackerspace. The terminology was different – they didn't use the language of hacking or making – and the group had been an informal hangout in a barn somewhere rather than a 'hackerspace', but they 'sat around and probably drank and hacked and had this culture similar to what we have here'. Communities for makers and hackers, and makers and hackers themselves, have been around long before maker and hackerspaces.

In all of these accounts what is emphasized is that hacker and makerspaces are not, in fact, particularly different from the outside world, but a part of it. 'I think there's not too much new about what we do, the more I think about it', Yan told us. 'There have always been co-ops and collectives and people trying to work together.' Hacking is exactly not new or revolutionary or a step-change in society; rather, it's an extension of wider attitudes and practices. It's a community like many others, focused on an approach – hacking – that is found in many other places.

'Hacking and making are buzzwords right now'

It is therefore not that easy to answer the question of whether hacker and makerspaces are hosting anything particularly new or different. On balance, those we spoke to would tend to say no: these spaces are just a slightly different way of 'getting people together' and of applying an approach – the hacker spirit – that is found in many other activities. At the same time, there are rather powerful voices making the argument that the maker movement is something that is extremely different from older ways of making, and that hacker and makerspaces are the seedbed for new ways of sparking innovation, creating businesses and, ultimately, making money. Among others, governments, universities and research funders are listening to those voices. Hacker and makerspaces are increasingly funded with the aim of boosting local entrepreneurial activity and fostering economic growth.[9] The jury is still out on these ambitions. Few of the hackers and makers we spoke to talked about their experiences of hacking and making in these terms. When they did emphasize the newness or innovation of hackerspaces, it was instead to argue that it was the hacker spirit of making and sharing that made hackerspaces different from wider society. Being a countercultural, active maker rather than a passive consumer was what makes hackers distinctive, not access to technology or new opportunities for innovation or entrepreneurship.

Does this matter? It would be possible to argue about whether the maker movement is genuinely innovative or not until the cows come home without reaching a definitive answer. In some ways, yes (digital fabrication tools are definitely becoming more accessible); in others, no (hacker and makerspaces foster tight-knit communities, but so do plenty of other kinds of organization). No one is policing hacking. If I decide that baking with sourdough involves the application of the hacker spirit, and want to call myself a hacker, then why not?

The distinctiveness of hacking and making matters for the same reason that many other questions of terminology matter. There is now social value, and increasingly actual money, attached to the idea of hacking and of the maker movement. There is a cachet attached to calling oneself a hacker. There is a sense of being in tune with the zeitgeist that comes from opening a makerspace in a library or museum. It is more attractive to fund a hacking programme that promises to boost the US economy than a quilting club or sourdough society. The nature of hacking has become something that governments care about and that venture capitalists are eager to get in on.

The questions of who is and isn't a hacker, and whether hacking is something new and distinctive or old and widespread, are therefore important because there is money and prestige at stake. This hasn't escaped the notice of hackers and makers. As one of our interviewees told us, there are regular and excitable discussions on hackerspace-associated email lists about what the word 'hacker' means and who gets to use it. My sourdough culturing is not an entirely spurious example here: one such discussion, on the hackerspaces.org discussion list in 2014, focused on the idea of 'food hacking'. The trigger seems to have been the activities of the group Food Hacking Base. This is not itself a hackerspace, but a loose collective of hackers and makers interested in 'experimenting with food and beverages'.[10] Such experiments – which are also found in hacker and makerspaces more generally, and particularly in biohacking spaces – can range from the traditional (culturing sourdough, making your own yoghurt) to the more radical (DNA-testing your sushi to check you are getting what you have been sold). 'Food hacking' might therefore involve anything from collecting and propagating food-related microbiological cultures[11] (like sourdough, miso or kombucha) to trying to match your food to your genotype.[12]

It was these kinds of activities that prompted the following comment on the hackerspaces.org discussion list, posted under the title 'Let's end the unnecessary joining of the words "food" and "hacker"'. The basic thesis is summed up by the title. Messing around with food, suggested the writer, is not hacking:

> I get the impression that people who call themselves 'food hackers' call themselves that because they want to be considered a part of the 'hacker movement'. Why don't those of you who identify with this moniker just call yourself a 'cook', 'chef', 'baker', 'maker', or whatever instead? Why don't you instead call the food 'food' or if you really want it to be associated with the hacker scene, 'food for hackers'? Is that hard? You're not a hacker and you dilute the term for those of us who are hackers.[13]

The author started their message by citing a definition of hacking that referred to computers; for them, hacking was something that was highly delimited, and the term should only be used to describe clever fixes and solutions in the context of computing.[14] As such, they were annoyed about what they saw as the proliferation of the term where it shouldn't be applied: anyone who picked it up and used it in other contexts was 'diluting the term'. These people should ask themselves why they were so eager to call themselves hackers. 'Why', the poster wrote, 'do people who are playing with their food want to be a part of the hacking scene?'

The resulting discussion thread involved some 70-odd messages, variously rejecting, supporting or commenting on food hacking and the notion of hacking in general (with many of the messages comprising a back and forth between the original poster and their critics, including various comments on their tone, intellectual capacity, and degree of what ended up being called 'troll-hacking'). Many of the posts explicitly disagreed with the narrowness of the original definition of hacking, with writers referring to sources such as the *New Hacker's Dictionary* and St Jude's emphasis on the circumvention of imposed limits (discussed in chapter 3). But many people, like the first poster, also expressed frustration with how 'hacking' was being used. One writer, who was sympathetic to others on the thread who were finding the attempt to defend 'true' hacker culture increasingly nonsensical, nevertheless commented:

> I know firsthand how frustrating it is that 'hacking' and 'making' are buzzwords right now and a lot of different people and organizations are trying to legitimize their own efforts by adopting them, or maybe just misunderstand the point, or maybe want to just take from an active community without giving anything back.[15]

In other words, however fruitless it might be to produce a narrow, tightly policed definition of hacking, it was still annoying that it was rapidly becoming a buzzword – a label to be slapped on everything and anything to make it sound hip, edgy and counter-cultural. The use of ideas of hacking and making outside particular 'active communities' is destructive, the writer suggests, in that these ideals are being used for 'legitimization' or to extract useful knowledge without giving anything back in return (something which is, of course, counter to the hacker spirit). Even if they're not limited to computing, or even to hackerspaces, hacking and making are unusual, special and counter-cultural activities. They are exactly not open to anyone to take up and claim as their own.

Hacking and making are in a state of change. So much excitement, so much growth: it's probably inevitable that there is disagreement about what these activities are, who has a stake in them, and who gets to own and define the movement. The questions 'is this anything new?' and 'can anyone call themselves a hacker?' are unlikely to be resolved. Rather, they form the context to a series of tensions that are emerging within hacking and making. Money, prestige, commodification and the instrumentalization of the movement by governments or educators all mean that imaginations of what hacking is – what I've expressed here as the hacker spirit – are increasingly unstable. The hacker spirit seems infinitely extendable. If curiosity, a commitment to learning and sharing, close-knit community and the desire to tweak one's circumstances are what mark out hackers and makers, then many of us are hackers without ever having heard the term. On the other hand, if the maker movement is defined by its access to technology and its entrepreneurial spirit, then many of the users of hacker and makerspaces we met during this research are not participants in it at all. Are hackerspaces clubs for hobbyists? Seedbeds for economic growth? Groups of counter-cultural technologists? Community centres? The answer might be all of these things, or none, depending on who you ask.

Whether sourdough baking, DIY home decor, or fixing your car are 'really' hacking thus seems less about the actual practices involved than about their context and the way in which they are discussed. In some small way, I am hacking my sourdough starter when I feed it spelt flour because I've run out of wheat, or when I test out a new bread mix of different flours and seeds. But that activity can be framed in totally different terms depending on whether I am in my kitchen, drawing on centuries of craft knowledge about baking; in a DIY bio space, working with other hobbyists as a fun leisure activity; or in a brand new, government-funded makerspace, trying to develop a product line to turn into a revenue-generating business. In any of those contexts there might be voices arguing that this is not genuine, 'real' hacking, that what I am doing, and the place I'm doing it in, is in some way inauthentic, a dilution or sell-out. At the moment hacking and making are simultaneously revolutionary and ancient; world-changing developments and intimate hobbies; open and accessible and cloistered and elite; and counter-cultural and anti-consumerist and mainstream business opportunities. It's not surprising that tempers can flare as ideas of hacking and making are extended and used in different communities and settings. What is at stake is the meaning of hacking itself.

11

Conclusion
Two Reasons Hacking Is Timely, and Three Reasons It Is Conflicted

During our research, we visited twelve US hackerspaces and spoke to dozens of people. We heard about projects as diverse as home-brewed servers and glow in the dark bacteria, flying robots and multi-coloured murals and kimchi. There was very little overlap in these projects. A hacker's projects are, as we've seen, deeply personal, invested with emotions and individual identity. Copying someone else, or following a step-by-step guide, was seen as derivative, lacking in the creativity and personalization that was part of the hacker spirit. But there was one exception – one project that multiple hackers and makers had in common, and that they told us they were committed to. That was the hackerspace itself.

That hacker or makerspaces themselves become projects – the focus of hackers' activities and energies and their making capacities – is perhaps unsurprising. Hackers and makers are passionate about the possibilities of their spaces. They are driven to ensure that hacker and makerspaces endure and spread. And, despite the vision of bottom-up organization and 'do-ocracy', hacker and makerspaces are undeniably time-intensive to run. Setting up and maintaining a space often requires the focused energies of a few members who are committed to ensuring that the space endures. Some of those we spoke to therefore told us that their personal projects were more or less on the back burner; instead, their energies were going into activities like setting up the space or equipping and maintaining it (building its furniture, sourcing tools, getting the 3D printer to work, keeping a temperamental laser cutter happy, setting up a Kickstarter project to gain additional funding).[1]

Some of these people were in the eye of the storm: they were a founder or co-founder of a space just getting off the ground. They talked ruefully about the times when 'the tools themselves become a project', and looked forward to having more space for their own projects. But others seemed more comfortable that their project was the space – or a space – itself. Tiah, for instance, was starting a hackerspace more or less single-handedly; she was also working on a large carpentry project and had a book project on the go. As she reflected on her long-term plans, she saw her interests going more in the direction of continuing to support and expand her hackerspace and others like it. Her vision, she said, was for her space to multiply; she would, perhaps, start a 'hackerspace business'. Tiah, and others for whom the hackerspace was their primary project, found that their real passion was for creating hacker and makerspaces themselves. What they hacked and made was communities and spaces: the focus of their creativity and craft and ingenuity was the people and structures that made hackerspaces possible. This could be hard work, but there was a general sense that the hackerspace-as-project was excitingly do-able – that hacker and makerspaces were, as Tiah told us, 'an idea whose time has come' and as such could readily slip into reality. In keeping with the hacker emphasis on getting on and doing things, those we spoke to were clear that they, or anyone, could start up a hackerspace if they wanted to. 'Wherever we go', Emil said, of himself and others in his space, 'if there's not a hackerspace there, we need to make our own, because I want to have that space.' 'If I go to a city without a hackerspace, I can always just make one', Winni told us.

The degree to which hacker and makerspaces became projects – the things that were hacked and made – is indicative of the excitement our interviewees expressed about them, and of how committed they were to their development. Hacking was experienced as transformative, whether that transformation involved becoming smarter, expressing one's authentic identity, or finding community. Hackers were passionate about creating spaces where such transformation could take place. But it is also indicative of the sense that – as Tiah said – hacker and makerspaces are an idea whose time has come. Hacking was viewed as being of the moment. It was the right time to develop these kinds of spaces: there was a general cultural hunger, we were told, for something like them. They represented the culmination of desires for community, for hands-on engagement, for creativity and experimentation, for self-governance or freedom from educational or professional structures. Thus, it was understood to be relatively easy to create a hackerspace from scratch, and to build a community in it. If you build it, they will come.

This is also, of course, the basic premise for this book. Hacker and makerspaces represent the zeitgeist in some way. They are an example of wider trends and developments, an ideal type of certain sociocultural cravings and norms. We know this not just because hackers and makers told us so, but because this movement is shooting to prominence in the public domain. Journalists write articles about hackerspaces. Mark Hatch publishes a Maker Manifesto. DARPA funds makerspaces. NHS Hack Day is about 'geeks who love the NHS' rather than computer hackers trying to access patient data.[2] Teenage maker Ahmed Mohammed is told, in a tweet from President Obama, that the US needs more kids like him because science 'makes America great'.[3] In this public discussion, hacking and making are both hip and hopeful: an exciting source of creative learning and the means of grassroots technological innovation.

In this final chapter I want to zoom back out to this scale, that of societies and nations, to reflect on what the rest of my discussion can tell us about why hacking and making are the focus of so much attention right now. Mark Hatch and Chris Anderson think that new technology is driving the maker movement; governments and educators see it as providing the educational tools that twenty-first-century employees need; the hackers and makers we spoke to talked more generally about a culture hungry for creativity and hands-on physical engagement with technology. What can the in-depth dive we have taken through the stories and practices of hackerspaces tell us about their rise to prominence and the way in which they capture the spirit of the age?

Community

Community, community, community. It's hard to emphasize enough how central the idea of community was to the conversations that we had with hackers and makers. We've seen this repeatedly throughout the book. Community was viewed as part of the hacker spirit: the characteristics of a hacker, such as doing things and learning by doing, were only meaningful when they were lived out around others. Doing was learning was sharing. It is community that animates a hacker or makerspace, to such a degree that we were told that franchised or impersonal makerspaces were not 'real' hackerspaces because they lacked community. A hacker or makerspace could only successfully function, in terms of its governance and administration, if it had a committed, sharing community. Spaces struggled because their communities were not tightly knitted or proactive enough – because they fell back on the hierarchies of the outside world, or were not sufficiently 'grassroots' in their priorities and administration.

We have also seen that there can be pathologies of community within hacker and makerspaces. At best, there were issues where erstwhile leaders or officers found themselves 'forcing people to be grassroots'. Individuals took on what they thought were largely nominal positions on a board or leadership group only to find that there was a constant struggle to encourage other members to step up, take decisions and live out 'do-ocracy'. At worst, community can function to exclude particular people, and to create a 'dominant culture' that is intimidating or unwelcoming. Many hackerspaces seem to fail at creating diverse community (just as the tech industry does more generally), an issue that has led to the rise of more focused communities that welcome those who are otherwise excluded or alienated. Community could even become a distraction. Some of those we interviewed spoke about their concerns that their space was too much a social environment, too much somewhere to hang out with your friends rather than a place to make and hack. Should hackerspaces be 'community centres'? Opinion was divided. For some, this was the whole point of their involvement; for others, too many members were 'coming here for the cool' (as Keira told us).

Community is not unproblematic. But its very centrality to the conversations we had suggests that it is something that is driving the growth of hacker and makerspaces. The experiences of community that hackers and makers had gained through their involvement in their spaces were described in all sorts of ways: community might be messy or exciting or life-changing or inspiring. But for many people, the sense of community they found in their hacker or makerspace had provided something profound that they had been looking for, perhaps even without knowing it. This experience of community met needs that they, as individuals of a hacker bent, had. It fed them where they were hungry. Their hackerspace community became, in some cases, their family, their home, their haven.

What to make of this? Public discussion of hacking and making often mentions community. John Baichtal, whose book *Hack This* offers a how-to guide to hackerspaces, writes that it's 'all about the community', suggesting that it's the sense of community that marks out hackerspaces from places like TechShop (as did some of our interviewees).[4] Mark Hatch – author of *The Maker Movement Manifesto* and co-founder of the aforementioned TechShop – describes community as a resource that hackers and makers can access to help them in their projects.[5] If you need specific information, or skills, or advice, then a makerspace community can help you find it. Media coverage (which often features the voices of high-profile makers like Hatch, Dale Dougherty or Mitch Altman, the founder of Noisebridge) also refers to the sense of community that is evident in hacker and makerspaces.[6] But none of these accounts view community as what is *driving* the growth of the maker movement. To them, it's an interesting – and useful – side effect of a movement that is primarily driven by the accessibility of fabrication technologies and the use of digital networks. This, in light of the encounters discussed in this book, is the wrong way around. It's not the technology that drives community, but the communities that happen to involve technology. Even without the nice tools and fancy 3D printers, we were told, users of hacker and makerspaces would participate in them. It was the sense of community, not the tools and technologies, that made a hackerspace.

This emphasis on community as defining hacker and makerspaces brings us back to the idea of social capital. Some of our interviewees complained about the digital nature of much contemporary life; all talked about the value of face-to-face interaction within the communities they had found in their hacker and makerspaces. It almost seems too trite, too simplistic, to say that the rise of hacker and makerspaces is about social capital and the opportunity to develop human connections in real-world environments, or about being able to access a 'third place' away from home and work.[7] But these dynamics do seem to be at least part of what is driving the use of and growth in hacker and makerspaces. Exactly what is happening with social capital in this digital era is a vexed question: while some argue that online connections can boost social capital,[8] others – such as the sociologist Sherry Turkle – suggest that digital connectivity simply involves being 'alone together'.[9] If this is true, then it is not surprising that our interviewees were hungry for a different way to connect with people. In this view, the use of hacker and makerspaces would be of a piece with other forms of online social networking that lead to real-world encounters (such as dating sites or MeetUp.com). Such meet-ups have become an increasingly important aspect of social networks over the last decade, to the extent that one group of scholars talks about an 'exodus to the real world'.[10] Online connectivity, they suggest, is good for developing weak ties around a shared interest (and thereby provides bridging capital). But once people 'find the friends they seek' they 'strengthen these loose ties and tend to stay embedded within closed social groups. Meetups...could be considered an accelerator of this process'.[11]

People need people. We function through being part of communities – communities that also give us a sense of purpose, of being part of something larger than ourselves. One driver behind the rise of hacker and makerspaces thus seems to be that, for many of us, it is not always easy to find a sense of community, and especially one that transcends the loose ties of Facebook or online discussion fora. This may be particularly the case if you are someone driven by the characteristics of the hacker spirit. Here we can return to Nick's words, quoted in chapter 6. 'It's hard to relate', he said, to 'people who don't see the production of original things as a priority in their life.' Hacker and makerspaces allow you to come together with people with the same interests as you, and to form deep bonds with them. Keith, a Bay Area hacker, told us how he valued being able to come to a games night at his hackerspace rather than playing Words with Friends at home online. The activity might be the same, but being at the hackerspace meant that he was collaborating with other people, getting involved in building something together. 'You're not just sitting at home watching the television', he told us, about his involvement. 'You're actually, like, going out and doing something.' Going out and doing something is almost a definition of how social capital is produced. 'Putnam implies', writes scholar David Gauntlett in a discussion of the term, 'that any kind of communal activity is better than slumping, isolated, in front of the TV.'[12] Or, as Lynn joked, involvement in hackerspaces 'keeps you off the streets'. It provides community in a world where it is all too easy to exist suspended in a digital miasma, surrounded by networks and connections but never having to genuinely engage with anyone else.

A spirit of the times

The simple desire for face-to-face community is one dynamic driving the growth of hacker and makerspaces, and ensuring that so many of their users find them timely. The second driver that emerges is more subtle, and is rooted in the troubled intersection between hacking's counter-cultural roots and its commodification. Hackerspaces are timely, I want to suggest, because the hacker spirit captures something of how we, as citizens, are meant to behave in contemporary minority world societies. The version of hacking and making that is celebrated by hackers themselves and by many public commentators is one that emphasizes self-reliance, being proactive and taking responsibility for one's own learning and development. This approach is one that accepts very few excuses and urges hackers and makers to do, not talk. Anything is possible, we were told. No hackerspace in your area? Start one! Want to work in tech? Learn by doing and teach yourself to program! Have a desire for a particular item of technology, or furniture, or clothing? Access tools and make it for yourself! Individual responsibility is key because it allows you to take control of your situation and reclaim agency. This message is of the moment, it seems to me, not only because it speaks to the satisfactions of a DIY approach in an age where we can seem to have very little control over our lives. It is also timely because it is exactly what we are asked to do by neoliberal governments and corporations. Assumptions about the necessity of individual responsibility are now replacing older expectations of collective action and social support in many countries around the world.

This aspect of the hacker spirit, and what it means to hack and make, returns us to the other kinds of active leisure discussed in chapter 2. The ethos of the hacker spirit – make, do, understand, tweak, care, learn, share – is shared by those who choose to spend their leisure in activities such as crafting, DIY or online creativity. All of these things involve doing something, rather than passively consuming. What it is that you do varies: make your own clothes as a response to concerns about factory conditions in Bangladesh, fix your coffee maker rather than buy a new one in order to contribute to sustainable consumption, create Star Wars fan videos in order to find community and personal satisfaction, hack together software that does what you want it to. But the version of the individual that is presented is one who consciously engages with the world around them, reflects on it, and acts accordingly. It is someone – to return to Faythe Levine's language, quoted in chapter 2 – who 'makes their own destiny'.

Trends such as the rise of the 'New Domesticity' that Emily Matchar charts, or serious leisure activities like those promoted by the *Guardian*'s 'Do Something' campaign, can therefore be seen as having key similarities with the use of hacker and makerspaces. All of these activities (largely leisure-based, but sometimes morphing into careers in their own right) involve the reclamation of agency and a sense of control in the world. They focus on tweaking your circumstances, such that they fit you better. This may result in self-actualization and the satisfactions of authentic identity, a feeling of control and empowerment, or simply getting something that you want: food without excessive processing, a home decorated with murals, a smartphone that you can program. These activities emphasize being proactive, rather than passive, and sidestepping authorities that might tell you what to do or how to feel. They are about effecting change. Hacking and making lead to solutions for your life. Crafting empowers you. The 'Do Something' campaign is about finding more fulfilling leisure activities. This change, however, tends to be within your immediate sphere. It is change on the small scale, on the level of individuals or small groups (such as hacker or makerspaces) rather than larger collectives or societies.

In many ways this is laudable. Personal empowerment – the feeling of being in control of one's own life – is something we all reach for. Resourcing people to take control of and grasp agency in their personal situations is an important aspect of the spirit of hacker and makerspaces, and something that is valuable in multiple ways. But it is important to notice that this emphasis on individual action and responsibility is not something that is in and of itself counter-cultural or emancipatory. In fact, the idea that it is individuals who are primarily responsible for their own lives and situations is a key theme of our neoliberal times. We live in an age which emphasizes the power of individual, rather than collective, actors, and we are increasingly asked to take personal responsibility for everything from our careers to our healthcare and the security of our neighbourhoods. The hacker ethos, with its central focus on individuals getting on and doing things, can be viewed as a distillation of this zeitgeist.

Over the past decades social researchers have traced the rise of the individual as the locus of responsibility and agency, a rise which has reached its peak in the dominance of neoliberalism in economic and political thought.[13] These developments are related to increased insecurity around structures, such as family, social class or the labour market, which might previously have dominated people's lives, making them predictable. As these expectations and structures disintegrate under the pressures of a globalized world, the onus is on the individual to make sense of the world and to find their way in it. Old certainties relating to one's participation in a social class, a profession or a community have vanished, leaving us adrift from wider social structures that define who we are and will be. The sociologist Deborah Lupton writes:

> In such arenas as education and work, for example, people are expected to make their destinies, to compete with others for credentials and employment and make their individualized careers, no longer relying on traditional expectation or social structures. Stable employment can no longer be taken as a given, and it is considered up to people to make their own opportunities. [...] Gender roles no longer rigidly structure the life course. As a result, there are greater possibilities for choice in the conduct of relationships, but this has required intense and continual negotiation and decision-making.[14]

In a world in which we are expected to 'make our own opportunities' we are faced with continual choices – choices which are liberating, but which may also be overwhelming. What work should I do? Who do I want to be intimate with, and how? Where should I live? Ultimately: who am I? The hacker spirit, and its expression in the maker movement and related forms of serious leisure like DIY or crafting, fits squarely into these dynamics in that it can help individuals consider these kinds of questions. Hacking allows you to curate your surroundings, tweaking your tools and technologies such that they are a better fit for your life. Crafting can enable you to 'find your people' and gain a better sense of your own identity. Web 2.0 platforms mean you can opt out of traditional broadcasting and become your own media curator and producer, personalizing the content you are interested in. DIY home-schooling or food production can allow you to ignore the mainstream and fit your family's education and nutrition exactly to your beliefs. These forms of active leisure thus continue our societies' emphasis on individual agency as the key way in which the world is made meaningful and, importantly, as something we can act upon to change.

Personal empowerment is a wonderful thing. Few of us would want to live in a world in which our gender, or place of birth, or social class rigidly determined our life course. But as Emily Matchar points out in her discussion of the New Domesticity, this emphasis on the individual as the primary means of change can lead to a neglect of collective action, solidarity and organizing for wider social good. She tells the story of progressive, middle-class professionals who, concerned about the quality of food available in North American grocery stores, turn to local, home-grown and organic produce to feed themselves and their families. They grow fruit and vegetables, can and preserve, keep chickens or pigs, and trade butter or honey with local farmers. Bread is homebaked from organic flour. But all this is done at the level of individual families or a small community of the like-minded: these people have, Matchar writes, essentially written off the possibility of government regulation or top-level business decisions as a way of ensuring the safety of the food chain. As a result, the change that they are interested in – better-quality, safer, less processed food – only happens for them. It excludes those who, because of lack of knowledge or resources or access, simply can't commit to a lifestyle which involves long hours of gardening, cooking and shopping. In practice, it excludes those who are poorer and less well educated.

This, then, is one aspect of individual empowerment that we should be alert to. Not everybody has the same access to resources to change their lives in the directions they want, or indeed to find self-actualization and satisfaction in their leisure activities. Many of the structures which are ostensibly dissolving in the contemporary world – gender, social class, race – still exert influence on the opportunities individuals have. This is why many groups and organizations continue to agitate for collective action, and seek to effect change at the level of whole societies. Not everyone is able to 'do something' with equal ease, just as not everyone automatically has the personal or social resources to craft a portfolio career, decide to live off the grid, or choose to experiment with gender identity. Hacking's call for people to be active, to do and make things or get out of the hackerspace community, runs the risk of making these kinds of structural inequalities invisible – as, indeed, we have already seen in discussing exclusion, in chapter 7. The suggestion that if women and minorities aren't in hackerspaces it's because they're not interested in hacking involves a similar elision of wider social circumstances. In both cases, the 'meritocracy' of hacker and makerspaces, the emphasis on individuals stepping up to claim their place, may mean that hackers and makers ignore the social and cultural resources that have got them to where they are.

Many of the hackers and makers we spoke to were clear that they were not political or concerned with their hackerspace being a 'cause'. They saw what they were doing as a hobby, not as a means of social justice, however empowering they personally found the practice of hacking to be. It may be unfair, then, to point out hacking and making's apparent self-exclusion from processes of collective action and social change: this was not what our interviewees said they were interested in doing. But hacking and making was also repeatedly described as something that is counter-cultural in its anti-consumption orientation. It was presented as the *solution* to contemporary capitalism, rather than a part of it. Running through the heart of hacking and making is the seeming paradox that something so counter-cultural and anti-authoritarian has been taken up so enthusiastically by the authorities. Governments are funding hackerspaces at the same time as users of those spaces talk about their activities as subversive and transgressive; businesses support makerspaces while hackers and makers unpick and unlock their products. Part of the reason that this is so is not just the parallel individualism of the hacker spirit and contemporary society (what Emily Matchar has called the 'hyperindividualism' of the twenty-first century), but a parallel emphasis on personal agency. In adopting the self-reliance and independence of the hacker spirit, hackers and makers are acting as ideal citizens.

A comparison with healthcare, and how we, as citizens, relate to it, is useful here. Increasingly, researchers have argued, we are being asked to take an active role in how our health is managed and cared for. This is not just about moving away from medical paternalism: the expectation that the doctor knows best and that we, as patients, should do as we're told. Rather, health scholars Daniel Hunt and Nelya Koteyko argue that:

> In promoting the rights and autonomy of the health-care consumer, neo-liberal discourse emphasizes the individual's responsibility for accessing relevant expert health information and proactively managing their health risks in order to decrease the demands on state health and welfare systems [...] accountability for health [is] devolved from the government to the level of the self-governing, responsible and enterprising individual.[15]

The starting point is the 'rights and autonomy' of patients. But this rapidly starts to involve the transfer of responsibility from medical professionals and national healthcare systems to individual 'healthcare consumers'; there is now a need, Hunt and Koteyko suggest, for us to be 'proactive' in accessing expert information and in managing health risks. It is not fair for us to rely solely on the knowledge or goodwill of government healthcare. In this neoliberal age we need to take responsibility for our health on ourselves, making good choices that will keep us healthy and which will, as we choose between different experts and healthcare providers, help hone the market. Good citizens are therefore active in looking after their health. They self-monitor, read up on any conditions they may suffer from, and decide who they want to be treated by and in what way. They are, as Hunt and Koteyko write, 'self-governing, responsible and enterprising'.

Such attitudes to health are just one way in which personal agency is becoming part of our expectations of citizenship: we find similar developments in, for instance, education and the provision of local services. But this description also has striking parallels with what is expected of hackers and makers – not so much in the context of healthcare (which almost none of our interviewees talked about hacking), but in the approach to life suggested by the hacker spirit. Hackers and makers should exactly be 'self-governing, responsible and enterprising'. They should be proactive and engaged, learning what they need for a particular task. They are self-reliant, governed through grassroots action rather than dictates from above. They need, as Kev told us, to 'bring something of value' to the communities of which they are part:

> Bring something of value with you. That's your exchange in the community. That's how you prove yourself, you bring your project, you

bring your knowledge, bring your skills with you. Don't just bring your ass and sit down.

For Kev, agency is everything. The hackerspace is not for freeloaders – just as, in the version of healthcare articulated above, responsible citizens do not take health (or healthcare) for granted, but actively participate in realizing it in their lives. No one is entitled to 'just bring your ass and sit down'. Whether the community in question is a hackerspace or a nation state, good citizens are active. They look after their needs. They take responsibility.

Governments, and the corporations that are increasingly entwined with them, now promote a model of society which emphasizes the personal responsibilities of citizens and consumers. What is demanded of us is not obedience or solidarity, but proactive engagement with the issues that define our lives: our health, education, welfare, employment. In this drive to inculcate self-reliance and responsibility, hackers are the ideal model. This is even more the case for the versions of hacking and making promoted most vigorously in public, which tell the story of making's potential not just for proactive, self-reliant engagement with the world but for innovation and entrepreneurial activity. Such entrepreneurial citizens show their agency in creating new technologies and the markets to sell them to. They don't rely on traditional education, or business hierarchies, or state support: they are creators who need only their ideas and some technological infrastructure – rapid prototyping, cheap manufacturing, international digital networks – to develop commercial opportunities. But even outside of these hacking and making entrepreneurs, the hacker encapsulates what is increasingly demanded of twenty-first-century global citizens. If hackers are self-reliant, proactive agents in a complex, choice-filled world, then we are all hackers now.

Faultlines and tensions

Why do governments fund hackerspaces, and business gurus laud books like Chris Anderson's *Makers*? Why are new hacker and makerspaces steadily opening up around the world? The interviews and visits described in this book suggest that there are two reasons for this growth: these spaces supply a kind of community that many people are hungry for; and, in promoting a hacker spirit of self-reliance and individual agency, they speak to the obsessions of a neoliberal era. They exemplify a model of personal agency that has the power to direct markets, ensure welfare and equality, and even organize government; as such, they offer a kind of ideal type of how all citizens should behave and interact.

Hacking may be prominent right now because it feeds into some of the less savoury dynamics of our times: a focus on individual change over collective action; an emphasis on the responsibility of individuals with no appreciation of wider circumstance. At the same time, it is impossible to doubt the enthusiasm, good-heartedness and generosity of the hackers and makers we spoke to. People were genuinely excited about the pleasures of creation and the possibilities of hacking the world around them. Whether talking about the pleasures of working recalcitrant materials or of doing messy community, hacking and making were practices streaked through with joy. While the movement as a whole may resonate in surprising ways with mainstream economic policy, it is clear that, for those we spoke to, participating in hacker and makerspaces was experienced as emancipatory and personally empowering. Hacking had changed these individuals' lives by telling them that anything was possible, and they were eager to see others' lives changed in the same way. Taken together, however, the conversations we had reveal not just resonances with mainstream culture but a set of tensions that run through the growing movement around hacking and making. There are contradictions and questions that sit in the background of most hackers' experiences, barely visible in the everyday life of hacker and makerspaces. These tensions will, I think, force themselves to the surface more and more, as the maker movement expands and is subject to increased critical attention. They are issues that deserve reflection from hackers and makers as well as from observers such as myself. They perhaps even demand decisions on some key questions. What is it that hackers and makers are engaged in? Who is it for? And what are its politics?

Gotkin's film *The Pleasure of the Hack* showed hackers talking about the pleasures of being counter-cultural and 'different'. Robert Stebbins, the scholar of serious leisure, has written about the 'marginality' of practitioners of serious leisure activities.[16] Practitioners, he suggests, show unusual commitment to their pursuits, and therefore view themselves as different from the vast majority of other people. In both cases we are given a hint of the satisfactions of being part of an exclusive community. One of the pleasures of being a hacker or maker is exactly that it is counter-cultural and unusual, different and separate from mainstream society. One of the pleasures of community is finding 'my people' – and avoiding the rest.

One question at stake as hacking and making develops is therefore the relation between community, exclusivity and openness. What will happen as hacker and makerspaces expand, open up in new places, and seek to engage broader swathes of society? Hacker and maker-spaces commonly operate a policy of being open to all comers. Everyone is welcome, we were told, and anyone can become a hacker. The hacker lifestyle is accessible to all. Hackers and makers were excited to see the movement grow, and to see different kinds of spaces open up around the US and worldwide. At the same time, the very emphasis on close-knit community that we've seen throughout this discussion should give us pause with regard to this ethos of openness. Is it possible, some of our interviewees wondered, to maintain this kind of community as hackerspaces reach 50, 100, 200 members? How could they manage do-ocracy and self-governance in spaces where not everyone knows each other? There are practical questions concerning the way in which individual spaces may grow and develop. How could this change governance, and the sense of community that currently dominates users' experiences and expectations?

We've also seen that, despite the rhetoric of radical openness, hackerspaces have serious problems with regard to the diversity of their membership. Clearly, not everyone feels welcomed into or able to join (some) hacker and makerspace communities. The sense of community that many of our interviewees experienced as comforting and empowering, even transformational, does not seem to be available to all. Hacker and makerspace communities therefore have some serious questions to ask themselves about what they mean when they talk about openness, or about being accessible to anyone in their local neighbourhood. What kind of community is modelled by their current membership? What effects might this have on newcomers? And does this matter? Many spaces may decide not: it is, after all, perfectly legitimate to run a hacker or makerspace as a private members' club or as a community centre for a particular type of person. But at the moment ideas of openness or meritocracy sit uneasily with a lack of acknowledgement of wider structural factors that may affect who is able to access hacking and making, under what circumstances. As the maker movement expands, it needs to reflect on what kinds of cultures are being nurtured within it, and what this means for who is included.

Finally, there is the issue of the pleasure of exclusivity itself. It is doubtless satisfying to portray hacking and making as an elite subculture, a haven of active resistance within a culture that takes passive consumption as the norm. As we saw in chapters 5 and 10, while hackers and makers were clear that anyone could become a hacker, they also told us that not everyone wants to do so. Those who were not 'our people' were better staying outside of hacker and makerspaces, where they could spend their spare time in casual leisure activities like watching TV or sports. But this distinction, this focus on the unusual and special nature of those with the hacker spirit, again raises questions as to what will happen as the movement around making and hacking expands and grows. Is it possible, or even right, to make hacking a mainstream movement? Where is the borderline between genuine, creative hacking and being passive and derivative? And to what extent does hacking's cultural value – and its current popularity – derive from its status as an elite, exclusive activity, rather than something that everyone does?

Emancipation and commodification

A second set of tensions circles around the ways in which hacking and making are becoming commodified, and the extent to which this is a problem. As we've seen, few of the hackers and makers we spoke to showed much concern about the commercialization of their activities, whether that was via their own (hypothetical) entrepreneurial enterprises or businesses such as MAKE. Most were happy to see their involvement in hacking and making as a personally meaningful lifestyle choice, something that they used as a means of self-development and the crafting of identity. For the most part the hackers and makers we talked with operated in a traditionally North American universe, one in which personal development was key, commercial markets were the ideal regulator, and individual autonomy was central to change.

At the same time, we were told that hacking was counter-cultural, anti-consumption and emancipatory. It allowed individuals to escape the straitjackets of corporate America. Hackers and makers spoke at length about the pleasures of hacking technologies that came with pre-determined settings: smartphones, cars, computers. We, the users, are not meant to be able to access these black boxes – but, through hacking, we can. We can impose our individual preferences onto systems that want to make us choose between blue and grey, Republican and Democrat, iOS and Android. We can therefore reject what multinationals choose to give us, and reclaim our technologies (and thereby the ability to define our own lives). Similarly, hackers spoke about the satisfactions of self-reliance, of 'making do and mending'. Being self-sufficient was the goal. Part of the power of hacking and making was the ability to fix or make your own tools and technologies, and thus not only to tweak them to suit your preferences but to escape the cycles of consumption and obsolescence that manufacturers have handed us. Hacking and making, we were told, were about independence.

There are therefore at least two contrasting stories about the nature of hacking and making in circulation today. One is exactly that hacking is anti-corporate and anti-consumption. It promotes radical independence from the materialistic mindset that structures our societies, and is therefore subversive and anti-authoritarian. The other maintains some of these ideas about hacking – it can lead to sustainable consumption; it builds on a history of tinkering and making do – but sets them within a framework where commercial development is the norm. The answer to the power of big corporations and cycles of consumption, this story says, is different kinds of corporation and consumption. Hacking and making will shake up manufacturing and production, but it will still lead to economic growth. Business, so to speak, as usual.

These rifts in how hacking and making are envisioned are not particularly surprising. The twinning of ideas about counter-cultural emancipation with commercial development has a long history in the rise of the computing industry.[17] Similarly, some of the more radical understandings of hacking as intrinsically anti-corporate can be traced to the pre-history of European hackerspaces and hacklabs.[18] But it seems to me that the presence, and mingling together, of these different imaginations of how hacking and making should develop requires some reflection from hackers and makers. Is mainstream commercial development the best approach for meeting the maker movement's potential for creating technologies, building communities and changing how we consume? Are entrepreneurship and the desire for economic productivity the natural endpoint for hacking and making activities? If so, then the commodification of hacking and making seems inevitable. Enterprises such as MAKE should be celebrated and imitated: hackerspaces should, indeed, become businesses with franchises, taking every opportunity to support the commercial activities of their members. If not – well, in that case even more reflection is needed. Disengaging from a universe in which business development is the natural outcome of good ideas will require the shedding of easy assumptions about hacking and making's implications for innovation and growth, and more discussion about how and why hacker and makerspaces are receiving funding from government and businesses. It may also require hackers and makers to stop having their cake and eating it – or at least to question whether hacking can simultaneously be subversively counter-cultural and a profitable business opportunity.

Collective action and individualism

A final set of tensions in how hacking and making are developing relates to the two central reasons I have suggested hackerspaces are timely: a desire for community, and an ethos of individual responsibility. How do these two things hang together? Or, to put it differently, how is it that the hacker spirit combines an emphasis on individualism with an emphasis on community?[19]

Hackers and makers are, as we've seen, expected to take responsibility for themselves. To quote Kev again, just sitting on your ass is not an option: your learning and growing is up to you. At the same time, this was not a selfish ethos. As we've also repeatedly seen, community was key. It was central to the hacker spirit that hackers did not exist in isolation, but were part of a community where they could share their interests and be inspired by others. A commitment to others in that community was taken for granted. If someone needed your help with a tool or technique, then you should give it. Learning from others was integral to how hackers and makers developed their projects and their skills. There were times when hackers talked about their communities as a kind of higher good, something for which they were prepared to sacrifice themselves. In the extract above, for instance, Kev talks about the need to bring 'something of value' to the community as a hackerspace member; similarly, Keira told us that the attitude in her space was 'not what I can do for myself, but what can I do for the [space], what can I do for the people'. Those we spoke to had made stringent efforts to nurture their communities in different ways, to the extent of neglecting their own projects and passions. They were responsible, yes, but responsible for their community as well as for themselves.

Hacker and makerspaces are therefore not hotbeds of individualistic striving. They are not solely about furthering one's own projects and pleasures – unlike, for instance, what we were told about commercial makerspaces. If spaces like TechShop lack community (we were told), then they are a resource for self-development rather than a site for generosity and altruism. But the hacker and makerspaces we visited were not like this. Their members were in some way concerned with the collective good. Their individual responsibilities were lived out through participation in these small, closely knit communities; they claimed agency in their own lives, but were also committed to the wellbeing of their space. There was a sense that hacking was a social project, and one that involved the promotion of social good. And again, as we've seen, hackers and makers were convinced that this way of life *is* a social good: that it helps individuals to better themselves, provides both pleasure and useful skills, and ultimately frees you to take control of your life. The issue I want to raise is that this concern for social good largely stops at the door of the hackerspace. Other than in the diversity-oriented space we visited, which took social change as part of its mission, hackers and makers generally saw collective action and change as relevant solely in the sphere of their space and its members. Hacker and makerspaces were not about social change. They were about building a strong community.

As it stands, the ethos of the hacker spirit seems poorly suited to pursuing social goods – empowerment, equality, justice – outside of hacker and makerspace communities. With its emphasis on individual agency and learning and sharing through the experience of close-knit community, it has little space for more traditional forms of collective action (such as agitating for policy change, or boycotting particular businesses). Perhaps this is not a problem. Many hackers and makers were explicit that they were not interested in doing politics through their hacking and making; instead, they were concerned with self-development and with growing a strong community. But we've also seen that our interviewees believed that hacking could 'change the world', and that it had the potential to improve people's lives in their own neighbourhoods and beyond. The question of how this is to happen inevitably raises the issue of politics. Should hackers and makers look beyond the bounds of their hackerspace, organizing and acting on a grander scale? What is their role in questions of social justice and equity? What part can the hacker spirit play in empowering not just individuals and small groups but whole neighbourhoods, communities and segments of society? I can't answer any of these questions. But it seems to me that it is important that hackers and makers, organized as communities of hacker and makerspaces, collectively reflect on them.

Hacking and making are awesome

I want to close by returning to the earliest stages of this research, and to my partner in it, Dr Dave Conz. Dave was, as I've said, a hacker and maker extraordinaire. He tinkered with his car, which ran on used cooking oil, with his food and drink (home-grown and home-brewed), and with his teaching, which was multidisciplinary, experimental and incredibly popular. Dave's enthusiasm for hacking and making was one trigger for this research, and it was infectious. As we visited hacker and makerspaces and carried out interviews he had many excited conversations about both the potential of this movement as a whole and specific, geeky aspects of it. Dave believed, as much as anyone, that hacking and making could change the world for the better. It seems fitting to finish with his words on the maker movement and this research. This extract is taken from the end of one of the interviews we carried out together, with the Arizonan hacker Yan. We've just thanked him for talking with us, and asked if he has any questions.

Yan: What's your hypothesis? What's your thesis?
Dave: I consider myself a participant observer. So I've been making biodiesel for almost ten years. Just built a MakerBot. Granted, of course, it comes in a kit form. But I didn't know what I was doing. It took me sixteen hours, and it worked after another three hours.
Yan: Only nineteen? You got lucky.
Dave: Yeah... Been making beer for a couple of years. I have pet chickens. I really like the hands-on hobby stuff. [...] So to answer your question, our hypothesis is that this is awesome. [Laughter]

Notes

1. Introduction

1 https://wiki.hackerspaces.org/List_of_planned_Hacker_Spaces
2 See, for example, https://en.wikipedia.org/wiki/Hackerspace: the definition given of a hackerspace is 'a community-operated workspace where
   people with common interests, often in computers, machining, technology,
   science, digital art or electronic art, can meet, socialize and collaborate'.
   Researchers at the University of Sussex say that they are 'community-
   oriented spaces dedicated to grassroots digital fabrication' (Hielscher, S.
   and Smith, A., 'Community-based digital fabrication workshops: A review
   of the research literature'. SPRU Working Paper Series, SPRU – Science
   and Technology Policy Research, University of Sussex, 2014).
3 http://www.theguardian.com/technology/2011/aug/24/inside-secret
   -world-of-hackers
4 Coleman, G., *Hacker, Hoaxer, Whistleblower, Spy: The Many Faces of Anonymous*. London: Verso, 2014.
5 Though some hackers, at least, embrace some of these stereotypes:
   http://www.outpost9.com/reference/jargon/jargon_50.html#SEC57
6 http://abcnews.go.com/blogs/politics/2013/06/obama-not-scrambling
   -jets-to-get-a-29-year-old-hacker-named-snowden/
7 http://www.urbandictionary.com/define.php?term=hacking
8 http://www.outpost9.com/reference/jargon/jargon_18.html#TAG365
9 The full definition is: 'to make one's day-to-day behaviors or activities
   more efficient. Also as a noun. Lifehacks apply the make-do, can-do, what-
   will-it-do attitude that originated in computer hacking.' http://www
   .americandialect.org/Words_of_the_Year_2005.pdf
10 Rosner, D. and Bean, J., 'Learning from IKEA hacking: I'm not one to
   decoupage a tabletop and call it a day'. In *Proceedings of the 27th International Conference on Human Factors in Computing Systems*. New York: ACM,
   2009, pp. 419–22.
11 Garrett, B., *Explore Everything: Place-Hacking the City*. London: Verso, 2014.
12 Haywood, D., 'The ethic of the code: An ethnography of a "humanitarian
   hacking" community'. *Journal of Peer Production* 3, 2013. Available from:

http://peerproduction.net/issues/issue-3-free-software-epistemics/
peer-reviewed-papers/the-ethic-of-the-code-an-ethnography-of-a
-humanitarian-hacking-community/
13 http://nhshackday.com
14 The 'civic hackathon' is now a relatively well-established practice, used by
social enterprises and governments around the world. See DiSalvo, C.,
Gregg, M. and Lodato, T., 'Building belonging'. *interactions* 21(4), 58–61,
2014.
15 See http://www.stupidhackathon.com; http://www.theguardian.com/
global/2016/feb/08/inside-stupid-hackathon-extremely-stupid-ideas
16 http://www.rigb.org/christmas-lectures/sparks-will-fly/media
17 http://www.3ders.org/articles/20151102-3ders-monday-warm-up-the
-top-3d-food-printers-that-will-feed-the-future.html
18 The dream of 'personal fabrication' is one aspect of this, in which manufacturing is democratized through everyone having access to their own means
of production. See Mota, C., 'The rise of personal fabrication'. In *Proceedings
of the 8th ACM Conference on Creativity and Cognition.* New York: ACM, 2011,
pp. 279–88. Available from: http://dl.acm.org/citation.cfm?id=2069665
19 http://www.mckinsey.com/insights/manufacturing/the_future_of
_manufacturing
20 http://www.iftf.org/uploads/media/SR1181_FutureofMaking_sm.pdf
21 Anderson, C., *Makers: The New Industrial Revolution.* New York: Crown
Business, 2012, p. 17.
22 Ibid., p. 103. Though, to be fair, Anderson is also interested in seeing
physical manufacturing on a large scale move back to the US, revitalizing
places such as Detroit.
23 http://media.wix.com/ugd/9bcbad_b72353cd3bed48f49391924d4a
7448a9.pdf
24 http://www.theguardian.com/lifeandstyle/2014/jan/19/3d-printer
-bomb-victim-new-arm-prosthetic-limb
25 http://www.wired.com/2014/05/3d-printed-guns/
26 http://www.theguardian.com/us-news/2015/sep/17/ahmed-mohamed
-is-tired-excited-to-meet-obama-and-wants-his-clock-back
27 http://www.wired.com/2015/09/heres-bomb-clock-got-ahmed-mohamed
-arrested/
28 https://www.whitehouse.gov/the-press-office/2015/06/12/fact-sheet
-new-commitments-support-president's-nation-makers-initiative
29 See, for example, https://www.theguardian.com/science/political
-science/2015/apr/04/tooling-up-civic-visions-fablabs-and-grassroots
-activism; http://www.theguardian.com/sustainable-business/2015/
dec/01/hacking-apple-samsung-smartphones-ewaste-fix-tech; https://
www.theguardian.com/science/2015/nov/18/biohackers-strange-
world-diy-biology; http://economictimes.indiatimes.com/news/interna
tional/world-news/co-working-grows-amid-search-for-new-office
-lifestyle/articleshow/50991730.cms; http://voices.nationalgeographic
.com/2016/02/13/how-citizen-science-changed-the-way-fukushima
-radiation-is-reported/
30 http://www.makerbot.com/faq/
31 Kostakis, V., Niaros, V. and Giotitsas, C., 'Production and governance in
hackerspaces: A manifestation of Commons-based peer production in the

physical realm?' *International Journal of Cultural Studies* 18(5), 555–73, 2015. 2016 figures from https://wiki.hackerspaces.org/List_of_Hacker _Spaces

32 Baichtal, J., *Hack This: 24 Incredible Hackerspace Projects from the DIY Movement*. Indianapolis, IN: Que Publishing, 2012, p. 3.

33 http://hackerspaces.org/wiki/Staff

34 http://hackerspaces.org/wiki/List_of_Hacker_Spaces

35 Baichtal, *Hack This*, p. 9.

36 Sometimes with an almost evangelistic fervour. Using funds raised on Kickstarter, the hackerspace entrepreneur Bilal Ghalib has set up spaces around the Middle East and describes himself as an 'Evangelist' for the desktop design software Autodesk. See bilalghalib.com

37 https://wiki.hackerspaces.org/List_of_planned_Hacker_Spaces

2. Craft, DIY and Active Leisure

1 Stoller, D., *Stitch 'N Bitch: The Knitter's Handbook*, 1st edn. New York: Workman Publishing, 2004.

2 There is also a parallel resurgence in academic and artistic interest in the crafts, with increasing numbers of artists using craft techniques in part or exclusively (e.g., the prize-winning British artist Grayson Perry) and with academic studies of craft as a practice that is distinct from, but as valuable as, 'fine art' also on the up. See Adamson, G., *Thinking Through Craft*. London: Bloomsbury Academic, 2007.

3 http://www.bbc.co.uk/programmes/b03myqj2

4 http://www.theguardian.com/lifeandstyle/2014/jan/11/do-something -hobby-upholstery

5 See Kuznetsov, S. and Paulos, E., 'Rise of the expert amateur: DIY projects, communities, and cultures'. In *Proceedings of the 6th Nordic Conference on Human–Computer Interaction: Extending Boundaries*. New York: ACM, 2010, pp. 295–304. Available from: http://dl.acm.org/citation.cfm?id=1868950

6 Williams, K.A., ' "Old time mem'ry": Contemporary urban craftivism and the politics of doing-it-yourself in postindustrial America'. *Utopian Studies* 22(2), 303–20, 2011.

7 Levine, F. and Heimerl, C., *Handmade Nation: The Rise of DIY, Art, Craft, and Design*. Princeton, NJ: Princeton Architectural Press, 2008, p. ix.

8 Adamson, *Thinking Through Craft*.

9 Charny, D., ed., *Power of Making: The Importance of Being Skilled*. London: V&A Publishing and the Crafts Council, 2011, p. 49.

10 https://www.craftandhobby.org/eweb/docs/2012.State.of.Craft .Industy_Key.Insights.pdf

11 http://www.hive.co.uk/book/a-girl-called-jack-100-delicious-budget -recipes/18105011/

12 http://www.seattlepi.com/business/article/New-customers-flocking-to -thrift-stores-1287767.php

13 http://repaircafe.org/about-repair-cafe/

14 Matchar, E., *Homeward Bound: Why Women Are Embracing the New Domesticity*. New York: Simon and Schuster, 2013.

15 Ibid., p. 233.

16 http://craftivism.com/about/what-is-craftivism-anyway/
17 Minahan, S. and Cox, J.W., 'Stitch'nBitch Cyberfeminism, a third place and the new materiality'. *Journal of Material Culture* 12(1), 5–21, 2007. Orton-Johnson, K., 'Knit, purl and upload: New technologies, digital mediations and the experience of leisure'. *Leisure Studies* 33(3), 305–21, 2012. Rosner, D.K., 'Mediated crafts: Digital practices around creative handwork'. In *CHI'10 Extended Abstracts on Human Factors in Computing Systems*. New York: ACM, 2010, pp. 2955–8.
18 Gauntlett, D., *Making Is Connecting*. Cambridge: Polity, 2011, p. 226.
19 http://www.theguardian.com/film/2014/oct/13/star-wars-fans-remake-the-empire-strikes-back
20 See Putnam, R.D., *Bowling Alone*. New York: Simon and Schuster, 2001.
21 Orton-Johnson, 'Knit, purl and upload'.
22 Shirky, C., *Here Comes Everybody: How Change Happens when People Come Together*. Harmondsworth: Penguin, 2009.
23 Miller, D., *Tales from Facebook*. Chichester: John Wiley & Sons, 2013.
24 Stebbins, R.A., 'Serious leisure'. *Society* 38(4), 53–7, 2001.
25 Stebbins, R., 'Serious leisure and work'. *Sociology Compass* 3(5), 764–74, 2009.
26 Levine and Heimerl, *Handmade Nation*, p. xi.
27 http://www.theguardian.com/lifeandstyle/do-something-blog/2014/jan/11/do-something-manifesto-oliver-burkeman
28 See http://www.theguardian.com/do-something
29 Wehr, K., *DIY: The Search for Control and Self-Reliance in the 21st Century*. London: Routledge, 2012.
30 Ibid., p.xii.
31 Ibid.
32 Atkinson, P., 'Do it yourself: Democracy and design'. *Journal of Design History* 19(1), 1–10, 2006.
33 Crawford, M.B., *Shop Class as Soulcraft: An Inquiry into the Value of Work*. Harmondsworth: Penguin, 2009.
34 Sennett, R., *The Craftsman*. Harmondsworth: Penguin, 2009.
35 Ibid., p. 21.
36 Atkinson, 'Do it yourself'.
37 Ibid., p. 6.
38 And indeed much academic interest in hacking, making and crafting more generally has been predicated on their ability to democratize production. See, e.g., Mota, C. 'The rise of personal fabrication'. In *Proceedings of the 8th ACM Conference on Creativity and Cognition*. New York: ACM, 2011, pp. 279–88. Available from: http://dl.acm.org/citation.cfm?id=2069665. Powell, A., 'Democratizing production through open source knowledge: From open software to open hardware'. *Media, Culture & Society* 34(6), 691–708, 2012. Tanenbaum, J.G., Williams, A.M., Desjardins, A. and Tanenbaum, K., 'Democratizing technology: Pleasure, utility and expressiveness in DIY and maker practice'. In *Proceedings of the SIGCHI Conference on Human Factors in Computing Systems, CHI'13*. New York: ACM, 2013, pp. 2603–12.
39 Atkinson, 'Do it yourself'.
40 Watson, M. and Shove, E., 'Product, competence, project and practice: DIY and the dynamics of craft consumption'. *Journal of Consumer Culture* 8(1), 69–89, 2008.

3. Histories of Hacking and Making

1   All the names of informants and interviewees have been changed to ensure anonymity.
2   Levy, S., *Hackers: Heroes of the Computer Revolution, 25th Anniversary Edition*. Sebastopol, CA: O'Reilly Media, 2010.
3   The latter activity continues to be an important, and celebrated, aspect of life at MIT, to the extent that the MIT Museum now maintains extensive documentation of pranks by MIT hackers. One of the most famous is the installation of a police car, complete with flashing lights and box of doughnuts, on the library roof.
4   Levy, *Hackers: Heroes of the Computer Revolution*.
5   Ibid., p. ix.
6   Turner, F., *From Counterculture to Cyberculture: Stewart Brand, the Whole Earth Network, and the Rise of Digital Utopianism*. Chicago, IL: University of Chicago Press, 2010.
7   Coleman, E.G., *Coding Freedom: The Ethics and Aesthetics of Hacking*. Princeton, NJ: Princeton University Press, 2013, pp. 17–18.
8   http://www.outpost9.com/reference/jargon/jargon_toc.html
9   http://www.well.com/conf/inkwell.vue/topics/190/St-Jude-Memorial-and-Virtual-Wak-page01.html
10 Hielscher, S. and Smith, A., 'Community-based digital fabrication workshops: A review of the research literature'. SPRU Working Paper Series, SPRU – Science and Technology Policy Research, University of Sussex, 2014.
11 Pettis, B. and Schneeweisz, A., eds, *hackerspaces @ the beginning*, 2011. Available from: http://blog.hackerspaces.org/2011/08/31/hackerspaces-the-beginning-the-book/
12 See Coleman, *Coding Freedom*.
13 http://www.monochrom.at/english/
14 http://www.monochrom.at/hacking-the-spaces/
15 See http://makezine.com/2013/05/22/the-difference-between-hacker spaces-makerspaces-techshops-and-fablabs/
16 Perhaps surprisingly, given hacking's roots in MIT and Californian computing culture. But it's important to note that this recent history is something of a simplification. There were some early hackerspace-like groups before the post-2007 spaces, dating back to the 1990s, but these tended to be private groups with closed membership. See the descriptions given of closed or inactive spaces in Pettis and Schneeweisz, *hackerspaces @ the beginning*.
17 Inspired by the regular meeting of 'Hackers on Planet Earth (HOPE)', a biennial conference organized by the magazine *2600: The Hackers Quarterly*.
18 Mitch Altman, founder of the San Francisco hackerspace Noisebridge, quoted in Baichtal, J., *Hack This: 24 Incredible Hackerspace Projects from the DIY Movement*. Indianapolis, IN: Que Publishing, 2012, p. 9.
19 Ibid., p. 3.
20 See http://www.thebaffler.com/salvos/the-meme-hustler
21 Dougherty, D., 'The maker movement'. *innovations* 7(3), 11–14, 2012.

22 Email, 14 August 2014.
23 For one discussion of *MAKE* Magazine and its relation to the maker movement as a whole, see Sivek, S.C., '"We need a showing of all hands": Technological utopianism in MAKE Magazine'. *Journal of Communication Inquiry* 35(3), 187–209, 2011.
24 http://makezine.com/2013/05/22/the-difference-between-hackerspaces-makerspaces-techshops-and-fablabs/
25 Hatch, M., *The Maker Movement Manifesto: Rules for Innovation in the New World of Crafters, Hackers, and Tinkerers*. New York: McGraw-Hill Professional, 2013.
26 http://www.techshop.ws/facilities_and_amenities.html
27 Hatch, *The Maker Movement Manifesto*, pp. 24–6.
28 Ibid.
29 http://www.techshop.ws/index.html
30 Hatch, *The Maker Movement Manifesto*, p. 29.
31 http://invest.techshop.com/corporate
32 Anderson, C., *Makers: The New Industrial Revolution*. New York: Crown Business, 2012.
33 Hatch, *The Maker Movement Manifesto*, p. 201.
34 http://cba.mit.edu/about/index.html
35 Gershenfeld, N., *Fab: The Coming Revolution on Your Desktop – From Personal Computers to Personal Fabrication*. New York: Basic Books, 2005.
36 http://www.fabfoundation.org/fab-labs/fab-lab-criteria/
37 Fab Labs thus balance a strongly coordinated and centralized network with specific local communities. For an account of how one Fab Lab has managed these dynamics in practice, see Kohtala, C. and Bosqué, C., 'The story of MIT-Fablab Norway: Community embedding of peer production'. *Journal of Peer Production* 5, 2014.
38 Maxigas, 'Hacklabs and hackerspaces – tracing two genealogies'. *Journal of Peer Production* 2, 2012.
39 Delfanti, A., *Biohackers: The Politics of Open Science*. London: Pluto Press, 2013. See also Curry, H.A., 'From garden biotech to garage biotech: Amateur experimental biology in historical perspective'. *British Journal for the History of Science* 47(3), 539–65, 2014.
40 http://openpcr.org
41 Delfanti, *Biohackers*, p. 116.
42 For a discussion of overlaps with start-ups and incubators, see Lindtner, S., Hertz, G.D. and Dourish, P., 'Emerging sites of HCI innovation: Hackerspaces, hardware startups & incubators'. In *Proceedings of the SIGCHI Conference on Human Factors in Computing Systems*. New York: ACM, 2014, pp. 439–48.
43 Fox, S., Ulgado, R.R. and Rosner, D., 'Hacking culture, not devices: Access and recognition in feminist hackerspaces'. In *Proceedings of the 18th ACM Conference on Computer Supported Cooperative Work & Social Computing*. New York: ACM, 2015, pp. 56–68.
44 Baichtal, *Hack This*.
45 See Kera, D., 'Hackerspaces and DIYbio in Asia: Connecting science and community with open data, kits and protocols'. *Journal of Peer Production* 2, 2012.

4. How Do Hackerspaces Work?

1 http://hackerspaces.org/wiki/Design_Patterns
2 http://blog.adafruit.com/2012/11/12/how-to-start-a-hackerspace/
3 Baichtal, J., *Hack This: 24 Incredible Hackerspace Projects from the DIY Move-ment*. Indianapolis, IN: Que Publishing, 2012.
4 https://wiki.hackerspaces.org/The_Landlord_and_Neighbourhood _Pattern
5 https://www.noisebridge.net/wiki/Do-ocracy
6 Alternatively, they might have needed a group to sign a lease on the build-ing, or to have their names on a bank account. In any of these cases it would become apparent that some set of individuals needed to 'own' the hackerspace as an organization for legal or financial purposes.
7 http://makezine.com/2013/05/22/the-difference-between-hackerspaces -makerspaces-techshops-and-fablabs/
8 http://hackerspaces.org/wiki/The_Plenum_Pattern
9 http://hackerspaces.org/wiki/The_Tuesday_Pattern
10 Location was often important in the choices that hackers made as to where they found their space. Though these were pragmatic decisions – who will rent us a suitable, affordable space? – hackers might also aim to be located somewhere with a high footfall, like a city's Main Street (or, alternatively, somewhere a bit more off the beaten track). They also saw themselves as being inflected by, and part of, their neighbourhood. Hackerspaces in high-tech, entrepreneurial regions, for instance, often mirrored that emphasis on entrepreneurialism. Exactly because hacker and makerspaces were seen as the sum of their members, and as part of their local communities, where you were could make a big difference to who you were.
11 Arduino is an open-source electronics platform based on easy-to-use hard-ware and software. It's intended for anyone making interactive projects.
12 I will discuss some of the potential consequences of these means of check-ing and crafting community in chapter 7, where I focus on the ways in which hacker and makerspaces can be experienced as exclusionary. Here it is worth noting that the language of the 'good fit' has a long history in feminist discussion of the tech industry as a way in which unspoken and unsavoury biases against, for instance, women, people of colour, or LGBT-identified people are expressed. For an account of one trans woman's experiences of tech interviews, interview discomfort and the sense that she was 'not a good fit', see Keeney, F., 'Gender bias in hiring: Interviewing as a trans woman in tech'. *Model View Culture* 23, 2016. Available from: https://modelviewculture.com/pieces/gender-bias-in-hiring-interview ing-as-a-trans-woman-in-tech
13 Coleman, E.G., *Coding Freedom: The Ethics and Aesthetics of Hacking*. Prince-ton, NJ: Princeton University Press, 2013, p. 107.
14 http://hackerspaces.org/wiki/The_Debate_Culture_Pattern
15 https://www.noisebridge.net/wiki/Mailinglist
16 https://schoolfactory.org
17 See https://www.noisebridge.net/wiki/Passport; http://www.adafruit .com/product/769
18 http://hackerspaces.org/wiki/Hackerspaces_Passport

5. The Hacker Spirit

1 http://www.outpost9.com/reference/jargon/jargon_23.html#TAG824

2 The furniture aspect seems to be a later addition: the online etymological dictionary says only that 'hacker', as a noun, is 'a chopper, cutter, perhaps also one who makes hacking tools', and that it dates from the early thirteenth century (http://www.etymonline.com/index.php?term=hacker).

3 Levy, S., *Hackers: Heroes of the Computer Revolution, 25th Anniversary Edition.* Sebastopol, CA: O'Reilly Media, 2010, p. vii.

4 Since we started our fieldwork, this emphasis on identity and community has become a widely recognized feature of hackerspaces and the maker movement. See, for instance, Rosner, D.K., Lindtner, S., Erickson, I., Forlano, L., Jackson, S.J. and Kolko, B., 'Making cultures: Building things & building communities'. In *CSCW Companion '14. Proceedings of the Companion Publication of the 17th ACM Conference on Computer Supported Cooperative Work & Social Computing.* New York: ACM, 2014, pp. 113–16.

5 This sense of hacking as generative was also, at times, contrasted with cracking, which was viewed as destructive and therefore not 'real' hacking. Hackers make new and interesting things; crackers (and others) destroy them.

6 Crawford, M.B., *Shop Class as Soulcraft: An Inquiry into the Value of Work.* Harmondsworth: Penguin, 2009.

7 Maybe: http://www.thedailymeal.com/fried-chicken-and-watermelon -cocktail. But I'm not entirely convinced.

8 It's here that there is a clear connection back to Levy's (and indeed Gabriella Coleman's) account of hacking. Levy views hacking as fundamentally tied to the notion that 'information wants to be free', and discusses the software freedom activist Richard Stallman as the 'last true hacker'. Some of this ethos, and commitment to free software, was present in the hackerspaces we visited, and in many cases there was a taken-for-granted assumption that sharing your products for free was a good idea – but this was by no means a universal (or clearly articulated) commitment.

9 Coleman, E.G., *Coding Freedom: The Ethics and Aesthetics of Hacking.* Princeton, NJ: Princeton University Press, 2013.

10 See also Grimme, S., Bardzell, J. and Bardzell, S., '"We've conquered dark": Shedding light on empowerment in critical making'. In *NordiCHI '14. Proceedings of the 8th Nordic Conference on Human–Computer Interaction: Fun, Fast, Foundational.* New York: ACM, 2014, pp. 431–40.

6. How Do Hackerspaces Really Work?

1 Also argued in Lindtner, S., Hertz, G.D. and Dourish, P., 'Emerging sites of HCI innovation: Hackerspaces, hardware startups & incubators'. In *Proceedings of the SIGCHI Conference on Human Factors in Computing Systems.* New York: ACM, 2014, pp. 439–48.

2 Putnam, R.D., *Bowling Alone.* New York: Simon and Schuster, 2001, p. 21.

3 Ibid.

4 Ibid., p. 28.
5 Ibid., p. 21.
6 Oldenburg, R., *Celebrating the Third Place: Inspiring Stories about the Great Good Places at the Heart of Our Communities*. Cambridge, MA: Da Capo Press, 2009, p. 2. See also Oldenburg, R., *The Great Good Place: Café, Coffee Shops, Community Centers, Beauty Parlors, General Stores, Bars, Hangouts, and How They Get You Through the Day*. St. Paul, MN: Paragon House, 1989.
7 Of course, hacker and makerspaces differ, and these ideals were expressed differently in different places. As discussed in chapter 4, at least some makerspaces, for example, were overtly hierarchical in their structure – though all spaces tended to emphasize that anyone could get involved in contributing to decision making even if they weren't part of a formal leadership team.

7. Exclusion

1 Baichtal, J., *Hack This: 24 Incredible Hackerspace Projects from the DIY Movement*. Indianapolis, IN: Que Publishing, 2012, p. 3.
2 https://archive.is/vVgZw
3 https://modelviewculture.com/pieces/the-rise-of-feminist-hackerspaces-and-how-to-make-your-own
4 http://makezine.com/magazine/make-40/where-are-the-women/
5 http://geekfeminism.wikia.com/wiki/Impostor_syndrome
6 Moilanen, J., 'Emerging hackerspaces – Peer-production generation'. In Hammouda, I., Lundell, B., Mikkonen, T., Scacchi, W., eds, *Open Source Systems: Long-Term Sustainability*. Heidelberg: Springer, 2012, pp. 94–111.
7 This emphasis on empowerment as central to hacker and makerspace use is also discussed in Grimme, S., Bardzell, J. and Bardzell, S., '"We've conquered dark": Shedding light on empowerment in critical making'. In *NordiCHI '14. Proceedings of the 8th Nordic Conference on Human-Computer Interaction: Fun, Fast, Foundational*. New York: ACM, 2014, pp. 431–40.
8 There is now a growing literature not just on feminist hackerspaces but on the practice of feminist hacking and making. A 2016 special issue of the *Journal of Peer Production* focuses on this topic, suggesting that there are two lines along which feminist hacking progresses: first, 'many feminist hackers and makers seek to redress the lack of gender diversity within these techno-communities through the designs of women, queer, and trans-friendly spaces for hacking and making or addressing women-centered concerns'. Feminist hackers and makers are thus concerned with making hacker and makerspaces (and related communities) more diverse and with supporting the inclusion of under-represented groups in tech generally. Secondly, hacking is viewed as 'both a method and a framework to introduce new kinds of expertise, such as craft and care, into conversations of information technology'. Feminist thought can thus open up hacking and making to languages, practices, and forms of knowledge (such as care practices or work on the body) that are otherwise elided within the largely 'heternormative masculine culture of hacking'. See Nagbot, S., 'Feminist hacking/making: Exploring new gender horizons of possibility'. *Journal of Peer Production* 8, 2016.
9 https://archive.is/vVgZw

10 https://modelviewculture.com/pieces/the-rise-of-feminist-hackerspaces -and-how-to-make-your-own

11 Much of which was evidenced in the 'Gamergate' controversy: see http:// www.bostonmagazine.com/news/article/2015/04/28/gamergate/. Gabriella Coleman also documents a fierce elitism amongst hackers with little regard for wider social dynamics; see Coleman, E.G., *Coding Freedom: The Ethics and Aesthetics of Hacking*. Princeton, NJ: Princeton University Press, 2013.

12 http://geekfeminism.org/2015/02/04/learning-how-to-hack-in-a-bros -world-a-womens-college-student-perspective

13 http://geekfeminism.wikia.com/wiki/Impostor_syndrome

14 More recently there have been efforts to 'hack' hackathons from a feminist perspective, for instance by working on issues of particular concern to women. See D'Ignazio, C., Hope, A., Metral, A., Brugh, W., Raymond, D., Michelson, B., Achituv, T. and Zuckerman, E., 'Towards a feminist hackathon: The "make the breast pump not suck!" hackathon'. *Journal of Peer Production* 8, 2016.

15 Also formulated as the Unicorn Law: http://geekfeminism.wikia.com/ wiki/Unicorn_Law

16 http://dpi.studioxx.org/en/feminist-hackerspaces-safer-spaces

17 Tautological but to the point.

18 This sense of community as itself something to be crafted and hacked is also emerging from more recent research on feminist hackerspaces. See Fox, S., Ulgado, R.R. and Rosner, D., 'Hacking culture, not devices: Access and recognition in feminist hackerspaces'. In *Proceedings of the 18th ACM Conference on Computer Supported Cooperative Work & Social Computing*. New York: ACM, 2015, pp. 56–68. Rosner, D.K. and Fox, S.E., 'Legacies of craft and the centrality of failure in a mother-operated hackerspace'. *New Media & Society* 18(4), 558–80, 2016.

19 A homeware and clothing store with a distinctive 'shabby chic', Bohemian aesthetic.

20 Putnam, R.D., *Bowling Alone*. New York: Simon and Schuster, 2001, p. 22.

8. Cool Projects

1 And indeed hobbyism and crafts more generally: Jackson, A., 'Understanding the home workshop: Project space, project time, and material interaction'. *Interiors: Design, Architecture and Culture* 4(2), 175–94, 2013.

2 Hielscher, S. and Smith, A., 'Community-based digital fabrication workshops: A review of the research literature'. SPRU Working Paper Series, SPRU – Science and Technology Policy Research, University of Sussex, 2014, p. 2.

3 Other hackerspaces, and particularly those in other cultural contexts, seem to function more formally as tech incubators or as sites for entrepreneurship. See Lindtner, S., Hertz, G.D. and Dourish, P., 'Emerging sites of HCI innovation: Hackerspaces, hardware startups & incubators'. In *Proceedings of the SIGCHI Conference on Human Factors in Computing Systems*. New York: ACM, 2014, pp. 439–48.

4   Frank, T., *The Conquest of Cool: Business Culture, Counterculture, and the Rise of Hip Consumerism*. Chicago, IL: University of Chicago Press, 1998. Pountain, D. and Robins, D., *Cool Rules: Anatomy of an Attitude*. London: Reaktion Books, 2000.

5   Culén, A.L. and Gasparini, A.A., 'Situated techno-cools: Factors that contribute to making technology cool in a given context of use'. *PsychNology Journal* 10(2), 117–39, 2012.

6   Ibid.

7   Coleman, E.G., *Coding Freedom: The Ethics and Aesthetics of Hacking*. Princeton, NJ: Princeton University Press, 2013, p. 118.

8   Joshua Tanenbaum and colleagues similarly argue that playfulness, and a delight in the material, is integral to maker practices. See Tanenbaum, J.G., Williams, A.M., Desjardins, A. and Tanenbaum, K., 'Democratizing technology: Pleasure, utility and expressiveness in DIY and maker practice'. In *Proceedings of the SIGCHI Conference on Human Factors in Computing Systems, CHI'13*, New York: ACM, 2013, pp. 2603–12.

9   This emotional register is also found more generally in the language and practices of hackerspaces, for instance around 'care' and caring. See Toombs, A., Bardzell, S. and Bardzell, J., 'The proper care and feeding of hackerspaces: Care ethics and cultures of making'. In *CHI '15. Proceedings of the 33rd Annual ACM Conference on Human Factors in Computing Systems*. New York: ACM, 2015, pp. 629–38.

10 See http://kevingotkin.com

11 See also 'newbie' in the *Hacker's Dictionary*: http://www.outpost9.com/reference/jargon/jargon_29.html#SEC36. Ideas about 'newbies' and 'script kiddies' derive from computer hacking culture specifically, discussed in Coleman, G., *Hacker, Hoaxer, Whistleblower, Spy: The Many Faces of Anonymous*. London: Verso, 2014.

12 http://www.urbandictionary.com/define.php?term=script+kiddie

9. Emancipation and Commodification

1   http://www.rigb.org/christmas-lectures/sparks-will-fly/media

2   Dougherty, D., 'The maker movement'. *innovations* 7(3), 11–14, 2012.

3   http://www.fabfoundation.org/about-us/

4   'GFP' stands for Green Fluorescent Protein: inserting its sequence and controlling its expression in cells is a central technique in biotechnology. See   http://makezine.com/2013/05/16/diy-synthetic-biology-making -your-own-glowing-plants/

5   Stebbins, R.A., 'The semiotic self and serious leisure'. *The American Sociologist* 42(2–3), 238–48, 2011.

6   I am indebted to Aubrey Wigner for highlighting this point to me.

7   http://www.monochrom.at/hacking-the-spaces/

8   http://makermedia.com

9   Ibid. Susan Currie Sivek has argued that *MAKE* magazine carefully cultivates a particular 'maker' identity for its readers, one which blends commitment to MAKE itself with national pride, a spirit of independence, and technological utopianism. See Sivek, S.C., ' "We need a showing of all

hands": Technological utopianism in MAKE Magazine'. *Journal of Communication Inquiry* 35(3), 187–209, 2011.

10 MAKE's resources – the magazine, the projects, the news – also display a slightly weird obsession with surveillance. They have, as I noted earlier, produced a special issue on homemade drone technologies; as I write, the 'weekend project' featured on the magazine homepage is a 'coffee cup spy cam' (http://makezine.com/projects/coffee-cup-spy-cam/). The instructions don't seem to include any reflections on how this would actually be used, or the rights or wrongs of doing so.

11 http://www.makershed.com/products/smart-sewing-basic-kit

12 Wehr, K., *DIY: The Search for Control and Self-reliance in the 21st Century*. London: Routledge, 2012.

13 Probably: http://makermedia.com/brands/make-magazine/

14 http://www.newyorker.com/magazine/2014/01/13/making-it-2?currentPage=all

15 http://bollier.org/blog/morozov-maker-movement. Others have similarly questioned the techno-utopianism inherent in discussion of the making 'revolution'. For a discussion of how this relates to 3D printing, see https://modelviewculture.com/pieces/questioning-the-3d-printing-revolution

16 Lindtner, S., 'Hackerspaces and the Internet of Things in China: How makers are reinventing industrial production, innovation, and the self'. *China Information* 28(2), 145–67, 2014. See also http://www.3ders.org/articles/20111124-hackerspaces-in-china.html

17 http://en.cncnews.cn/news/v_show/43702_2014_Beijing_maker_carnival.shtm

18 http://hackaday.com/2011/11/27/chinese-hackerspaces-or-what-happens-when-a-government-is-run-by-engineers/

19 Lindtner, 'Hackerspaces and the Internet of Things in China'.

20 http://www.wsj.com/articles/SB100014240527023037226045791112534 95145952

21 Though see the debate in the comments here: http://hackaday.com/2011/11/27/chinese-hackerspaces-or-what-happens-when-a-government-is-run-by-engineers/; strikingly, one comment reads, 'this is a hacker sight [sic] and it is not in our area to discuss politics'.

22 http://makezine.com/2012/01/19/darpa-mentor-award-to-bring-making-to-education/

23 http://makezine.com/2012/04/04/makerspaces-in-education-and-darpa/

24 http://www.nytimes.com/2012/10/06/us/worries-over-defense-dept-money-for-hackerspaces.html?_r=1

25 http://makezine.com/2012/04/04/makerspaces-in-education-and-darpa/

26 http://owni.eu/2012/04/10/darpa-pentagon-hackers-us-maker-faire/

27 Military research has an illustrious history of co-opting the hackers who resist and subvert it, as evidenced by the DARPA programme manager involved in reaching out to MAKE and to hackerspaces more generally: a former computer hacker known as Mudge. See http://www.nytimes.com/2012/10/06/us/worries-over-defense-dept-money-for-hackerspaces.html?_r=1: the before and after photos of him are quite something.

28 For one higher education example of this, see Kolko, B., Hope, A., Sattler, B., MacCorkle, K. and Sirjani, B., 'Hackademia: Building functional rather than accredited engineers'. In *PDC '12. Proceedings of the 12th Participatory Design Conference: Research Papers*, Volume 1. New York: ACM, 2012, pp. 129–38.

29 http://www.edutopia.org/blog/6-strategies-funding-makerspace-paloma -garcia-lopez

30 http://makered.org/wp-content/uploads/2014/09/Makerspace-Playbook -Feb-2013.pdf

31 Hamilton, M. and Schmidt, D.H., *Make It Here: Inciting Creativity and Innovation in Your Library*. Santa Barbara, CA: ABC-CLIO, 2014.

32 http://tinkering.exploratorium.edu/about

33 Gutwill, J.P., Hido, N. and Sindorf, L., 'Research to practice: Observing learning in tinkering activities'. *Curator: The Museum Journal* 58(2), 151–68, 2015.

34 Hamilton and Schmidt, *Make It Here*, p. 3.

35 Sims, C., 2015. 'Progressive educational reform as neoliberalism by other means'. Society for Social Studies of Science Annual Meeting, Denver, CO.

10.   Who Is a Hacker?

1 In fact, 'food hacking' is a recognized term, with at least a couple of meanings – one being quick and easy 'food hacks' (like using dental floss to cut soft cheese) that make your life better, and the other referring to more traditional hackers' experiments with food and drink. See http://www.buzzfeed.com/readcommentbackwards/42-clever-food-hacks-that -will-change-your-life-dmjk and https://foodhackingbase.org

2 http://www.virtuousbread.com/bread-and-conversation/refreshing-the -1857-sourdough/

3 In the context of baking, this is often about avoiding the 'Chorleywood process', by which most mass-produced bread is now made and which involves a high number of additions to bread's basic ingredients of flour, yeast, water and salt. See http://www.independent.co.uk/life-style/food -and-drink/features/the-shocking-truth-about-bread-413156.html

4 Kostakis, V., Niaros, V. and Giotitsas, C., 'Production and governance in hackerspaces: A manifestation of Commons-based peer production in the physical realm?' *International Journal of Cultural Studies* 18(5), 555–73, 2015.

5 Smith, A., Hielscher, S., Dickel, S., Söderberg, J. and van Oost, E., 'Grassroots digital fabrication and makerspaces: Reconfiguring, relocating and recalibrating innovation?' SPRU Working Paper Series, SPRU – Science and Technology Policy Research, University of Sussex, 2013, p. 1.

6 Dougherty, D., 'The maker movement'. *innovations* 7(3), 11–14, 2012.

7 Institute for the Future, *The Future of Making*. Palo Alto, CA: Institute for the Future, 2008.

8 Hence, similarly, the emphasis on self-made tools in hackerspaces. See Bardzell, J., Bardzell, S. and Toombs, A., ' "Now that's definitely a proper hack": Self-made tools in hackerspaces'. In *CHI '14. Proceedings of the SIGCHI Conference on Human Factors in Computing Systems*. New York: ACM, 2014, pp. 473–6.

9   Holm, E.J.V., 'Makerspaces and contributions to entrepreneurship'. *Procedia – Social and Behavioral Sciences* 195, 24–31, 2015. http://reicenter.org/upload/documents/colearning/benton2013_report.pdf

10   https://foodhackingbase.org

11   For instance, see http://biologigaragen.org/kulturkollektionen/

12   Kera, D. and Tuters, M., 'Social stomach: Performative food prototypes'. In *Workshop Proceedings of the 7th International Conference on Intelligent Environments*. Amsterdam: IOS Press, pp. 279–89, 2011. http://dces.essex.ac.uk/Research/iieg/papers(2011)/CS11_Kera(16).pdf

13   http://lists.hackerspaces.org/pipermail/discuss/2014-January/008922.html

14   They also had a screen name which was that of a well-known black-hat hacker – though their signature noted that they 'may or may not be the person you think I am'.

15   http://lists.hackerspaces.org/pipermail/discuss/2014-January/009039.html

11.   Conclusion

1   See the following on, for instance, the importance of making and maintaining tools within hackerspace culture: Bardzell, J., Bardzell, S. and Toombs, A., ' "Now that's definitely a proper hack": Self-made tools in hackerspaces'. In *CHI '14. Proceedings of the SIGCHI Conference on Human Factors in Computing Systems*. New York: ACM, 2014, pp. 473–6. Toombs, A., Bardzell, S. and Bardzell, J., 'The proper care and feeding of hackerspaces: Care ethics and cultures of making'. In *CHI '15. Proceedings of the 33rd Annual ACM Conference on Human Factors in Computing Systems*. New York: ACM, 2015, pp. 629–38.

2   http://nhshackday.com

3   http://www.theguardian.com/technology/2015/sep/16/istandwith-ahmed-obama-zuckerberg-internet-rally-texas-student

4   Baichtal, J., *Hack This: 24 Incredible Hackerspace Projects from the DIY Movement*. Indianapolis, IN: Que Publishing, 2012.

5   Hatch, M., *The Maker Movement Manifesto: Rules for Innovation in the New World of Crafters, Hackers, and Tinkerers*. New York: McGraw-Hill Professional, 2013, p. 52.

6   http://www.nytimes.com/2013/05/02/garden/the-rise-of-the-hacker-space.html?_r=0

7   See Oldenburg, R., *The Great Good Place: Café, Coffee Shops, Community Centers, Beauty Parlors, General Stores, Bars, Hangouts, and how They Get You Through the Day*. St. Paul, MN: Paragon House, 1989.

8   Gauntlett, D., *Making is Connecting*. Cambridge: Polity, 2011.

9   Turkle, S., *Alone Together: Why We Expect More from Technology and Less from Each Other*. New York: Basic Books, 2011.

10   Shen, C. and Cage, C., 'Exodus to the real world? Assessing the impact of offline meetups on community participation and social capital'. *New Media & Society* 17(3), 394–414, 2015.

11   Ibid., p. 410.

12   Gauntlett, *Making is Connecting*, p. 159.

13 Harvey, D., *A Brief History of Neoliberalism*. Oxford: Oxford University Press, 2005.
14 Lupton, D., *Risk*. London: Routledge, 1999, p. 71.
15 Hunt, D. and Koteyko, N., ' "What was your blood sugar reading this morning?" Representing diabetes self-management on Facebook'. *Discourse & Society* 26(4), 445–63, 2015.
16 Stebbins, R.A., 'The semiotic self and serious leisure'. *The American Sociologist* 42(2–3), 238–48, 2011.
17 Turner, F., *From Counterculture to Cyberculture: Stewart Brand, the Whole Earth Network, and the Rise of Digital Utopianism*. Chicago, IL: University of Chicago Press, 2010.
18 Maxigas, 'Hacklabs and hackerspaces – tracing two genealogies'. *Journal of Peer Production* 2, 2012. Grenzfurthner, J. and Apunkt Schneider, F., 'Hacking the spaces', n.d. Available from: http://www.monochrom.at/hacking-the-spaces/
19 One answer to this question is that hackerspace members choose to *care* for each other. For an extended discussion of how practices of care interact with a libertarian hacker ideology, see Toombs et al., 'The proper care and feeding of hackerspaces'.

Index